WORLD STATE

Introduction to the United Federation of the World

How a democratically-elected World Government can replace the UN and bring peace

Nicholas Hagger

First published by O-Books, 2018
O-Books is an imprint of John Hunt Publishing Ltd., No. 3 East St., Alresford, Hampshire SO24 9EE, UK
office1@jhpbooks.net
www.johnhuntpublishing.com

For distributor details and how to order please visit the 'Ordering' section on our website.

ISBN: 978 1 78099 964 7
978 1 78099 972 2 (ebook)
Library of Congress Control Number: 2017950789

A CIP catalogue record for this book is available from the British Library.

Design: Stuart Davies

Printed and bound by CPI Group (UK) Ltd, Croydon, CR0 4YY, UK

WORLD STATE

Introduction to the United Federation of the World

How a democratically-elected World Government can replace the UN and bring peace

Nicholas Hagger

BOOKS

Winchester, UK
Washington, USA

Also by Nicholas Hagger

The Fire and the Stones
Selected Poems
The Universe and the Light
A White Radiance
A Mystic Way
Awakening to the Light
A Spade Fresh with Mud
The Warlords
Overlord
A Smell of Leaves and Summer
The Tragedy of Prince Tudor
The One and the Many
Wheeling Bats and a Harvest Moon
The Warm Glow of the Monastery Courtyard
The Syndicate
The Secret History of the West
The Light of Civilization
Classical Odes
Overlord, one-volume edition
Collected Poems 1958–2005
Collected Verse Plays
Collected Stories
The Secret Founding of America
The Last Tourist in Iran
The Rise and Fall of Civilizations
The New Philosophy of Universalism
The Libyan Revolution
Armageddon
The World Government
The Secret American Dream
A New Philosophy of Literature
A View of Epping Forest
My Double Life 1: This Dark Wood
My Double Life 2: A Rainbow over the Hills

Selected Stories: Follies and Vices of the Modern Elizabethan Age
Selected Poems: Quest for the One
The Dream of Europa
Life Cycle and Other New Poems 2006–2016
The First Dazzling Chill of Winter
The Secret American Destiny
Peace for our Time

"Unless we establish some form of world government, it will not be possible for us to avert a World War III in the future."
Winston Churchill, 1945

"Human society can be saved only by Universalism."
Emery Reves, *The Anatomy of Peace*, 1945

"Mankind can be saved only if a supranational system, based on law, is created to eliminate the methods of brute force."
Albert Einstein, 1950

"History is now choosing the founders of the World Federation. Any person who can be among that number and fails to do so has lost the noblest opportunity of a lifetime."
Carl van Doren

*

To the Presidents of the USA, China, the Russian Federation and the EU, who as a quartet could lay this introduction to a United Federation of the World, a democratic, partially-federal World State, before the UN General Assembly and request a World Constitutional Convention (see pp.106, 116-120, 156-163, 165, 187-188, 193 and 214).

CONTENTS

Author's Note

The World Government (2010) was, I believe, a ground-breaking, pioneering work. It was subtitled 'A Blueprint for a Universal World State'. As a work of philosophical Universalism it was necessarily to some extent exploratory, and focused on the process of arriving at a World State.

Since then I have been awarded the Gusi Peace Prize for Literature and in my acceptance speech in Manila have called for a democratic World State. *World State* (2018) is subtitled 'Introduction to the United Federation of the World', a 'democratically-elected World Government' that 'can replace the UN', and is more straightforward and more of a presentation of a finished idea. It seeks to offer an objective, definitive and authoritative account. It inevitably overlaps with the earlier book in places, and I have deliberately not sought to amend overlapping passages that still hold good and do not need updating, on which I cannot improve.

I have prepared a Constitution for the United Federation of the World, which is being published separately by O-Books in 2018.

To the memory of Truman, Einstein, Churchill, Eisenhower, Russell, Gandhi, J.F. Kennedy and Gorbachev, who all called for a democratically-elected World State following the first atomic bombs and in whose tradition I may be the only Western literary author to follow. I am grateful again to my publisher John Hunt, who urged me to present my political Universalism in an authoritative work on a coming World State and whose penetrating, perspicacious vision has again seen the way forward. And I am again grateful to my PA Ingrid Kirk, who has again kept up with my gruelling pace and the vastness of this project and whose research has helped me assemble the data in the appendices.

Prologue

The Need for a World State

A World State is "a state comprising the whole world; a state possessing world-power" (*Shorter Oxford English Dictionary*). There has never been such a state, and although there have been attempts to create one we are used to nation-states and so a state comprising the whole world seems difficult to imagine. Yet our television cameras take us to the United Nations and show us the representatives of all nations in the UN General Assembly.

A Democratic World State and its Early Supporters

A democratic World State's lower house will resemble the UN General Assembly. It will be a Parliamentary Assembly representing all nations like the UN General Assembly, and indeed will possibly initially meet in the great hall of the UN General Assembly.

However, unlike the UN General Assembly it will have a partly-federal, partly-supranational structure that will allow nation-states to be internally independent. Through its federal power it will impose disarmament; abolish war, famine, disease and poverty; and govern the world in accordance with internationalist thinking and principles. It will run the world for the benefit of humankind and will bring peace and prosperity to all.

This book is about a State that will cover the whole world and exercise world-power. The two atomic bombs dropped on Hiroshima and Nagasaki in Japan in 1945 shocked and appalled the world, and many of the world's leaders and prominent men called for such a democratic World-State.

President Harry S. Truman was among the first, in 1945:

> It will be just as easy for nations to get along in a republic of the world as it is for you to get along in the republic of the United States. When Kansas and Colorado have a quarrel over the water in the Arkansas River, they don't call out the National Guard in

> each state and declare war over it. They bring a suit in the Supreme Court of the United States and abide by the decision. There isn't a reason in the world why we can't do that internationally.
> Dedication of war memorial in Omaha, Nebraska on 5 June 1948

Winston Churchill, Prime Minister of the UK, called for a democratic World State in 1945:

> Unless we establish some form of world government, it will not be possible for us to avert a World War III in the future.

Also:

> Unless some effective world supergovernment for the purpose of preventing war can be set up... the prospects for peace and human progress are dark.... If... it is found possible to build a world organization of irresistible force and inviolable authority for the purpose of securing peace, there are no limits to the blessings which all men enjoy and share.

Albert Einstein, whose scientific papers contributed to the splitting of the atom and therefore the explosion of the atomic bomb, added his voice in 1945:

> There is no salvation for civilization, or even the human race, other than the creation of a world government.

Also:

> A world government with powers adequate to guarantee security is not a remote ideal for the distant future. It is an urgent necessity if our civilization is to survive.

And in 1946:

> A world government must be created which is able to solve

> conflicts between nations by judicial decision. This government must be based on a clear-cut constitution which is approved by the governments and nations and which gives it the sole disposition of offensive weapons.[1]

The philosopher Bertrand Russell spoke in 1946:

> It is entirely clear that there is only one way in which great wars can be permanently prevented, and that is the establishment of an international government with a monopoly of serious armed force.[2]

And:

> A scientific world society cannot be stable unless there is a world government.[3]

Also:

> Our goal should be the creation of a world government.

The Indian leader Mahatma Gandhi was of the same view in 1947:

> I would not like to live in this world if it is not to be one world.[4]

Atomic scientists through a 1948 UN Resolution supported their view:

> The emergency committee of atomic scientists, having explored for two years all means other than world government for making responsible the control of atomic energy [meaning nuclear weapons, really, and by implication, all weapons of mass destruction], has become convinced that no other method than world government can be expected to prove effective, and that the attainment of world government is therefore the most urgent

problem now facing mankind.

In 1955 Russell and Einstein made common cause in their call for world peace in the Russell-Einstein Manifesto:

> We invite this Congress, and through it the scientists of the world and the general public, to subscribe to the following resolution: 'In view of the fact that in any future world war nuclear weapons will certainly be employed, and that such weapons threaten the continued existence of mankind, we urge the governments of the world to realise, and to acknowledge publicly, that their purpose cannot be furthered by a world war, and we urge them, consequently, to find peaceful means for the settlement of all matters of dispute between them.'[5]

Subsequently other prominent people called for a democratic World State.

President Dwight D. Eisenhower added his voice:

> The world no longer has a choice between force and law; if civilization is to survive, it must choose the rule of law.

And:

> We have been warned by the power of modern weapons that peace may be the only climate possible for human life itself.... There must be law, steadily invoked and respected, for without law, the world promises only such meagre justice as the pity of the strong upon the weak.

Jawaharlal Nehru, the first Prime Minister of India, called for the world to unite:

> Either the world will unite or it will perish.

John F. Kennedy called for a world-wide law:

> We must create... world-wide law and law enforcement as we outlaw world-wide war and weapons.

Ronald Reagan echoed Kennedy in his address to the UN General Assembly on 26 September 1983:

> Our goals are the same as those of the UN's founders, who sought to replace a world at war with one where the rule of the law would prevail, where human rights were honoured, where development would blossom, where conflict would give way to freedom from violence.

And more recently Mikhail Gorbachev expressed the same sentiment:

> There is an increasing awareness of the need for some form of global government.

Pope John Paul II also envisaged a World State:

> The international community should support a system of laws to regularise international relations and maintain the peace in the same manner that law governs national order.

In 1946 Einstein saw the need for new thinking to take humankind beyond nationalism to supranationalism:

> A new type of thinking is essential if mankind is to survive and move toward higher levels. The fundamental problems we face cannot be solved at the same level of thinking with which we created them.[6]

New thinking in Europe and America

Europe implemented this new thinking regarding a democratic

World State immediately after the war. Churchill called for a United States of Europe at Zurich University on 19 September 1946:

> We must build a kind of United States of Europe.... We must re-create the European family in a regional structure called, it may be, the United States of Europe, and the first practical step will be to form a Council of Europe.

And from 1946 to 2016 Europe enjoyed 70 years of peace after being riven by wars between nation-states every 30 years or so for two thousand years – through conflicts between the Romans and the Gauls and the Germanic tribes, the Anglo-Saxons, the Normans and the wars of the Middle Ages – and most recently in 1870, 1914 and 1939. Devised by Jean Monnet in conjunction with the Council on Foreign Relations in the early 1920s, first the European Economic Community and the Common Market, then the European Community and most recently the European Union and the Single Market implemented and progressively constructed a European system of governance that brought peace and prosperity to the EU's 510 million out of Europe's 739 million citizens and absorbed 28 member states with another 22 waiting to join, making 50 in all:

> 28 members of the EU: Austria, Belgium, Bulgaria, Croatia, Cyprus, Czech Republic, Denmark, Estonia, Finland, France, Germany, Greece, Hungary, Ireland, Italy, Latvia, Lithuania, Luxembourg, Malta, Netherlands, Poland, Portugal, Romania, Slovakia, Slovenia, Spain, Sweden, the UK (which in March 2017 triggered Article 50 to leave the EU).
>
> 22 states not yet members of the EU: Albania, Andorra, Armenia, Azerbaijan, Belarus, Bosnia and Herzegovina, Georgia, Iceland, Kazakhstan (Kazakhstan's bilateral agreement with the EU secures Kazakhstan's common foreign policy and trade relations with the EU), Kosovo, Liechtenstein, Macedonia, Moldova, Mo-

naco, Montenegro, Norway, Russia, San Marino, Serbia, Switzerland, Turkey, Ukraine.[7]

America also implemented this new thinking in the 1960s. An American-led New World Order called for a world government of free liberal democracies. It was advanced by Nelson Rockefeller, who had called for world federalism in his *The Future of Federalism* (1962), claiming that current events demand a "New World Order", "a federal structure of the free world", and echoed by Richard Nixon in 1967 and by George Bush Sr on 11 September 1990 after the pulling-down of the Berlin Wall and the end of the Cold War ("a New World Order can emerge"), and used secrecy and deception. The New World Order favoured liberal interventionism to overthrow the dictatorships of the Middle East and Asia. It worked to create a world-wide liberal democracy and sought to cover the earth with oil and natural-gas pipelines. These pipelines benefited élitist families who were more interested in making fortunes for themselves than in benefiting humankind, and who were responsible for many local wars. My view of a World State has no truck with these élitist families.[8]

Populism and Nationalism

The rise of populism in Europe and America in 2016 challenged the European and American élitist Establishment, which was entrenched on both sides of the Atlantic. In Europe populism took the form of a revolt against the EU and the flow of refugees from wars in East Asia, the Middle East and North Africa which threatened livelihoods. Populists called for anti-immigrant nationalistic policies and challenged supranationalism. There was a similar revolt against the US Establishment that saw Trump come to power. 'UK First' policies in the UK and 'America First' policies in the US (whose Statue of Liberty symbolised America's welcoming of immigrants) sought to strengthen nation-states' borders with walls and block the free movement of peoples.

European populism spread to the 'France First' policies of the neo-Fascist Front National of Marine Le Pen, the 'Netherlands First' policies of the Party for Freedom of Geert Wilders (who did not win the Dutch election), the 'Italy First' policies of Five Star, the 'Germany First' policies of the Alternative for Germany (AfG) party and the 'Hungary First' policies of the Fidesz party. Populism's roots in Fascism, itself a 'national socialism' (a combination of ultra-nationalism and improving the people's working and social conditions), were pointed out by the Archbishop of Canterbury. The eurozone was divided between rich northern states like Germany and indebted southern states such as Greece, Italy, Portugal and Spain.

Although all the anti-Establishment parties had relatively minor support and it was statistically unlikely that they would take power like Trump, it seemed the EU might collapse before the UK had completed its exit, that there would be no EU from which the UK could exit. A European Golden Age looked as if it might disintegrate into a new Dark Age, and the feeling among supranationalist defenders of the European Union seemed elegiac. As at the end of Camelot, a noble Arthurian world seemed as if it was coming to an end.

Revival of calls for a democratic World State

As a result of this populist and nationalistic revolt against supranationalism, the 20th-century calls for a democratic World State are no longer heard. Today I believe I am the only Western literary author and thinker to continue the tradition of those 20th-century calls. I called for a democratic World State in my acceptance speech when I received the Gusi Peace Prize for Literature in Manila in November 2016.[9] In that speech I pointed out that since 1945 the United Nations has failed to prevent 162 wars[10] and the manufacture of (at the time, autumn 2016) 15,375 nuclear weapons, a total that had fallen to 14,900 in spring 2017 (see Appendix C9):[11]

> In my lifetime I've seen the world go through a miserable period and we could be heading for a *Third* World War. Since 1945 the

> UN has failed to prevent 162 wars – *162 wars* – and the world has accumulated 15,375 nuclear weapons: *15,375 nuclear weapons*. There were none when I was born. In my books I've tried to analyse what's gone wrong, and find solutions. I've concluded that ideally we need a *democratic* World State with the nation-states staying as they are and a partly-federal government that's *strong* enough to prevent wars and control nuclear weapons. The present United Nations lacks overall authority, and nation-states go to war too readily.
>
> The first two atomic bombs left many international figures in shock and calling for such a democratic peace-bringing World State. These included Churchill, Truman, Einstein and Eisenhower. I have the same vision, and so I'm carrying on this call in *my* works.
>
> As I see it, the UN General Assembly could eventually be turned into a lower house of democratically-elected Representatives in a partly-federal government that includes a World Senate, as set out in my work *The World Government*. I see the UN eventually becoming a UF, a United Federation. A *UF*.
>
> Such new thinking could create a world government with enough authority to abolish war, enforce disarmament and alleviate famine, disease and poverty.

However, there were signs of a reawakening regarding the need for some sort of world government. There was now an increasing feeling among many that, with Europe under threat, the noble supranational European idea should be applied to the world, and a revival of calls for a strong central authority could be detected in the international reactions to IS (Islamic State), or Daesh. It was asserted that IS had captured 40 tonnes of nuclear material from Mosul University and was trying to convert it into a 'dirty' bomb that could be delivered by drone and contaminate a Western capital with radioactive material, creating Western refugees.[12] President Obama was so worried about this prospect that he summoned 50 Western leaders to a conference in Washington from 31 March to 1 April 2016, and asked them what they would do if a drone-borne dirty-bomb spread nuclear material on their territory.[13] IS was defeated in Mosul in July 2017.

Threat of a Third World War

There was talk of the world's being on the verge of a Third World War. It looked as if a proxy Third World War had already broken out in the Middle East, with the superpowers on opposite sides and fighting each other through intermediaries. If a new front opened with a Russian invasion of the Baltic states of Estonia, Latvia and Lithuania then there would be a World War on two fronts – a Baltic front as well as a Middle-Eastern front – and technically the Third World War, a world war on more than one front, would have broken out. The retreat of European states into the nation-statehood of the past brought no solutions to the world's problems, and a democratic World State, a State covering the whole world and exercising world-power, is much needed today.

In each region of the world humankind lives under the threat of war and annihilation, and the lives of many are blighted by famine, disease and poverty, especially in parts of Africa, Asia and South America.

Dream of a strong supranational authority

There seems to be a recognition that there should be a stronger central authority than the UN so that wars can be stopped, including the interventionist wars involving pipelines in Afghanistan (the Trans-Afghan Pipeline from the Turkmen Dauletabad fields through Afghanistan to Multan in Pakistan and then India); in Iraq (the Kirkuk–Haifa pipeline); and in Syria (the Qatar–Jordan–Syria–Turkey pipeline and the Iran–Syria pipeline).

Under a stronger central authority full nuclear disarmament can happen, and there can be global drives on famine, disease, poverty and global warming to benefit the lives of all humankind. To achieve this there must be supranational planning, and so the UN General Assembly needs to be turned into the lower house of a World State with democratically-elected representatives. Supranationalist supporters of Europe who are bruised by the populist movement's successes may now look beyond Europe to the world itself and throw their weight behind a movement that can bring all 193 nation-states under one global governance with democratically-elected representatives.

An objective study of history's civilizations shows that 'sovereign' nation-states are competitive and self-interested, and that their obsession with borders and walls inevitably leads to war as wars begin out of fear. Einstein understood this:

> As long as there are sovereign nations possessing great power, war is inevitable.

And:

> With all my heart I believe that the world's present system of sovereign nations can only lead to barbarism, war and inhumanity, and that only World law can assure progress towards a civilized peaceful community.

Dr Sarvepalli Radhakrishnan, the second President of India, grasped that some sovereignty must be surrendered to achieve a World State:

> There will be one central authority to which the instruments of coercion will be surrendered and a fraction of the sovereignty of independent nation-states will have to be given up for the security of the whole world.

Jan Tinbergen, Nobel Laureate in Economic Sciences, saw the need for a World State:

> Mankind's problems can no longer be solved by national governments. What is needed is a world government.

The next few years may see the beginning of a general disillusionment with nation-states as Trump's ban on immigrants is seen to be unconstitutional, reactionary and not conducive to economic growth while Brexit nation-statism is seen to lead to a lowering of living standards. It may become very evident that the solutions to the world's problems of wars, disarmament, famine, disease, poverty and global warming can be found through a co-operative democratic World State rather than economic self-interest, protectionism and isolationism.

Political Universalism

My championing of a World State came out of my philosophy. In *The New Philosophy of Universalism* I set out Universalism, which sees the universe and humankind as a unity in terms of several disciplines. I maintain that history should be about the history of humankind as a whole and all civilizations; that philosophy should be about humankind's place in the universe; that literature should be about the fundamental theme of world literature, which I stated in *A New Philosophy of Literature*; and that international politics and statecraft should be about humankind as a political unity – in other words, a democratic World State. It was appropriate that, to show that a World State can be created, when chairing the World Philosophical Forum's Constitutional Convention in 2015 I brought in a World State, the Universal State of the Earth.[14]

Political Universalism holds that all humankind can be organised under a World State and that this is the best structure for solving the world's problems, which have not been solved by nation-states and the UN. The UN is 'inter-national', and hosts meetings of nation-states, some of which have vetoes, and it has no supranational power to impose an abolition of war and an enforcement of disarmament. Political Universalism sees a stronger authority running the world. The League of Nations was seen to have failed when the Second World War broke out, and its replacement the United Nations may now be seen to have failed as the war in Syria has lasted longer than the First and Second World Wars and seems to have no end in sight; and as according to many a Third World War has already begun. Political Universalism sees the UN as being replaced by a 'UF', a United Federation of the World.

Despite populist nationalism, political Universalism has our world-wide lifestyle on its side. Air travel, satellite television and instant communications via the internet have all brought humankind together. Globalisation – the expansion of global linkages, the organisation of social life and trade on a global scale and the growth of a global consciousness – has spread and integrated different countries' ideas, values, norms, behaviour and ways of life. The way the world is linked is Universalist, and our globalised way of life, with goods coming from China and all parts of the world, lends itself to a Universalist political structure.

In short, the time of the World State is approaching and the concept and model of the World State can be expected to receive increasingly serious attention in the next two decades. Hence this objective study.

Surprisingly there has been no accessible study of the concept of a World State until my pioneering (and therefore necessarily tentative) book *The World Government* (2010). This current book describes the evolution of the World State, the longings for it and attempts to impose it by force, and the nation-states' failures that have made it possible. It sets out the World State's supranationalist identity; the new structure it requires which goes beyond the structures of the UN and regional unions; and its ideal form, supranationalist structure and agenda. It seeks to be sufficiently comprehensive and authoritative to last for several decades while a coming World State can be formed. This book is therefore a manifesto for a World State, and implementing its principles can unite humankind and bring in a Golden Age of peace and prosperity.

PART ONE

Beyond the Nation-State

Nationalism is an infantile disease. It is the measles of mankind.

Albert Einstein, 1929[1]

1

Transient Forms of Government and the Drift towards a World State

There are many histories of the 193 individual nation-states that are members of the United Nations. There are few histories that show the rise and fall of all civilizations and consider how a World State might emerge. (Toynbee's *A Study of History* and my own *The Rise and Fall of Civilizations* are two of these.) There are no histories that show humankind as a whole drifting in one direction from the primitive to globalisation like a river flowing towards the open sea: humankind advancing from simple family groupings to tribal states, to more complex city-states, to feudal baronial states, to nation-states with national governments to colonial empires and colonies, to confederations and federations, to regional organisations and eventually widening into a World State.

Transient Old Forms of Government

Homo sapiens sapiens emerged from Africa less than 100,000 years ago and probably between 70,000 and 50,000 years ago (after 13 previous species of *Homo* and a previous 9 intermediate forms), and co-existed with Cro-Magnon man who occupied the Dordogne until c.10,000BC.

Tribal states

In Neolithic times (c.10,200–4500/2000BC) there were groups of families, and from at least c.10,000BC the tribe emerged, a loose association of families who were nomadic. They wandered the steppes seeking new pastures for their domesticated animals, and they fought other tribes and conquered their territories. A conquering tribe imposed its leadership on the tribes it subjugated, and the first primitive government was within the tribe.

Subjugated tribes could continue as they were, so long as they acknowledged the victorious tribe's leadership. Tribes therefore exercised loose control over their subjects, and in some tribal states tribes negotiated how they would be governed. At some stage nomads began to settle in villages as farmers.

The Celtic tribes emerged. In the UK there were Celtic tribal states: the Trinovantes, the Catuvellauni and the Iceni (who resisted the Roman occupation under Boudicca).

City-states

Primitive government had become enmeshed in primitive religion, which had expressed itself in shamanism and the painting of animals in dark caves. This can be traced back to c.40,000BC. Tribal leaders encouraged primitive religion as it strengthened their control of their tribes.

A more sophisticated form of government came into being within city-states. Tribes had been brought together round religious buildings as in early Sumer. The Sumerians appeared c.3500BC and by 2500BC built ziggurats, stepped towers surmounted by a temple, man-made mountains from which they practised their religion. Tribes came from far and wide and camped round these religious buildings, and primitive cities were formed that were really enlarged villages. Their tribal leader turned himself into a monarch and ruled by one-man rule.

Over time he became a priest-king who led religious rites that brought rain and guaranteed good crops and harvests. Village councils practised division of labour, and tribal villagers specialised as warriors, farmers, tax collectors and priests who protected their city from attacks and natural disasters. Fields were cultivated and agriculture was settled round the city-states. In Sumerian cities there were arguments as to which city owned the nearby water of the river Tigris and the river Euphrates. Nomads envied the wealth of the new cities and stormed their walls.

The Greek city-states had monarchies ruled by tribal kings.

Over time they developed into military aristocracies and plutocracies, and democracies. There were conflicts between the aristocratic, plutocratic and democratic factions within city-states, and different Greek city-states had different emphases. Athens became a democratic power whereas Sparta remained an aristocratic power, and the Peloponnesian Wars of 431–404BC between Athens and Sparta represented a collision between these two rival forms of government that weakened the Athenian Empire and Greek power.

Rome's city-state also had conflicts between aristocratic, plutocratic and democratic factions. It was referred to as *res publica*, a "public thing", and its legislative Senate was at first drawn from the aristocratic classes, but eventually from all classes of citizens. The unity of the city-state's factions was advertised in letters on Rome's buildings and battle standards: "SPQR", *Senatus Populusque Romanus*, the Senate and the People of Rome. The city-state's executive power was invested in two consuls, and after the end of the Republic it was headed by divine Caesar, who commanded the legions, the military. By the 3rd century AD Italian city-states were heavily taxed by the imperial administration, and many were eventually bankrupted. The Roman State and the Church, brought together under Constantine, were eventually separated in Roman law. The Caesars who ruled the Roman Empire became tyrants and the Roman Empire eventually fell to barbarian Visigoths from the steppes.

Baronial states

Now the baronial states came into existence. After the collapse of the Roman Empire barons became crucial to government. There were uprisings by landless peasants and attacks by invaders from neighbouring lands, and day-to-day living was often dangerous. A feudal system evolved in the Frankish kingdom of the 8th century and spread with the Frankish conquests. It came to France, and the Normans brought the system to England.

Under this system all lands were owned by the king. Feudal lords or barons held lands from the king, for which they paid scutage, a tax to the king. A baron "held lands or property from the sovereign or a powerful overlord" (*Concise Oxford Dictionary*). Barons gave protection in their territory. All had a role in feudal society, and the lord provided safe living conditions. In peacetime landless freemen and small landowners went to the most powerful lord in their neighbourhood and were granted protected shelter. In return their services were required in times of war.

A feudal lord, or baron, had financial, juridical and military sovereignty over his subject's land, and he had power to tax, try and arm his subjects. A subject gave himself and his land to a lord and received food, shelter and protection; and equipment in times of war. In return he tilled the baron's soil, paid taxes and fought his battles. Both vassal and lord were bound by their contractual relationship, and the lord, or baron, was a vassal of the king and an aristocrat.

The medieval and Renaissance baronial states were run by kings and their military aristocrats, the barons or feudal armoured lords – warlords – who provided standing armies for kings. The kings were unable to tax for wars like Roman emperors and could not afford armies. There were strong monarchies in England, France and Spain. Trade brought wealth to cities that could be spent on fortifying walls, and the city-state revived in Italy, the Rhineland and Low Countries.

Nation-states

The nation-state was born in West Europe in the 16th–18th centuries. The concepts of the 'nation' and 'state' were strengthened by the writings of Machiavelli, Bodin and Hobbes, who supported the authority of secular governments against that of the Church. Monarchies became territorial, and kings sought to impose uniformity on their peoples. The English kings fought the Welsh, Scots and Irish to bring them under their sovereign rule. The French kings drove into the Alps, Pyrenees and Rhine valley. The Spanish kings forced Christianity on their Jewish and Moorish subjects. Absolute monarchs made royal decrees that were administered by a class of bookkeepers, letter-writers and analysts, a new bureaucracy.

In the 17th and 18th centuries absolutist monarchies fell. In England the absolutist monarchy became a constitutional monarchy with an executive, legislature and judiciary and eventually an electorate. In France the absolutist monarchy became a republic whose monarch-free structure brought the nation-state to maturity. In America the Constitution opened the way to liberal democracy. In all three countries the idea of the sovereign nation-state was reinforced. Nation-states received their power from their peoples to protect their citizens, guarantee their safety and maintain law and order.

Nation-states have been able to develop societies and economies in which democracies can grow. A state is unified, there is national self-assertion and a constitution is established that gives control over the government. Nation-states tend not to increase their territory and so their trade, industries and capital investment lead to economic prosperity in which a civil and cultural identity becomes nationality. The source of the legitimacy of a nation-state's political system is its nationality. A list of the 193 nation-states is in Appendix C4.

Colonial empires and colonies

Twelve of the European nation-states developed colonial empires whose colonies were a new form of government. The British, French, German, Dutch, Belgian, Italian, Spanish, Portuguese, Danish, Swedish, Russian and Ottoman nation-states all set up colonies and empires in the Americas, Africa, Asia, Oceania and many other parts of the world. These started in the 16th century in Latin America and continued in the 17th century in America and in the 18th and 19th centuries, when India became an empire. These colonial territories were throwbacks to the early Phoenician and Greek colonies and the Roman *coloniae*. In all these colonies, the colonial power pumped money to a colony's leadership and in return transferred its natural resources for use in its own country. The benefits colonies acquired from the arrangement varied, but in some colonies and empires the people lived in poverty and derived little or no benefit from the colonial contract, which merely enriched the few who surrounded the leadership.

The colonialist and imperialist nation-state was nationalist. It asserted its nation-statehood against other nations in imperial competition, and its competing ambitions led to war. While these colonialist and imperialist constitutional monarchies and republics vied for empire, some European nation-states turned totalitarian. The 20th-century totalitarian dictatorships of Stalin and Hitler embodied government by constraint of largely unconsenting peoples. Such dictatorships were copied in smaller states, especially during the Cold War between the USSR and the West.

In the 20th century clashes between nation-states led to the First and Second World Wars, and to the Cold War, and similar clashes may be taking place in our own time. There are fears that collisions in Syria between Russia, Iran and Turkey on the one hand, and Saudi Arabia, Britain, France, the EU, the US, Qatar and Jordan, with Israel in the background, on the other hand may lead to a wider war, and that, having absorbed Georgia, Crimea and East Ukraine, Russia will re-invade Baltic states such as Estonia. There are fears that incompatibility between the ambitions of nation-states may lead to a Third World War just as incompatible claims of city-states ruined ancient Greece.

New Forms of Regional and Global Governance

During the rise of the nation-states new forms of government have emerged: federations, regional organisations and the functional organisations of global governance, all of which, collectively, indicate a drift towards a World State.

Confederations and federations

A confederation (or confederacy or league) is a union of sovereign states for the purpose of common action in relation to other states. It is an organisation that consists of a number of groups that are united in an alliance or league. One of the first confederations in the West was the Hanseatic League, which was formed in the time of the city-states of the Middle Ages and lasted from the 13th to the 17th centuries. Confederations formed during the rise of nation-states, for example the seven United Provinces of the Netherlands from 1581 to 1795 and the US under the Articles of Confederation from 1781 to 1789. For a full list of confederations see Appendix A1.

A federation is a union of partially-self-governing states or regions under a central (federal) government. A federation unites distinct ethnic, cultural and lingual regions under a common government. Federations began with the US states in 1776 and the US Constitution which was drafted in 1787 and ratified in 1788. The US federation was followed by Switzerland in 1848 and Canada in 1867, both of which began as 'confederations' with sovereign provinces (Canada) and cantons (Switzerland) – reflecting the first US *Articles of Confederation and Perpetual Union between the States* (1777), which was replaced by the second US Constitution in 1787–1788 – and became 'federations' when their provinces and cantons lost their sovereign status. Brazil followed in 1889, Australia in 1901 and Austria in 1920. Since then another 20 federations have been formed. The total federations in chronological order of formation are in Appendix A2.

Devolved states are a kind of 'federation in reverse'. In federal systems the powers of the sub-units of states cannot be withdrawn unilaterally by the central federal government. In devolved states the powers delegated from the central government to a subnational, regional or local level may be temporary and are reversible, and can be withdrawn by the central government. Devolution began with Denmark in 1849. Finland followed in 1919 and the United Kingdom in 1922. Now three of the four constituent countries of the United Kingdom (excluding England) have devolved governments. Since 1922 another 31 devolved states have been formed. The total devolved states in chronological order of formation are in Appendix A3.

Regional organisations

In our time the flow of government has widened into regional organisations. Regional organisations foster co-operation and political and economic integration. They have international memberships with boundaries and have unique geography that confines them to continents or geopolitical economic blocs, and they operate in ways that transcend single nation-states.

Regional organisations began with the Commonwealth of Nations in 1931, followed by the Organization of American States in 1948 and the North Atlantic Treaty Organization (NATO) in 1949. The European Union or EU, the regional organisation that most immediately comes to mind, began in an earlier form in 1957.

Competing European nation-states had led to two world wars, and the aim of the EU was to prevent yet another European war by enmeshing Germany, France and the other warring European nation-states within peaceful institutions. Following the Monnet Plan, which was developed in conjunction with the US Council on Foreign Relations and announced on 4 December 1945, Winston Churchill in his speech at the University of Zurich on 19 September 1946 called for "a kind of United States of Europe" and declared that the first step was to form "a Council of Europe".

Amid the chaos of post-war Europe these moves led to a European Economic Community of six members, and now the EU region has its own legal personality and 28 member states (from which the UK has decided to withdraw), with 20 more European nation-states ultimately eligible for membership; potentially 48 member states.[1]

The regional European Union has kept peace in Europe since 1945 along with NATO, and has reunified Eastern and Western Europe following the collapse of the USSR. It is the only union recognised as being a fully supranational union.

A full list of the world's 34 regional organisations that, though not supranational unions like the EU, have policies that will lead to similar integration is as follows:

- the African Union (AU): established in 2001, consisting of all 55 nation-states on the African continent totalling 0.85 billion, formerly the Organisation of African Unity (OAU);
- the Arab League (AL): established in 1945, formerly the League of Arab States, consisting of 8 nation-states in North Africa and Arabia totalling 0.423 billion, set to become an Arab Union;
- the Asia-Pacific Economic Cooperation (APEC): established in 1989, consisting of 21 Pacific Rim member nation-states totalling 2.7 billion, growing into an Asian Economic Community and set to pass into an Asia-Pacific Union;
- the Association of Caribbean States (ACS): established in 1994, consisting of 25 member nation-states and 12 associate members totalling 0.237 billion;
- the Association of Southeast Asian Nations (ASEAN): established in 1967, consisting of 10 nation-states in South-East Asia totalling 0.625 billion;
- the Caribbean Community (CARICOM): established in 1973, having grown out of the Caribbean Free Trade Association (CARIFTA), consisting of 15 Caribbean nation-states and dependencies totalling 0.016 billion, set to become a Caribbean Federation;
- the Central-American Integration System (SICA): established in 1993, consisting of 8 nation-states in Central America totalling 0.51 billion;
- the Collective Security Treaty Organization (CSTO): established in 1992, consisting of 6 post-Soviet nation-states, a military alliance including Russia;
- the Commonwealth of Independent States (CIS): established in 1991, consisting of 9 of the 15 former Soviet republics and 2 associate members totalling 0.282 billion, set to become a Russian Union;
- the Commonwealth of Nations: formerly the British Commonwealth, established in 1931, consisting of 52 nation-states, mostly former British colonies, across all continents, totalling 2.3 billion;

- the Community for Democracy and Rights of Nations (CDRN, also known as the Commonwealth of Unrecognised States): established in 2006, consisting of 4 nation-states in the former Soviet Union;
- the Community of Latin American and Caribbean States (Spanish abbreviation, CELAC): established in 2010, consisting of 33 nation-states in the Americas totalling 0.591 billion, set to become a Latin American Union;
- the Cooperation Council for the Arab States of the Gulf (CCASG): established in 1981, consisting of 6 nation-states in Arabia totalling 0.50 billion;
- the East-African Community (EAC): established in 1967 and again in 2000, consisting of 6 nation-states in East Africa totalling 0.169 billion, a proposed political Union;
- the Economic Cooperation Organization (ECO): established in Tehran in 1985, consisting of 10 nation-states totalling 0.463 billion;
- the Eurasian Economic Union (EAEU): established in 2015, consisting of 5 nation-states in Northern Eurasia including Russia totalling 0.183 billion;
- the European Union (EU): established in 1993, having grown out of the European Community (EC), whose roots were in the European Economic Community (EEC) and before that the European Coal and Steel Community (ECSC), consisting of 28 member nation-states totalling 0.510 billion and 20 potential members, the only fully supranational Union in the world with a legal personality that overrides its 28 member nation-states;
- the European Economic Area (EEA): established in 1994, consisting of 28 European nation-states totalling 0.510 billion;
- the Inter-Parliamentary Union (IPU): established in 1889, consisting of the national parliaments of 170 nation-states;
- Mercosur or Mercosul (Southern Common Market): established in 1991, consisting of 4 nation-states (Venezuela was suspended in 2016) and 6 associate members, totalling 0.288 billion in 2011;

- the North American Free Trade Agreement (NAFTA): established in 1994, consisting of the US, Canada and Mexico totalling 0.478 billion, set to become a North American Union (NAU), and also in conjunction with 31 additional Western nation-states a Free Trade Area of the Americas (FTAA), which also incorporated the Central American Free Trade Agreement (CAFTA) and the Latin America Free Trade Association (LAFTA, created in 1960 and replaced in 1980 by the Latin American Integration Association, LAIA), all opposed by President Trump;
- the North Atlantic Treaty Organization (NATO): established in 1949, a regional military alliance consisting of 28 member nation-states across North America and Europe totalling 0.88 billion;
- the Organization of American States (OAS): established in 1948, consisting of the 35 nation-states of the Americas totalling 0.910 billion;
- the Organization of Ibero-American States (Spanish abbreviation, OEI): established in 1949, consisting of 22 Portuguese- and Spanish-speaking nation-states totalling 0.713 billion;
- the Organization of Islamic Cooperation (OIC): established in 1969, consisting of 57 member nation-states across the Muslim world totalling 1.6 billion;
- the Organization of the Petroleum Exporting Countries (OPEC): established in Baghdad in 1960, consisting of 13 nation-states totalling 0.451 billion;
- the Pacific Islands Forum (PIF): formerly the South Pacific Forum (SPF), established in 1999, consisting of 18 nation-states in the Pacific Ocean totalling 0.040 billion, set to become a Pacific Union;
- the Shanghai Cooperation Organisation (SCO): established in 2001, consisting of 6 Eurasian nation-states including China and Russia totalling 1.57 billion;
- the South Asian Association for Regional Cooperation (SAARC): established in 1985, consisting of 8 nation-states in South Asia totalling 1.7 billion;

- the South Asian Free Trade Area (SAFTA): established in 2006, consisting of 8 South Asian nation-states including India totalling 1.8 billion in 2011, growing into an Asian Economic Community (AEC) and set to pass into an Asia-Pacific Union;
- the Trans-Pacific Partnership (TPP): established in 2016, consisting of 12 nation-states including the US, which withdrew on 23 January 2017;
- the Turkic Council (TurkKon): established in 2009, consisting of 4 nation-states in the Turkic countries, including Turkey;
- the Union of South American Nations (USAN or UNASUR): formerly the South American Community of Nations, established in 2008, having replaced the South American Community of Nations (created in 2004), consisting of 12 South American nation-states totalling 0.418 billion and set to pass into an American Union; and
- the Union State: established in 1996, consisting of Belarus and Russia totalling 0.156 billion.

The regional organisations have extended the federal principle throughout North America, Latin America, Europe, Africa and Asia. The many regional trade groupings and unions await federal linkage into a global network.

Global governance

A further widening of government towards a new stage, partial global governance, has been a consequence of superpowerdom. There will be no complete system of global governance of the military, executive, legislature or judiciary covering the entire earth until there is a World State. There are now institutions, unions, coalitions and agreements between nation-states which act in a partially supranational way.

Following the fall of the Berlin Wall in 1989 and the collapse of the USSR (one of the two world powers) in 1991, the US was left as the world's only remaining superpower in a partially globalised humankind nurtured by functional organisations:

- some 20 UN organisations affiliated to the UN's Economic and Social Council such as
    - the World Health Organization;
    - UNESCO;
    - the International Labour Organization;
    - the International Telecommunications Union; and
    - the World Trade Organization
- the World Bank;
- the IMF (International Monetary Fund, see Appendix E7 for members);
- the International Criminal Court (and treaty signed by 139 nation-states) and the International Court of Justice;
- NATO;
- Interpol (an international police force);
- secretive agencies such as
    - the Round Table;
    - the Royal Institute of International Affairs;
    - the Council on Foreign Relations;
    - the Bilderberg Group;
    - the Club of Rome; and
    - the Trilateral Commission
- the meetings of ministers:
    - G6 nations (United Kingdom, France, Germany, Italy, Spain and Poland), interior ministers of EU nation-states with the largest populations;
    - G7 nations (United Kingdom, France, Germany, Italy, Japan, US and Canada), the 7 nation-states with the highest gross domestic products which have 64 per cent of the net global wealth of $263 trillion;
    - G4 nations (Brazil, Germany, India and Japan), nation-states seeking permanent seats at the UN, heads of government or heads of state;
    - G8 nations (the G7 nations and Russia), the 8 most highly-industrialised economies in democracies, heads of government or heads of state; and
    - G20 (the G8 nations and Argentina, Australia, Brazil,

China, India, Indonesia, Republic of Korea, Mexico, Saudi Arabia, South Africa, Turkey and the EU), 20 major economies, heads of government or heads of state, finance ministers and governors of central banks
- multi-national (or trans-national or trans-border) corporations, including those dealing with digital communications and mass-media distribution such as the internet and satellite television.

These meetings of ministers collectively formed a network of global governance.

In this partially globalised world the US was dominant until 2016. Globalised consumers followed American films, bought American clothes and aspired to the American way of life, the American dream in which any immigrant had a chance to succeed. After 1991 there were not many parts of the world which did not look to America as a model for the way of life they admired.

President Trump's clamp-down on immigration has changed this perception. Now there are parts of the world – notably within the more primitive tribal regions of Islam – which actively dissent from having anything to do with the American way of life. Russia under Putin has sought to restore Russia's pre-1991 superpowerdom, and Russian bombing in Syria added to the columns of refugees trudging through Europe and causing former Eastern-European countries in the Schengen Area to seal their borders to migrants. Russia has successfully sown division within the EU.

All this has encouraged populism: politicians in European nation-states such as the UK, France, Germany, Italy and Holland claiming to speak for their people who (they assert) are alarmed by immigrants taking jobs and benefits in European nation-states and filling their schools and hospitals.

In our time there have also been splinter trends as emerging peoples hail their newly-fledged nation-states and resent being "regionalised" into large blocs or globalised. When Yugoslavia fragmented, nationalism swept through the Balkans and was behind wars involving Serbia, Bosnia and Kosovo. The Taliban are such a splinter group, fighting to regain control of Afghanistan, expel US puppets and restore Sharia law. Such nationalistic roots have poured into the current of history and slowed its flow.

Such nationalistic groups may find they do not succeed in resisting wider grouping and global governance. It can be expected that in due course there will be a Middle-Eastern Union, a region that will subsume Islamic nation-states. The populism of Trump's US and the UK's Brexit may come to be seen as a backward phenomenon that will be overtaken by the onward flow of history just as the backwash of a tributary into an estuary is swept out towards the open sea.

None of the first three forms of government – the tribal state, the city-state and the baronial state – would endure. Each proved to be transient and ephemeral, and the nation-states, colonies and regions are no exception.

World State

A World State, a "state comprising the whole world", is the next form of government. The idea behind it is that all nation-states will become states within one World State. It will be a United States of the World. Each nation-state will be internally independent like the 50 American states, but all 193 nation-states will be under federal rule which will abolish war and control nuclear weapons. The nation-state is no more of an enduring form than the tribal state, city-state or baronial state, and, like the federations and regional organisations, the World State will replace the nation-state as the most widely followed form of government.

The constructionist school of international relations theory sees the formation of a World State as inevitable. It sees international relations as being socially constructed and transformed by social practice, not governed by human nature which promotes national self-interest that leads to war. The German social constructionist Alexander Wendt has argued[2] (using Aristotelian and Hegelian insights) that a World State with a global monopoly on the legitimate use of force is "inevitable". Wendt traces the development of world order from anarchic states to a World State, broadly the course of this chapter. He argues that the "logic of anarchy" contains within it the seeds of transformation towards a "global monopoly on the legitimate use of organised violence – a World State".[3] Wendt sees nation-states as being at the mercy of weapons of mass destruction (destructive technology) and, following Kant, he sees the development of a World State as teleological: purposive.

The formation of a World State would protect nation-states from nuclear weapons and serve as "a universal security community" whose members resolve conflict peacefully rather than through the use of force. A World State would be a "universal collective security" system that would protect each member. A "universal supranational authority" could make binding authoritative decisions about the collective use of force.[4]

Wendt sees a World State as taking various forms. It would collectivise organised violence but need not collectivise culture, economy or local politics on a global scale. It would require a structure that "can command and enforce a collective response to threat", but it need not abolish national armies, or require a single UN army. It would require a procedure for making binding choices, but "it would not even require a world 'government', if by this we mean a unitary body with one leader whose decisions are final".[5]

Government, then, evolves and develops from primitive forms to a global model which may become a World State, which to some is inevitable.

Three schools of international relations theory doubt whether world government is a good thing:

- Neo-realists hold that world government is not feasible and is impractical; that a world government would pursue its own interests at the expense of the interests and freedom of states, and that an atomistic order of sovereign states is better.[6]

- 'International society' theorists hold that world government is unnecessary as sovereign states can relate to each other in a non-lawless way.[7]
- Liberal internationalists combat global ills such as poverty, denial of human rights, threat of war, environmental degradation and lack of democratic accountability without calling for world government. They have seen humanity as a common, cosmopolitan moral community of free and equal persons and have not seen a World State as being part of a liberal ideal world order.[8] Communitarian liberals have seen centralised world government as a threat to social pluralism.[9] Many liberals have seen a world government as politically tyrannical and inefficient, homogeneous (in obliterating distinct cultures and communities) and soulless, and have called for a global politics of non-domination.

Supporters of world government can counter these arguments. Constructivists like Wendt do think world government may be a good thing. In my view, it all depends on who is doing the governing. If a World State is organised by oligarchs for their own financial benefit, dictatorially, so they can hijack and profit from selling the earth's natural resources, notably its oil and natural gas, then world government is a bad thing. On the other hand, if a World State is organised altruistically and philanthropically for humankind's benefit, it may be a good thing. The process in itself is neutral, and whether it is good or bad depends on who is running the world government, and the motivation and integrity of those who serve it.

To prevent a World State from falling into the wrong hands, into the hands of bad, autocratic and dictatorial incumbents, the structure of the World State should strengthen the regions at the expense of the rulers. In other words, a World State must be democratic with built-in safety measures to prevent abuse of power.

History has taken humankind from primitive tribal groups to federations, complex regional organisations, and a World State is inevitably and inexorably ahead – just as the open sea is ahead of the widening river. However, as I have shown in *The Rise and Fall of Civilizations*[10] the world's civilizations since 3000BC pass through similar stages, and a World State will only last for a while. In due course it will disintegrate back into the civilizations that have flowed into it. It would be more accurate to see the river of history as flowing into a great lake, from which it will emerge the other side; just as the Nile flows from Tanzania into Lake Victoria through an anabranch river, the Bahr el Zeraf, and emerges the other side near Jinja, Uganda.

The trend, the flow, is inexorably in the direction of a World State, and world government. We have reached a point where globalisation is so strong a force that it would not be surprising if a World State were suddenly declared. Populism, the backward-looking revival of nation-states and their competitive national self-assertion, is like the transient and illusory 'branchings-off' of tributaries that actually flow into a steadily gliding river and widening estuary before being absorbed into a World State whose unification of all humankind will one day seem as obvious and all-embracing as the unification of all the individual seas that encompass our globe.

2

Longings for a World State

It is only relatively recently that it has been possible to think of the governance of the *whole* world. Past empires governed the *known* world.

Pre-Renaissance Longings to Rule the Known World

The Macedonian Empire of Alexander the Great controlled regions from the Balkans to India, which at that time was considered to be the end of the world. The Roman Empire ruled the world that was known. The Ch'in (now written Qin), Han and Tang dynasties of the Chinese Empire conquered the known world of the Chinese civilization. The Mongol Empire at its greatest extent in 1279 extended from the Danube to the Sea of Japan and from the Arctic to Cambodia. It covered 22 million square kilometres, a fifth of the earth's total land area, and ruled a population of over a 100 million. The Inca Empire encompassed virtually all of the world known to the Incans, but was confined to South America. The British Empire conquered a quarter of the world's land surface and a third of the world's population, and of all the empires of the past was the nearest the world has come to achieving total political unification.

All these empires ruled massive parts of the world in their different times. No complete world government has ever existed. Before the era of US superpowerdom the British came nearest to realising the ideal of world government. Within the limited knowledge and relatively near horizons of past civilizations humans longed for perpetual peace and yearned for a government, citizenship and State that would encircle the whole of the known world.

The ancient world

Longings for a World State can be found in ancient Egyptian

thought. Such longings were present in the world of the ancient Egyptians. From at least c.2600BC the Pharaoh embodied the sun and ruled where the sun shone, "all that the sun encircles"[1] (all the known world), as Ra, the sun-god. Hence the two sons of Khufu, who built the Great Pyramid, were named after Ra: Djedefra (also written Djedefre) and Khafra (also written Khafre or Chephren). In the Pharaonic sun-cult the Pharaoh as the sun-god ruled the known world.

Such longings can be found in ancient Mesopotamian thought. Sargon of Akkad, who conquered the Sumerian city-states in the 24th and 23rd centuries BC, ruled "all from the sunrise to the sunset", the whole known world. When revolts broke out during the last years of his rule, the *Chronicle of Early Kings* reports that "from the rising of the sun unto the setting of the sun they opposed him and gave him no rest".[2]

Longings for a World State were also present in ancient Indian thought. In the earliest sacred literature in India, in *Rig Veda*, the oldest of the four Vedas (c.1500–1200BC), *rta*, unity and cosmic order, is universal.[3]

Vedic man knew the oneness of the universe in all its levels, including the social level. This oneness extended to all the people on earth, who could open to the cosmic order's "universal Light", which was reflected in universal harmony. The Vedic notion of the One illumining all humankind passed into later Brahmanism (c.600BC), the *Upanisads* (5th century BC) and the *Bhagavadgita* (5th or 3rd centuries BC, or 1st and 2nd centuries AD). In this last work Arjuna tells Krishna that he is reluctant to fight in the battle of Kurukshetra as he does not want to kill his kinsmen who may be absorbed in Brahman and may thus be illumined. Krishna explains that he must fight and can still be illumined, but it is clear that universal peace is a better reflection of the oneness of the cosmic order than war, as its follower Mahatma Gandhi recognised by proclaiming non-violence.

Longings for a World State pervade ancient Chinese thought. The Chinese Emperor ruled "all under Heaven", *Ti'en-hsia*,[4] the whole known world. In many Chinese texts the Emperor was mediator between Heaven, *T'ien*, the Earth and Man, all of which are within cosmic unity. The *I Ching* reflects the oneness of Heaven, Earth and Man in the Chou (or Zhou) dynasty (from 1046 to 221BC), which included Confucius and Lao-Tze. In Confucian and Taoist philosophy, Heaven and Earth denote the Great Whole of the universe, and the world of Man denotes the Great Whole of man's society.[5] The Great Whole is the One, and as the universe within the cosmic order of Heaven, Earth and Man is one, all known mankind is one.

The illumined man was mediator between Heaven and Earth. To Confucius, "Without knowing the Mandate of Heaven, one cannot become a superior man."[6] Mo-Tzu (or Mozi, 5th century BC) taught "universal love" and denounced war, arguing that it is the will of Heaven that men should love universally. By now the cosmic order involved Heaven, Earth and all Man, not just Chinese man. "All under Heaven" was a Great Unity, or *da yi tong*, literally "large scale unification". In 113BC the Han dynasty erected an altar of the Great Unity.[7]

Longings for a World State can be found in Graeco-Roman thought. Socrates said in the 5th century BC, according to Plutarch, "I am a citizen, not of Athens, or Greece, but of the world."[8] Socrates saw humankind as one, to which he belonged. Plato's *Republic*, which featured Socrates, focused on a utopian city in a time of city-states that by implication has universal applications, but the "Republic" described is an ideal city-state rather than a World State. Plato's philosopher-king ruled a city-state. In contrast, the Greek Stoic school founded in Athens by Zeno of Citium in the early 3rd century BC saw the universe as a whole in which all individual persons, natural phenomena and objects are parts, and preached one monarch over all humankind. The Greek historian Polybius, writing in the 2nd century BC in *Histories*, book 1, saw Rome's achievement of one government over the Mediterranean world during the period 264–146BC as the "marvellous" achievement of "Fortune".

By the time of Roman Stoic thought, the world was seen as a unity, one great city. Man as a world citizen must live according to the unity and orderly arrangement of Nature and the world design, and with a sense of the universal brotherhood of mankind. The Graeco-Roman Stoics were close to supporting the idea of a world government. Their thinking rubbed off on St Augustine, whose *De Civitate Dei* or *City of God*, 415–420, saw the world as filled with Christian souls who all had equality before God.

Different civilizations in the ancient world produced thinking that reflected the concept of unity. It was felt that as the universe was regarded as a unity in Eastern thought, this unity should be expressed in a political form – a view that has also shaped the thinking of Universalism. In Western thought, Stoic ideas about the oneness of the universe inspired medieval Christian proposals for a global political authority.

Dante's Universal Monarch

The Roman Empire was a government of the known world, and the *Pax Romana*'s world government survived as an ideal into the Middle Ages. In the 14th century the Italian poet and philosopher Dante expounded the Christian ideal of human unity and its expression in a world governed by a universal monarch or Emperor. In *Convivio (The Banquet,* 1304), Dante argued that wars and their causes would be eliminated if "the whole Earth and all that humans can possess be a monarchy, that is one government under one ruler. Because he possesses everything, the ruler would not desire to possess anything further, and thus, he would hold kings contentedly within the borders of their kingdoms, and keep peace among them".[9]

Dante had been offered hospitality in his exile by the ruler of Verona, Can Grande della Scala, and he became his guest in 1315–1316. The new Holy Roman Emperor, Henry VII, had conferred the title Imperial Vicar on Can Grande. Pope John XXII challenged this title. Dante was asked to write in defence of Can Grande and prove to the clergy of Verona that the Pope's decree was without authority. Dante was a persecuted White Guelf seeking aid from the Ghibelline Can Grande, and he supported the Emperor. Their opponents, the Black Guelfs, supported the

Papacy, and the Popes reciprocally supported the Black Guelfs and opposed the White Guelfs.

It is likely that Dante wrote *De Monarchia (On Monarchy,* sometimes translated as *On World Government)* in 1317–1318, when he was starting *Paradiso*. We know this because a reference to *Paradiso*, recently confirmed as being authentic,[10] spoke of monarchy as "the greatest gift conferred by God on human nature: *sicut in Paradiso Comedie iam dixi* ('as I have already said in the *Commedia Paradiso*')".

In *De Monarchia* Dante lamented the fall of the *Pax Romana*:

> But what has been the contention of the world since that day the seamless robe [of *Pax Romana*] first suffered mutilation by the claws of avarice.... Nor dost thou heal thy affection by the sweetness of divine persuasion, when the voice of the Holy Spirit breathes upon thee, 'Behold, how good and how pleasant it is for brethren to dwell together in unity.'
>
> (*De Monarchia*, 16:1)

Dante argued for a universal Emperor whose temporal power was distinct from the Pope's religious power, and he envisaged that Pope and Emperor would forge a co-operative rather than a competitive relationship. At one level he was undoubtedly thinking of the Holy Roman Emperor Henry VII and the Pope John XXII, but he probably hoped that Can Grande della Scala, ruler of Verona, would act as universal Emperor. He sent him batches of cantos from his *Paradiso* after moving to Ravenna in 1319 until his death in 1321, in the hope that Can Grande would take on the role of universal Emperor.

De Monarchia was a political treatise affirming universal monarchy. Drawing on Aristotle, Dante argued that human unity stems from a shared effort to develop humankind's intellectual potential. Peace is vital to realise this end, and cannot be maintained if humanity is divided. Just as "every kingdom divided against itself shall be laid waste", since humankind shares one goal, "there must therefore be one person who directs and rules mankind, and he is properly called 'Monarch' or 'Emperor'. And thus it is apparent that the well-being of the world requires that there be monarchy or empire."

When conflicts arise between two rulers who are equals, "there must be a third party of wider jurisdiction who rules over both of them by right" (i.e. Can Grande). A universal monarch is necessary as "a first and supreme judge, whose judgment resolves all disputes either directly or indirectly". In the absence of a universal monarch, humankind is "transformed into a many-headed beast", striving after "conflicting things". Humankind ordered under a universal monarch "will most closely resemble God, by mirroring the principle of oneness or unity of which he is the supreme example". The Roman Empire was "a part of God's providential plan for humanity".[11]

By "monarchy", Dante does not merely mean the rule of a single individual, the Holy Roman Emperor, although he did believe that legitimate monarchy, as opposed to tyranny, is the most perfect form of government. He is referring to the structure of the international system. Universal government is necessary because it is the way to universal peace, the only way humankind can attain its end or purpose – which is the realisation of "possible intellect". Dante insists that the ideal political order is a universal polity. The universality of a universal monarch requires that he should bring in universal law, which would guarantee freedom as the perfect condition of humankind.

We shall see that Dante's reasoning is similar to Kant's and to Francis Fukuyama's view that liberal democracy satisfies all aspects of human nature and is therefore the Hegelian end of history (see pp.58, 61). The Holy Roman Empire thus guarantees the highest level of human freedom that is possible. Dante argues from first principles, but his conclusions have much in common with Kant's Enlightenment thinking.[12]

Dante urges that the Holy Roman Emperor should be universally accepted as the temporal sovereign authority who could unite the world in peace under one rule of law. Several passages in *De Monarchia* reinforce the message that humankind needs unity and peace:

> Since individual men find that they grow in prudence and wisdom when they can sit quietly, it is evident that mankind, too, is most free and easy to carry on its work when it enjoys the quiet and tranquillity of peace. (1:4.)
>
> Justice has greatest power under a unitary government; therefore the best order of the world demands world government. (1:11.)
>
> The human race is at its best when most free. (1:12.)
>
> All concord depends on a unity of wills; the best state of mankind is a kind of concord, for as a man is in excellent health when he enjoys concord in soul and body, and similarly a family, city or state, so is mankind as a whole. Therefore, the well-being of mankind depends on the unity of its wills. (1:15.)
>
> Behold, how good and pleasant it is for brethren to dwell together in unity. (1:16.)[13]

These sentiments are reflected by Dante's contemporaries Marsilius of Padua, who completed *Defensor Pacis* (*The Defender of Peace*) in 1324, three years after Dante died, and by Petrarch, who met Dante in 1310:

> The fruits of peace or tranquillity, then, are the greatest goods, as we have said, while those of its opposite, strife, are unbearable evils. Hence we ought to wish for peace, to seek it if we do not already have it, to conserve it once it is attained, and to repel with all our strength the strife which is opposed to it. To this end individual brethren, and in even greater degree groups and communities, are obliged to help one another, both from the feeling of heavenly love and from the bond or law of human society.
>
> Marsilius of Padua, *The Defender of Peace* (1:1:4)

> The authority to make or establish the laws, and to give a command with the guard to their observance, belongs only to the whole body of the citizens or to the weightier part thereof as efficient cause, or else to the person or persons to whom the aforesaid whole has granted this authority.
>
> Marsilius of Padua, *The Defender of Peace* (1:13:8)[14]

> Just as the love of the people is gained more easily by mercy and generosity than by any other quality, so, conversely, nothing is more guaranteed to provoke a people's hatred than cruelty and greed.
>
> Petrarch, 'How a Ruler Ought to Govern His State'

> My song, be humble, for you are addressed to haughty folk, ever hostile to the truth. Speak then to those few high hearts that love virtue. Say to them: "Who gives me strength to speak, as I go crying: 'Peace! Peace! Peace!'"
>
> Petrarch, 'My Italy'[15]

In the early 14th century, then, there was a great longing for unity and peace within the known world, and there were clear views as to how this could be achieved.

Post-Renaissance Longings for a Perfect Society and Federations

From the 16th to the 18th centuries the focus was on creating a perfect society rather than a World State.

Sir Thomas More based his *Utopia* on the works of Plato. He modelled *Utopia* on the island of Atlantis (its topography, its plain, harbours, mountains, baths, temples, army, government, population, products and bull-sacrifice) which Plato described in *Critias*. More took the idea of an ideal state from Plato's *Republic*, and was also indebted to Plato's *Timaeus* and *Laws*. He followed Plato in borrowing his communism, contempt for gold and championing of equality in training and pursuits between men and women.

However, More's purpose was not to portray an ideal commonwealth, as Plato had done, but to expose the social and political evils of England satirically. In this aim he was close to Erasmus's *In Praise of Folly* (also translated as *Praise of Folly* or *The Praise of Folly*), and he borrowed techniques from Plutarch's *Instituta Laconica* and from Tacitus' *Germania*. Tacitus described the manners and customs of uncivilized Germans and while doing so by implication satirised the evils of Roman life in his own time.

Utopia was probably suggested by a narrative of the voyages of Vespucci, which was printed in 1507. Its subject is the search for the best possible form of government, the perfect society. In Antwerp More meets a traveller, Raphael Hythloday, who has discovered the "island of Utopia", "Nowhere land". Its best possible form of government is one that a world government would be proud of. Its communism offers equality to all, there is a universal system of education for men and women, and there is toleration of religion. More anticipates Sir Francis Bacon's *New Atlantis*, Defoe's *Robinson Crusoe* and Swift's *Gulliver's Travels* in using a remote island – Swift used Lilliput – to present a society that by implication satirises English society.

These Utopian works held up a representation of a perfect society by which the author's own imperfect society could be judged. They were by definition about specific places with good government, and did not advocate a universal World State. No hint of world government can therefore be found in More's *Utopia*, or in Bacon's *New Atlantis*, which was set in the New World. However, it may be implied that the principles of the ideal states were to be followed by states throughout the world.

The Spanish Renaissance Roman Catholic philosopher, theologian and jurist, Francisco de Vitoria, writing after Bacon – he died in 1546 – founded the philosophical School of Salamanca and was the father of international law. He was ahead of his time and conceived of a *res publica totius orbis*, "a republic of the whole world": a World State. He is now regarded as the founder of global political philosophy.

The Dutch jurist Hugo Grotius, living in the turmoil of warfare during the Eighty and Thirty Years' Wars, was concerned to resolve international conflicts. Grotius came up with the idea of having a system of international law. After the Peace of Westphalia (1648), which concluded the exhausting Thirty Years' War, the system of sovereign states was strengthened as states pledged not to interfere in each others' affairs. To Grotius the aim was to create a perfect society within a sovereign nation-state. Uniting humankind under one monarch or Emperor became a remoter possibility.

Soon afterwards, the English philosopher Thomas Hobbes anticipated the development of international law and collective security organisations such as the League of Nations and the UN: "Leagues between Common-wealths, over whom there is no humane Power established, to keep them all in awe, are not onely lawfull [because they are allowed by the commonwealth], but also profitable for the time they last."[16] Hobbes argued that a world government or World State is unnecessary, but held that a lawful interstate order is both possible and desirable.

Interstate links between sovereign nation-states led to the development of the concept of a federation. Charles-Irénée Castel, Abbé de Saint-Pierre, an inspirer of Rousseau and Kant, held in *Project for Making Peace Perpetual in Europe (Extrait du projet de paix perpétuelle,* 1713) that Europe's princes should form a federation of states by social contract. The contracting sovereigns would form a perpetual alliance and establish a permanent Diet or Congress. This would adjudicate all conflicts between the contracting princes. The decisions of the federation would be enforced by armed action.[17] In other words, the European princes would surrender their sovereign rights to make war or peace to a superior, federal body that would guarantee their protection. In the work of Abbé de Saint-Pierre the concept of a federation of a number of nation-states pointed the way forward towards a World State.

Abbé de Saint-Pierre's federal idea was a serious attempt to prevent war by international law. Jean-Jacques Rousseau, in *A*

Lasting Peace through the Federation of Europe and The State of War (1756), supported the idea in principle: "Realise this Commonwealth of Europe for a single day, and you may be sure it will last forever; so fully would experience convince men that their own gain is to be found in the good of all." However, Rousseau held that societies had corrupted humans' natural innocence. He thought that the Abbé's proposals would not be followed "because men are crazy". Furthermore, the European sovereigns would be unlikely to volunteer to liquidate their power: "No Federation could ever be established except by a revolution."[18]

To Rousseau, the best way of abolishing war was to establish well-governed societies as he outlined in *The Social Contract* (1762). Thus to achieve perpetual peace, states should be made morally perfect. According to Rousseau, the moral perfection of states would establish perpetual peace, not a world government. A world of ideal states or societies would have no cause for war, and therefore would not need a world government. All states should be perfect societies linked federally.

In the late 18th century the idea of a federation gained momentum after the American Declaration of Independence of 1776, and the first modern democratic federation, the US, was established (i.e. finally ratified) in 1788. The US's multi-state federation of 1788 looked back to Rousseau's ideal, morally perfect states.

Nevertheless, it must be said that Rousseau's view was excessively idealistic as there will never be a world of ideal, morally perfect states. Therefore there is a need for a world government and World State.

Kant's Federation of Free States

The philosopher Immanuel Kant, writing in the mid-1790s, saw the need for an "international state (*civitas gentium*)", a World State, but settled for a federation of free states, believing that an "international state" would take a long time to create.

Kant thought deeply about a world government. In his *Idea for a Universal History with a Cosmopolitan Purpose* (1784)[19] – "cosmopolitan" suggests "relating to world citizens" – he linked the development of the domestic state to the "slow development of man's original [rational] capacities". He argued that war logically leads to an international state. War moves states "to take the step which reason could have suggested to them even without so many sad experiences – that of abandoning a lawless state of savagery and entering a federation of peoples in which every state, even the smallest, could expect to derive its security and rights not from its own power or its own legal judgment, but solely from this great federation (*Foedus Amphictyonum*, a federation like the Amphictyonic League of Greek tribes), from a united power and the law-governed decisions of a united will".

The federation Kant envisaged would be the "inevitable outcome" of human history. Soon afterwards, in a treatise, *Perpetual Peace: A Philosophical Sketch* (1795), a title that owes much to Abbé de Saint-Pierre, he reinforced the idea of the inevitability of such a federation. He argued that rationality dictated the formation of "an international state (*civitas gentium*), which would necessarily continue to grow until it embraced all the peoples of the Earth".[20] This international state would be a world government. However, Kant conceded that "the positive idea of a world republic cannot be realised" in the conditions of his day, the 1790s when Europe was still reeling from the French Revolution.

In *Perpetual Peace* Kant argued that in a world of distinct but interacting states the threat of a future war could be abolished by following a three-step plan. First, the civil constitution of each state should be republican and guarantee the freedom and equality of citizens through the rule of law and representative political institutions.

Secondly, the law of nations should be founded on a federation of free states, a "federation of peoples" which is distinct from an "international state". A "pacific federation (*foedus pacificum*)... does not aim to acquire any power like that of a state, but merely to preserve and secure the freedom of each state in itself, along with that of the other confederated states". He argued that a federal Union of free and independent states "is still to be preferred to an amalgamation of the separate nations under a single power which has overruled the rest and created a universal monarchy". Kant believed that a universal monarchy would be a world government that seemed to be all-powerful but would in fact be powerless: "For the laws progressively lose their impact as the government increases its range, and a soulless despotism, after crushing the germs of goodness, will finally lapse into anarchy." A "universal despotism" would end "in the graveyard of freedom".

The third step for permanently abolishing war is the observance of cosmopolitan right, which Kant limits to universal hospitality. The rights of people as citizens of the world should be limited to the conditions of universal hospitality. In other words people should be allowed to visit other countries, but not to stay unless invited. For although humans share a right to the Earth's surface, strangers require the inhabitants' agreement to settle on their territory. There is thus no right to conquer foreign lands as, Kant states, happened in "America, the negro countries, the Spice Islands, the Cape" and East India.[21]

Kant, then, writing in the mid-1790s when Europe was in turmoil, saw the need for an "international state" (*civitas gentium*)", and he saw it as a process, for it would "necessarily continue to grow until it embraced all the peoples of the Earth". But realistically this world republic was not going to happen overnight, and so he focused on a second-best, a "pacific federation" (*foedus pacificum*) between states, an intermediate means of abolishing war immediately, and his principle of "universal hospitality" was undoubtedly conceived with French revolutionary troops in mind. (In early 1795 the French republican armies conquered Belgium and then the left bank of the Rhine and the United Provinces, which would have alarmed Kant in Köningsberg, East Prussia.) They should withdraw back to France, for humans had the right to visit other countries but not conquer them and occupy them. Kant thus had world government as an aim but was clear that it should not be a "universal despotism" under a despot like Napoleon. (Napoleon declared to Benjamin Constant before the Battle of Waterloo, "I wanted to rule the world, and in order to do this I needed ultimate power.... I wanted to rule the world – who wouldn't have in my place? The world begged me to govern it."[22])

Kant thus endorsed the ideal of human unity and saw a world republic of free and equal individuals as an ideal end of the progress of human history. He was opposed to a universal monarchy as he felt that monarchy, as distinct from a republic, does not guarantee the freedom and equality of individual citizens: "Under a constitution where the subject is not a citizen, and which is therefore not republican, it is the simplest thing in the world to go to war."[23] Writing in 1795, Kant saw world citizenship as being vital to establishing world peace. A world republic remained his political ideal, but his short-term "realistic utopia"[24] would comprise a federation of free republican states short of a World State, the nearest achievable approximation, he felt, to the ideal of a world republic.

A contemporary of Kant's, the radical political cosmopolitan Anarcharsis Cloots (Jean-Baptiste du Val-de-Grâce, Baron de Cloots), who died in 1794, basing his thinking on the social-contract theory outlined in Rousseau's *The Social Contract* (1762), went further than Kant. He argued that the sovereign-state system should be abolished in favour of a universal republic that embraced all humankind.[25]

Soon afterwards the German philosopher, Johann Gottlieb Fichte, writing in 1806 when Napoleon overwhelmed Prussia, appealed to the German nation "to look at the deceptive vision of a universal monarchy", which he associated with Napoleon's tyrannical rule.

World Federation and Federalists in the 19th–21st centuries

The idea of a world republic was taken up by the German philosopher, Karl Krause, in an essay, 'The Archetype of Humanity' (1811). He proposed the formation of five regional federations: Europe, Asia, Africa, America and Australia – and that they should all be under a world republic.[26]

The idea of a world federation and universal law that would bring perpetual peace was in the thoughts of Englishmen when the British army was fighting in Afghanistan from 1838 to 1842. In 1842 the English poet Tennyson published 'Locksley Hall' (written in 1837–8), which included the lines:

> For I dipt into the future, far as human eye could see,
> Saw the Vision of the world, and all the wonder that would be; ...
>
> Till the war-drum throbbed no longer, and the battle-flags were furled
> In the Parliament of man, the Federation of the world.
>
> There the common sense of most shall hold a fretful realm in awe,
> And the kindly earth shall slumber, lapt in universal law.

We have seen (on p.9) that there were federations in Switzerland in 1848 and Canada in 1867. Although there had been International Peace Congresses in Europe every two years from 1843 to 1853 the momentum for further federalism was temporarily lost after the outbreak of first the Crimean War and then the American Civil War. Ulysses S. Grant, the Northern US Civil-War general, with the carnage of the American Civil War of the 1860s fresh in his mind, said:

> I believe at some future day, the nations of the Earth will agree on some sort of congress which will take cognizance of international questions of difficulty and whose decisions will be as binding as the decisions of the Supreme Court are upon us.[27]

Bahá'u'lláh founded the Bahá'i Faith between 1852 and 1892. He saw a global commonwealth of nations – a global federation of nations that would establish world unity – as being fundamental to the new religion. It would have a world legislature, an international court and an international executive. The Bahá'i religion advocated universal weights and measures, currency unification and a global language.

There was now a surge of internationalism in Europe. Many international organisations were formed, starting with the International Red Cross in 1863, the Telegraphic Union in 1865, the Institute of International Law in 1873 and the Universal Postal Union in 1874. There was growing interest in world government. James Lorimer explored the idea of a world government establishing a global rule of law in *The Institutes of the Law of Nations* (1883). An embryonic world parliament, the Inter-Parliamentary Union, was founded in 1889 by Cremer and Passy. There were around 450 international organisations by 1914.

The author H.G. Wells was a champion of world government. In *Anticipations* (1900) Wells foresaw "a New Republic dominating the world" that must ultimately become a "World State". He had been the first to foresee the dangers of an "atomic bomb" in his novel *The World Set Free* (1914), which in 1932 inspired the scientist Leo Szilard to work out how to start the nuclear chain reaction needed to build an atomic bomb. Wells foresaw the consequences of nation-states' developing atomic weapons and using them against each other. *The Outline of History* (1920, revised 1931) presented the world's history in one volume. At the end of his *Outline*, in a section headed 'Some Possibilities of a Federal World State', Wells called directly for world federation:

> A federation of all humanity, together with a sufficient measure of social justice to ensure health, education and a rough equality of opportunity, would mean such a release and increase of human energy as to open up a new phase in human history.[28]

In *The Shape of Things to Come* (1933, the year Hitler came to power) Wells saw a dictatorship to enforce world government as beneficial to humankind. This is not a view that democratic world federalists would share.

Aldous Huxley in *Brave New World* (1932) wrote of a World State, a unified government, ruled by a World Controller, that administers the entire planet except for a few isolated areas. Set in 2059 following a Nine-Years' War that broke out in 2049, the novel shows a world economy regulated by the State. Humans live in racial, social and economic harmony. The vision is dystopian and there is no place for individualism in regimented living conditions.

There had been various attempts to establish global institutions to resolve international disputes and to regulate the conduct of wars by laws. The Hague Conferences of 1899 and 1907 failed to prevent the First World War, and the League of Nations failed to prevent the Second World War.

Towards the end of the Second World War two federalist books appeared.

Wendell Willkie's *One World* (1943) sold over 2 million copies. Most of the book is Willkie's description of his wartime tour of the Middle East, the Soviet Union and China as Roosevelt's personal representative in 1942. Willkie, a Democrat, had lost to Roosevelt in the 1940 presidential campaign, and then worked with Roosevelt, rousing the US from isolationism. It is only at the very end of his book that he touches on the federal theme:

> America must choose one of three courses after this war: narrow nationalism, which inevitably means the ultimate loss of our own liberty; international imperialism, which means the sacrifice of some other nation's liberty; or the creation of a world in which there shall be an equality of opportunity for every race and every nation. I am convinced the American people will choose, by overwhelming majority, the last of these courses.[29]

Emery Reves' *The Anatomy of Peace* (1945) argued that the United Nations should be replaced by a federal world government as an association of nation-states can never prevent a new war: "What chance have we to create a world government before the next war? Not much."[30] This book became the "bible" of world federalists and was commended by Einstein in 1947.[31]

The first world federalist organisation had been launched in 1937: the Campaign for World Government. A Federal Union was set up in the UK in 1938, and another Federal Union (now the Association to Unite the Democracies) followed in the US in 1939. This called for a Federation of Atlantic Democracies. In 1940 a *Mouvement populaire suisse en faveur d'une fédération des peuples* was established in Geneva. Altiero Spinelli's plan for a European federation was circulated among the anti-Fascist resistance movements during the Second World War. In 1945, the Committee to Frame a World Constitution convened at the University of Chicago and drafted a Constitution for the World.[32]

The Second World War was responsible for over 60 million dead, 90 million according to some estimates. The atomic bombings of Hiroshima and Nagasaki were deeply shocking, and atomic scientists lobbied for the international control of atomic energy as the main function of a world federalist government. The United Nations was established by charter in 1945, when it had 51 members, and adopted the Universal Declaration of Human Rights in 1948. Many felt that it presided over discussions and co-ordination between sovereign governments, and as we saw on pp.xiii-xvi such prominent thinkers as Harry S. Truman, Albert Einstein, Winston Churchill, Bertrand Russell and Mahatma Gandhi called for the forming of a federal world government.

In 1947 grassroots federalists formed the United World Federalists (UWF), later renamed World Federalist Association, and then Citizens for Global Solutions. They called for the transformation of the United Nations into a universal federation of states with powers to control armaments. States should surrender their sovereign rights to stockpile weapons and wage war, and they should submit their disputes to authoritative international institutions of adjudication and enforcement. World peace would only be achieved by establishing world law.

At the same time similar movements formed in many countries. In 1947 a global coalition, now known as the World Federalist Movement – Institute for Global Policy (WFM-IGP), was formed in Montreux, Switzerland. This body was created when five small world federalist organisations agreed to merge in Asheville, North Carolina. In August 1947 more than 51 organisations from 24 countries attended the Conference for the World Movement for World Federal Government, which made the Montreux Declaration. The World Movement met again in Luxembourg in 1948 and founded an association of parliamentarians for world government, which came into existence in 1951.

In 1948 Garry Davis renounced his US citizenship, declared himself a "citizen of the world" and called for world government from the balcony of the UN General Assembly in Paris,[33] until he was dragged away by guards. Davis founded a Registry of World Citizens. Opinion polls carried out by UNESCO in 1948–49 found world government was preferred in six European countries, and rejected in the US. On 4 September 1953 Davis, speaking from the City Hall of Ellsworth, Maine, announced the formation of the "World Government of World Citizens". He based this on three "World Laws": One God (or Absolute Value); One World; and One Humanity. Claiming that his mandate was article 21(3) of the Universal Declaration of Human Rights, he founded the United World Service Authority in New York City as the administrative agency of the new world government. It then designed and issued a "World Passport" based on article 13(2) of the Universal Declaration of Human Rights. Some 800,000 passports have been issued and these have been recognised by over 151 countries.[34]

Some federalists did not reject the nation-state, only authoritarian, non-democratic states. In 1949 Clarence Streit founded the Atlantic Union Committee (AUC), which called for a federal Union of democratic states that would be the genesis of a "free-world government, as nations are encouraged by example to practice the principles which would make them eligible for membership, namely the principles of representative government and protection of individual liberty by law".[35]

In 1954 E. Adamson Hoebel, a legal anthropologist, broadened the legal realist tradition to include non-Western nations:

> Whatever the idealist may desire, force and the threat of force are the ultimate power in the determination of international behaviour, as in the law within the nation or tribe. But until force and the threat of force in international relations are brought under social control by the world community, by and for the world society, they remain the instruments of social anarchy and not the sanctions of world law. The creation in clear-cut terms of the corpus of world law cries for the doing. If world law, however, is to be realized at all, there will have to be minimum of general agreement as to the nature of the physical and ideational world and the relation of men in society to it. An important and valuable next step will be found in deep-cutting analysis of the major law systems of the contemporary world in order to lay bare their basic postulates – postulates that are too generally hidden; postulates felt, perhaps, by those who live by them, but so much taken for granted that they are rarely expressed or exposed for examination. When this is done – and it will take the efforts of many keen intellects steeped in the law of at least a dozen lands and also aware of the social nexus of the law – then mankind will be able to see clearly for the first time and clearly where the common consensus of the great living social and law systems lies. Here will be found the common postulates and values upon which the world community can build. At the same time the truly basic points of conflict that will have to be worked upon for resolution will be revealed. Law is inherently purposive.[36]

This call for all nations to pool their laws and create from them a system of international law is just as relevant today, fifty-five years on, as it was in 1954.

In 1962 the Secretary-General of the United Nations, U Thant, called for world government in a speech at Uppsala, Sweden.

The world movement for World Federal Government had

hoped that a UN review conference in 1955, planned under article 109 of the UN Charter, would turn the UN into a world federal system. Due to the Cold War, there was no political will for such a conference. In 1965 the movement established offices near the UN, and appointed a UN observer and advocate. The focus was on amendments to the UN Charter with a view to making the Security Council more representative, creating a World Court with compulsory jurisdiction and authority to conduct judicial reviews, and to turn the General Assembly into a democratically-elected world parliament. Federalists proposed a commission on sustainable development, an international development authority, a standing peacekeeping corps and an international criminal court.

In 1969 the American landing on the moon brought a new perspective to the Earth. The first astronauts on the moon's surface saw the Earth as a blue ball against a black sky, and it seemed a unity, one. Film they took was relayed to Earth and humankind saw the Earth as seen from the moon. Suddenly millions of people thought it inconceivable that there could not be a World State with a world government. Nelson Rockefeller called for a World Federation in 1962 (see p.139).

Support for multinational federalism led to the formation of the European Union. However, the intensification of the Cold War (1946–1991) had divided the world into two ideologically opposed camps, led by the US and the USSR, and world government came to be seen as one of the two opponents ruling the world by conquering the other. Progress towards global federation was halted and, indeed, went into reverse. The US was accused of attempting to impose "American monopolistic capitalism" on the world, and universal federation faced the same accusation. Public discussion of world government ceased.

Now the Soviet Union became the historical conveyer of socialist or communist thinking. Socialist ideas were linked to the French Revolution, and the state was held up to be coercive on behalf of the proletarian class. It was to coerce and oppress the bourgeoisie. Such notions of the state crowded out the concept of a philanthropic World State. There was talk of a world socialist economy governed by a "Bolshevik World State".[37] Soviet apologists argued that the real cause of war was capitalism. In practice, Soviet Communism was based on repression and had little to do with socialist ideals.

In spite of the Cold War recent world leaders had continued to urge world government, notably Dwight D. Eisenhower, John F. Kennedy, Mikhail Gorbachev and Ronald Reagan.

Following the dissolution of the USSR in 1991, there was a revival of interest in federal world government and in the global protection of human rights. In 1992 the Maastricht Treaty paved the way for the European Union (EU), which was enlarged to include half a billion people in 27 member nation-states. In 1998 the Rome Statute led to the establishment in 2002 of the International Criminal Court. The African Union was founded in 2002 and the Union of South American Nations in 2008 (replacing the 2004 South American Community of Nations).

The concept of world government has seeped throughout Western culture. Robert A. Heinlein's *Starship Troopers*, a literary work adapted into a series of films, presents a world government with a socialist ideology. Orson Scott Card's *Shadow of the Giant* shows a "Hegemon" over the Earth. The TV series *Star Trek* presents the Earth as united under one government in the 22nd century. It is called United Earth following the unification of Earth in the 22nd century. United Earth is a political subdivision of the United Federation of Planets, which was founded in 2161. The concept of world government also appears in comics, animation and video games.

Today a number of international organisations promote world government. The World Federalist Movement (WFM) is a movement of global citizens with 23 member organisations and 16 associated organisations around the globe. It seeks to establish a federated world government. The US member organisation is Citizens for Global Solutions. The Centre for International Governance Innovation (CIGI) is a research and education centre in Canada. It is creating a global online research community to strengthen governance around the world. One World Trust (OWT) is a UK-based charity and member of the World Federalist Movement. It seeks to make existing global organisations more accountable. Civitatis International is a UK-based non-governmental organisation. It does legal research and promotes increased systems of global governance to policymakers. The Committee for a Democratic UN is a network of parliamentarians and non-governmental organisations from Germany, Switzerland and Austria. It has a world federalist philosophy. Democratic World Federalists is a San-Francisco-based civil-society organisation. It promotes a democratic federal system of world government. Vote World Government (VWG) is a Canadian non-governmental organisation which has embarked on a global referendum that asks, "Do you support the creation of a directly-elected, representative and democratic world government?"

The Japanese-based World Party campaigns for a world parliament with seats allocated in proportion to the populations of nation-states. It co-operates with the World Government Institute, which is the theoretical wing of the world-government movement, and with the World Citizen Network.

The World Philosophical Forum (WPF), which meets annually in Athens, has been a place where a World State could be debated. In October 2015 I chaired the WPF's Constitutional Convention and with Igor Kondrashin brought in the Universal State of the Earth and the Supreme Council of Humanity to show that a World State *can* be created.[38]

Once again there is a consensus for global governance, and a renewed longing for a World State. In every part of the world people long for a world government that stops short of being coercive, authoritarian and dictatorial, but which can put an end to war. In a time when images of wars in Iraq, Afghanistan and Syria fill television screens, there has never been a greater need for a supranational World Authority.

What can the Universalist deviser of a World State take from the long yearning for one world? Eastern unity reflected in humankind's oneness. Dante's universal monarchy to bring peace. Grotius' international law. Abbé de Saint-Pierre's federation by social contract. Rousseau's morally perfect states. Kant's federation of free states. Cloots' universal republic to replace sovereign states. Federations like the US are a step towards world government. Krause's five federations to become a world republic. H.G. Wells' world federation and a federation of all humanity. Groups of world federalists. The European Union. All these are seeds from the past that could bear fruit in a coming World State.

3

Attempts at Imposing a World State on the Known World by Conquest

Many conquerors of the past conquered nearby territories. Some aspired to rule the whole of the known world and tried to achieve this by conquest. None succeeded. The attempts to impose a World State on the known world by conquest accounted for many of the wars in past generations.

It is only relatively recently that the known world was the whole world. America was not discovered until 1492, and Australia not until 1770.

When the Known World was *not* the Whole World

The farther back in history we find conquerors, the more their conquests seem – to them – to have conquered most of the known world. Most of the early conquerors wanted to conquer the known world, and in some cases thought they had conquered the known world, as we can see now.[1]

Sargon of Akkad, the Akkadian Emperor, conquered the Sumerian city-states in the 23rd and 22nd centuries BC. Cuneiform sources confirm that he rose from cup-bearer in charge of wine and may have replaced King Ur-Zababa of Kish as 'Great King' to conquer large parts of Mesopotamia, modern Iran, Asia Minor and Syria. As his capital he built or renovated Akkad (which was associated with *The Epic of Gilgamesh*), and his dynasty controlled Mesopotamia and much of the known world to Akkadians.

Thutmose III of the Egyptian 18th dynasty was co-regent with his stepmother and aunt Hatshepsut. After her death in 1458BC he fought 17 campaigns and created the largest empire Egypt had known. It stretched from north Syria to Nubia (the fourth waterfall of the Nile), much of the known world to the

Egyptians. He became co-regent with his son Amenhotep II two years before he died.

Cyrus the Great founded the Persian Empire under the Achaemenid dynasty. He conquered most of South-West Asia and much of Central Asia, and ruled from Egypt and the Hellespont to the Indus River: the largest empire the world had then seen, consisting of 2.09 million square miles.

Darius I of Persia reigned from 522BC to 486BC. He refounded the Achaemenid empire and extended it to Thrace and India so it reached its greatest extent.

Philip II of Macedon ruled from 359BC to 336BC. In 340BC he besieged Perinthus and in 339BC Byzantium, and the following year he defeated the Thebans and Athenians, destroyed Amfissa and brought most of the Greek city-states under Macedonian hegemony. In 337BC he led the League of Corinth, whose members agreed never to fight each other, and he was elected leader of the army to invade the Persian Empire. He was assassinated at an early stage in the invasion, and was replaced by his son Alexander the Great, having extended Macedon's conquests to leave Alexander the basis for a known-world empire.

Alexander III of Macedon, Alexander the Great, was tutored by Aristotle and created one of the largest empires known to the ancient world by the time he was 30. It stretched from the Ionian Sea to the Himalayas, most of the known world, after he invaded Persian-ruled Asia Minor and conquered the entire Persian Empire, and consisted of 2.18 million square miles.

Chandragupta Maurya founded the Mauryan Empire and was the first to subjugate the Indian subcontinent and unify India into one state. He ruled from 322BC to 298BC, and his empire extended from Bengal and Assam to Afghanistan, Balochistan and eastern and south-eastern Iran, and from Kashmir to the Deccan Plateau. It was the largest empire yet known in Indian history and covered much of the world known to Indians.

Ashoka the Great, Indian Emperor of the Mauryan dynasty, ruled from 269BC to 232BC. He extended the Mauryan Empire through military conquests to most of present-day India and ruled from Afghanistan to Assam. His empire included most of the world known to Indians in the 3rd century BC.

Qin Shi Huangdi (traditionally known as Ch'in Shih Huang-ti, the ruler who gave his name to China), the modern Chinese name for King Zheng of Qin, 246BC–221BC, completed his conquest of China in 221BC and became the first Emperor of China as Emperor of the Qin dynasty from 220BC to 210BC. He expanded China to include Hunan and Guangdong, unified diverse state walls into one Great Wall of China and created the Terracotta Army for his mausoleum. He conquered most of the world known to the Chinese of the 3rd century BC.

The time of the Roman Republic saw some great conquerors such as Hannibal of Carthage, who marched an army and war elephants from Iberia (Spain) over the Alps into northern Italy. He occupied much of Italy for 15 years during the Second Punic War. (His father Hamilcar Barca was the leading Carthaginian commander in the First Punic War.) But neither he nor Scipio Africanus, the Roman general who defeated Hannibal at Zama in 202BC, can be described as conquering the known world, the extent of which had grown in the Roman time. Likewise, Mithridates VI, king of Pontus and Armenia Minor (now in modern Turkey), who ruled from 119BC to 63BC, fought battles against Roman generals, one of whom was Pompey, a brilliant Roman military leader who fought a civil war against Julius Caesar. Pompey was defeated at the Battle of Pharsalus. Neither Mithridates nor Pompey could claim to have fought to conquer the known world.

Julius Caesar, however, became ruler of the Roman Empire. He had armies in Gaul, Germany, Spain and Britain, and fought Pompey for control at home. He had a romance with Cleopatra, the Egyptian ruler. In 45BC he was named dictator of Rome for life and had the Roman Empire at his feet. He was assassinated the next year. He ruled much of the known world, and his name 'Caesar' is reflected in the modern 'Kaiser' and 'Tsar'. Under his great-nephew and protégé Augustus, the first Roman Emperor, the Roman Empire expanded into Hungary, Croatia and Egypt, and secured Spain and Gaul. Augustus added more land than Julius Caesar.

During the 3rd century AD there were wars on the fringes of the Roman Empire that threw up conquerors, but they did not rule the known world. Ardashir I overthrew the Parthian Empire, which the Romans had tried to subjugate, and founded the Sasanian Empire. Queen Zenobia of the Palmyrene Empire in Syria revolted against the Romans and expanded into Egypt, which she ruled.

Emperor Aurelian ruled much of the known world. He defeated the barbarian Alamanni, Goths, Vandals, Juthungi, Sarmatians and Carpi, and restored the Roman Empire's eastern provinces after conquering the Palmyrene Empire of Queen Zenobia in 273. He reunited the Roman Empire by conquering the Gallic Empire but lost Dacia. He presided over much of the known world and was known as '*Restitutor Orbis*' ('Restorer of the World') and was publicly hailed as '*dominus et deus*', 'overlord and god'.

Attila, Emperor of the Huns from 434 to 453, ruled the Hunnic Empire which extended from Germany to the Ural River and from the Danube to the Baltic. He invaded the Balkans twice and marched through Gaul (modern France) to Orléans, and was Rome's main enemy before he was defeated by the Romans and Visigoths. He had a large empire consisting of 1.45 million square miles, but there were many territories in the known world of the 5th century that he did not conquer.

The spread of Islam threw up military leaders. The first Muslim caliph Abu Bakr As-Siddiq, the prophet Mohammed's father-in-law, ruled the Rashidun Caliphate from 632 to 634, after Mohammed had conquered Mecca. The second caliph Umar (Omar) ibn Al-Khattab, Mohammed's companion, expanded the Rashidun Caliphate to rule the whole Sasanian Empire and two-thirds of the Byzantine Empire. These early caliphs dominated Asia Minor but not the known world.

Charlemagne ('Charles the Great'), King of the Franks from 768 to 814, expanded the Frankish kingdom into an empire that incorporated much of Western and Central Europe. He conquered Italy and in 800 was crowned *'Imperator Romanorum'*, 'Emperor of the Romans', by Pope Leo III. He was Charles I of Germany, the Holy Roman Empire, and France, but much of the known world was outside his domains.

The Holy Roman Emperor Otto I extended his German kingdom. He conquered the Slavs to the east, made Bohemia pay tribute and gained influence in Denmark and Burgundy. He ruled the Lombards and married the queen of Italy. He was crowned Holy Roman Emperor in 962 and subdued Rome. He defeated the Magyars and betrothed his son to a Byzantine princess. He created the most powerful state in Western Europe and laid the foundation of the later Holy Roman Empire.

The 11th century saw conquerors of regions rather than the known world. William I, the Conqueror, a descendant of Viking raiders who became Duke of Normandy, claimed the English throne because his first cousin once removed, Edward the Confessor, died childless. He built a fleet and launched the Norman Conquest of England and he spent the rest of his life securing England and his continental lands.

Roger I, the Norman conqueror of Sicily, took Sicily from the Arabs between 1066 and 1091. Roger became the most powerful lord in Sicily. His son Roger II united all the Norman conquests in Italy into one kingdom with a central government.

Mahmud of Ghazni (971–1030) founded the Ghaznavid Empire. He ruled much of the Middle East, including Iran, Afghanistan, Pakistan, part of India and a number of smaller countries, in all consisting of 0.68 million square miles.

Alp Arslan, the 2nd Sultan of the Seljuq Empire, took Anatolia from the Byzantines and became Sultan of Great Seljuq and sole monarch of Persia from the river Oxus to the Tigris. He invaded Cappadocia and Armenia, and conquered Georgia in 1064. He invaded the Byzantine Empire and drove the Turks across the Euphrates.

Saladin, the Kurdish first Sultan of Egypt and Syria, founded the Ayyubid dynasty. He led the Muslims against the Christian

Crusaders who had invaded the Levant and created the Crusader Kingdom of Jerusalem. In 1187 he recaptured Palestine from the Crusaders and at its height his sultanate included Egypt, Syria, Mesopotamia, Hejaz, the Yemen and part of North Africa.

Genghis Khan founded and was Great Khan (Emperor) of the Mongol Empire which consisted of 4.86 million square miles. He united the nomadic tribes of north-eastern Asia in the 12th century and started the Mongol invasions (and massacres) that conquered most of Eurasia. He came to control much of Central Asia and China, and united the terrain of the Silk Road. His descendants created vassal states in modern China, Korea, the Caucasus, Central Asia, Eastern Europe, Russia and the Middle East.

His grandson Kublai Khan, the fifth Khan of the Mongol Empire, founded the Yuan dynasty in 1271, a division of the Mongol Empire limited to China and Mongolia, and became Emperor of China, the first non-Chinese Emperor to conquer all China. His summer garden at Xanadu is celebrated in Coleridge's poem 'Kubla Khan'. Although he did not rule the known world his empire extended from the Pacific to the Black Sea, and from Siberia to Afghanistan, a fifth of the world's inhabited land.

Also the 13th-century Hulagu Khan, another of Genghis Khan's grandsons and Kublai Khan's brother, a Mongol ruler, expanded the Mongol Empire south-west into much of South-West Asia. He founded the Ilkhanate of Persia (a precursor of the Safavid dynasty), destroyed Baghdad, weakened Damascus and shifted Islamic influence to the Mamluks of Cairo.

Tamerlane (Timur), Marlowe's Tamburlaine the Great, founded the Timurid Empire in the 14th century and conquered much of western and central Asia. His empire extended from the modern south-eastern Turkey, Syria, Iraq, Kuwait and Iran through Central Asia: Kazakhstan, Afghanistan, Armenia, Azerbaijan, Georgia, Turkmenistan, Uzbekistan, Kyrgyzstan, Pakistan, North-West India and Kashgar in China. At its height it consisted of 2.145 million square miles.

Mehmed II, the conqueror, was the Sultan of the Ottoman

Empire. He ended the Byzantine Empire by capturing Constantinople in 1453 and other Byzantine cities in Anatolia and the Balkans, and the Ottoman State was now recognised as an Empire.

Selim I, Sultan, Ottoman Emperor and 'Caliph of Islam', conquered the Middle East, and on his death in 1520 the Ottoman Empire consisted of 1.5625 million square miles. The Ottoman admiral Hayreddin Barbarossa secured Ottoman dominance of the Mediterranean through naval victories in the 16th century, and the Ottoman Empire reached its zenith and became a world power under Sultan Suleiman I.

Babur, a Muslim conqueror from Central Asia who was descended from both Genghis Khan and Tamerlane, founded the Mughal dynasty in India, and was, again, a conqueror of a region rather than the known world.

In Spain, James I of Aragon, King of Aragon from 1213 to 1236, had expanded his kingdom into Valencia, Languedoc and the Balearic Islands, and had annexed Catalonia from the French.

Ferdinand II, King of Sicily from 1468, became King of Castile by marrying Isabella I in 1474. In 1479 he became King of Aragon. He became King of Naples as Ferdinand III and King of Navarre. By sponsoring Columbus's voyage he was responsible for discovering the New World and he fought Granada to expel the Muslims from Spain and end the *Reconquista*.

Francisco Pizarro, the Spanish *Conquistador*, seized the Inca Empire for Spain and named it Peru. His empire consisted of 0.48 million square miles. Cortés, another Spanish *Conquistador*, ended the Aztec Empire and extended the rule of Castile over much of Mexico.

All these were conquerors to extend an empire, not to rule the world. Something similar had begun in England when Edward I conquered Wales and kept Scotland under English domination. Again, foundations were being laid for expansion.

When the Known World *was* the Whole World

Napoleon Bonaparte, Emperor of the French from 1804 to 1814, fought two coalitions during the Napoleonic Wars and seized control of most of continental Europe totalling 0.72 million square miles. He had control of a region rather than the known world for his last two defeats, at the Battles of Leipzig (1813) and Waterloo (1815).

Adolf Hitler, Chancellor of Germany from 1933 to 1945, wanted a New Order of German hegemony. He extended his German Empire throughout Europe, most of northern Africa, east and south-eastern Asia and the Pacific Ocean, in territory totalling at its greatest extent 1.37 million square miles.

Hitler had aspirations to rule the world. He selected Nuremberg, the city of the Holy Roman Emperors, to be his seat after the Second World War, when he planned to be crowned Kaiser Adolf I, Emperor of Germany. After accepting the surrender of the Soviet Union, the US, the British Empire including India and in due course his ally Japan, he would be Emperor of the whole world, whose representatives would meet in Nuremberg.

In Nuremberg he began an impressive building program modelled on ancient Rome. He built the Coliseum, an open New Congress Hall modelled on Rome's Coliseum, which would seat 50,000 world representatives. Near this was the grandstand of the Zeppelinfeld from which Hitler addressed 1.6 million people one day in 1938. A nearby lake was gouged out and turned into a Stadium to accommodate a crowd of 350,000 to 450,000 people. A two-kilometre-long route was constructed to lead to the Castle where electors would meet to elect Hitler Emperor. Nuremberg would be the centre of the world, and Hitler's new buildings there, which can now be visited, would be the seat of his world government, which would be imposed by conquest, not voluntary association.

George W. Bush, US President from 2001 to 2009, led the War on Terror in Afghanistan and Iraq and elsewhere in the Middle East to eliminate the Taliban and al-Qaeda, on territory totalling 0.423429 square miles (putting him, at no.10, in the top 10 conquerors in history when measured by the square mileage he conquered). But by the 21st century the known world was the whole world, and Bush merely conquered a region.

Most of the above conquerors would have ruled the whole world and imposed a World State if they had been able to do so.

Attempts at Achieving a World State by Consent

In the 20th century, following the cataclysmic First World War and ruin of Europe, a peace treaty, the Treaty of Versailles, brought World War I to an end.

The League of Nations

As a result of the Treaty of Versailles (1919–1920) the League of Nations was set up in Geneva on 10 January 1920. It was an inter-governmental organisation to resolve international disputes between its member nation-states.

At its height the League of Nations had 58 members whose delegates met in the Assembly. Each country had three representatives and one vote. Besides an Assembly it had a Council and Permanent Secretariat, and numerous agencies. Delegates met by consent to resolve their disputes by discussion. The League of Nations had no armed forces of its own and depended on the Great Powers to enforce its resolutions, economic sanctions and military strengths.

The League of Nations received a setback when in October 1933 Hitler ordered the German delegates to leave the Disarmament Conference in Geneva and withdrew Germany from the League. Soon after that the League of Nations failed to prevent Japan from occupying Manchuria, part of China, in 1932. It failed to prevent war in Abyssinia in 1935–1936 (the second Italo-Ethiopian War when Italy invaded Abyssinia). In the coming years it failed to prevent the Second World War and could not cope with Hitler's invasion of Poland. The Japanese world view during its imperial period (1868–1945) was "*Hakko ichiu*", "eight corners of the world under one roof" – establishing a Greater Asian Co-prosperity Sphere that would result in world domination, and the League of Nations was powerless to prevent Japan's wartime activities towards this end. The League of

Nations ceased operations – ended – on 18 April 1946.

The League of Nations failed because it lacked supranational powers. It was 'inter-national', 'between nation-states', and had no authority to ban war and enforce disarmament. It provided a forum for 58 members and tried to get them to resolve their disputes through discussion, by consent.

The Atlantic Charter

The Atlantic Charter was a joint declaration released by US President Franklin D. Roosevelt and British Prime Minister Winston Churchill on 14 August 1941 following a meeting in Newfoundland. It set out US and British war aims.

It offered a blueprint for the postwar world. The Atlantic Charter derived its name from a report in the British newspaper *Daily Herald* which referred to "an Atlantic charter", and this was widely adopted after Churchill used the phrase in parliament on 24 August 1941. The joint declaration was a succession of telegraphed drafts, and no formal document exists.

The declaration made it clear that the US supported the UK in the war, and although American involvement looked likely the US had not entered the war when the declaration was issued. Its main points were: the US and UK would seek no territorial gains; territorial adjustments must be in accordance with the wishes of affected peoples; all peoples had a right to self-determination; trade barriers should be lowered; there should be global economic co-operation and advancement of social welfare; the US and UK would work for a world free from want and fear, and for freedom of the seas; and aggressor nations should be disarmed and all nation-states should disarm after the war.

The Atlantic Charter laid the foundations for the main international agreements that have shaped the world including the General Agreement on Tariffs and Trade (GATT) and the granting of independence to British and French colonies, and it paved the way for the creation of the United Nations.

The United Nations

The Second World War had been catastrophic. Over 60 million had been killed, two atomic bombs had caused horrific loss of life and German concentration camps had perpetrated crimes against humanity. A shocked world called for institutions that could permanently prevent the recurrence of such an international conflict.

The United Nations was founded in 1945 and, after the dissolution of the League of Nations in 1946, adopted the Universal Declaration of Human Rights in 1948. Like the League of Nations, the United Nations was a forum to resolve disputes through discussion, by consent. All participating nation-states were sovereign and could dissent, and the five permanent members of the UN Security Council (China, France, Russia, the UK and US) had a veto.

The emergence of a Cold War between the Soviet Union, the Allies' wartime partner, and the US was an immediate setback to the work of the UN. The Soviet Union wanted world-wide Communism, which was theoretically a stateless society with no government. In fact, international Communism threatened world domination by one government, the totalitarian government of the Soviet Union. The division of the world into East and West led to frequent vetoes in the UN and the paralysis of the UN's working institutions.

It was soon clear to such prominent thinkers as Einstein, Churchill, Russell and Gandhi (see pp.xiii-xvi) that sovereign governments could continue to do what they wished and that there should be a federal world government with sufficient federal authority to abolish war.

In 2017 the United Nations had 193 member nation-states (see Appendix C4). These nation-states sought to resolve all disputes through discussion, by consent. Good work was done on promoting international law, international security, economic development, human rights, social progress and the goal of world peace, but the United Nations lacked supranational authority as did the League of Nations, and it was just as powerless to prevent wars. Since 1945 the UN has failed to prevent 162 wars (see Appendix C8) and has stood by while vast numbers of nuclear weapons have been amassed in the world.

According to the Federation of American Scientists (FAS), in early 2017 there were approximately 14,900 warheads of which 5,500 were awaiting dismantlement, leaving about 9,400 in military stockpiles, of which more than 3,900 were deployed with operational forces; of which nearly 1,800 US, Russian, British and French warheads were on high alert. Some 93 per cent of all nuclear weapons were Russian or US, and both Russia and the US had 4,000–4,500 warheads in their stockpiles. The Arms Control Association (ACA) puts the figure in January 2017 as 15,000, and gives a country-by-country breakdown. (See Appendix C9 for both FAS and ACA estimates of the world's nuclear weapons.) The number is steadily reducing. The world had 69,401 nuclear weapons in 1985, 24,000 in 2009,[2] and 15,375 in autumn 2016. According to the Federation of American Scientists the world had 15,350 in 2016 and 14,900 in early 2017.[3] Nevertheless, despite the reduction the UN has still failed to prevent 14,900 nuclear weapons (see Appendix C9) as we have just seen.

Like the League of Nations, the United Nations has failed to keep the peace by consent.

A UN Parliamentary Assembly

The federal movement (see pp.34-42) and interest in multinational, supranational federalism had led to the formation of the European Union. However, the Cold War (1946–1991) divided the world and prevented the spread of world federalism. International politics became dominated by containing an expanding and totalitarian Communism that appeared to threaten the Western world with an oppressive regime that sought to replace democratic governments.

The dissolution of the Soviet Union in 1991 renewed interest in federal world government and the global protection of human rights, and it is no coincidence that the Maastricht Treaty which named the EU and paved the way for its enlargement followed soon after, in 1992. The Rome Statute of 1998 led to the establishment of the International Criminal Court in 2002. The African Union (2002) and the Union of South American Nations (2008) continued the trend.

The revival of interest in the world federation has renewed the idea of a UN Parliamentary Assembly (UNPA), to which representatives could be elected by the world's citizens. The idea of a League of Nations parliament was raised in 1920, and again in1945. The idea was dormant during the setting-up of the United Nations and during the Cold War, but since 1991 the globalisation of trade and the regional and global organisations that govern it (see pp.10–16) have led to calls for a World Parliamentary Assembly that can scrutinise their activities. The Campaign for the Establishment of a UN Parliamentary Assembly was formed in 2007, and is supported by 21 Nobel and Right Livelihood Laureates. It remains to be seen whether anti-globalist populism has arrested calls for a world parliament.

The creation of a UN Parliamentary Assembly with representatives elected by world citizens would be a dramatic step towards setting up a World State by consent. I have always seen this – it was the driving force behind my book *The World Government* (2010) – and I had in no way abandoned my view that the UN General Assembly should be turned into a World State's democratically-elected lower house when, in an act of statecraft, I brought in the Universal State of the Earth (USE) on 7 October 2015 to show that a World State *can* be set up. (See p.43.) It was largely to draw the UN's attention to the need to create a democratic World State that I brought in the USE. It is now time to create a UN Parliamentary Assembly that can be a fully democratic World Parliamentary Assembly within a coming World State.

4

The Failure of the Old Order

Modern history began c.1500 with the Renaissance, and our 'old order' – our Western system of capitalism and nation-states – can be dated back to that early Renaissance time. The Enlightenment saw history as progressing in one direction, and it was Kant who first stated the Enlightenment view of the progress of history to a goal, a new order, like the flow of a river towards an estuary. He dreamt of a universal history that would show the progressive evolution of humankind. Hegel also saw history as an evolutionary process.

Universal History as Progress towards a New Order

In 1992 I heard Francis Fukuyama, a follower of Hegel, speak in London. In *The End of History* he claimed that in a Hegelian sense history as an evolutionary process has a direction and will reach an end when it achieves a form of society that satisfies humankind's deepest longings. For Hegel this meant a liberal state, for Marx a communist society. Fukuyama suggested that history reached its "end" with the end of the Cold War as there would now be permanent liberal democracy. He seemed to be saying that the world was about to pass very soon into a permanent World State. In support of this view, it is worth noting that while there were no liberal democracies with universal suffrage in the world in 1900, in 2017 125 out of the 193 nation-states were deemed to have an electoral liberal democracy (see Appendix D1).[1] However, there are indications that world-wide democracy has weakened since then. (See pp.74–75.) As I have already intimated (see p.20), my view of the permanence of a World State differs from Fukuyama's.

Kant's Enlightenment view of history as progress can be found in his 1784 essay of 16 pages, *An Idea for a Universal History from a Cosmopolitan Purpose*, to which I have already referred.

The title, *Idee zu einer allgemeinen Geschichte in weltbürgerlicher Absicht*, is variously translated as ending "Cosmopolitan Purpose" and "Cosmopolitan Point of View", Fukuyama's preference, and "purpose" is arguably the better translation. That is the translation I have adopted, and it is supported by a short notice in the twelfth number of the *Gothaische gelehrte Zeitungen* for 1784, which said:

> A favourite idea of Professor Kant's is that the ultimate *purpose* of the human race is to achieve the most perfect civic constitution and he wishes that a philosophical historian might undertake to give us a history of humanity from this *point of view*, and to show to what extent humanity in various ages has approached or drawn away from this final *purpose* and what remains to be done in order to reach it [my italics].

Kant is saying that the purpose of the human race is to achieve a perfect civic constitution – for a World State. This constitution would enshrine the "freedom of the human will". History has "a regular movement" in it that carries the human race to this end-point. History, and Nature, are therefore teleological, for their purpose is to bring about this "natural end": the "goal" of a "society with the greatest freedom". Kant believed that history was a progressive evolution with an end-point, a final purpose that made the whole of history intelligible, in which "the human race finally achieves the condition in which all the seeds planted in it by Nature can fully develop and in which the destiny of the race can be fulfilled here on Earth".

An Idea for a Universal History with a Cosmopolitan Purpose is really a list of nine theses and exegeses. The fifth thesis asserts, "The greatest problem for the human race, to the solution of which Nature drives man, is the achievement of a universal civic society which administers law among men." The sixth thesis asserts, "This problem is the most difficult and the last to be solved by mankind." The seventh thesis asserts, "The problem of establishing a perfect civic constitution is dependent upon the problem of a lawful external relation among states."

The eighth thesis asserts, "The history of mankind can be seen, in the large, as the realisation of Nature's secret plan to bring forth a perfectly constituted state as the only condition in which the capacities of mankind can be fully developed, and also bring forth that external relation among states which is perfectly adequate to this end." The ninth thesis speaks of the "union of the human race": "A philosophical attempt to work out a universal history according to a natural plan directed to achieving the civic union of the human race must be regarded as possible, and, indeed, as contributing to this end of Nature."

The accompanying exegesis asserts that it can be assumed "that Nature, even in the play of human freedom, works not without plan or purpose". The idea that history has a plan and purpose that challenges the work of "empirical historians" is "only a suggestion of what a philosophical mind... could essay from another point of view". "A philosophical history" can see Nature and history as having a plan and purpose.[2]

Writing after the American Declaration of Independence and in the run-up to the French Revolution, then, Kant saw the end-point of history as the realisation of human freedom. A Universal History would determine whether history is a general human progress in the direction of republican government, which today we think of as liberal democracy.[3] Kant believed that Universal History is both philosophical and empirical. He called for a Kepler or Newton who could explain the universal laws of the evolution of human history. "We leave it to Nature to produce the man capable of composing it."

Kant was looking for a Universal History that showed the progressive evolution of humankind within the societies the civilizations have thrown up. He was looking for the idea of progress, an Enlightenment idea rather discredited by two world wars and the wars of our time:

> If one follows the influence of Greek history on the construction and misconstruction of the Roman state which swallowed

> up the Greek, then the Roman influence on the barbarians who in turn destroyed it, and so on down to our times; if one adds episodes from the national histories of other peoples in so far as they are known from the history of the enlightened nations, one will discover a regular progress in the constitution of states on our continent (which will probably give law, eventually, to all the others).

To jump ahead H.G. Wells' *Outline of History* came close to charting the progress of humankind and answering Kant's call. But Wells stopped at the end of the First World War when, despite the League of Nations, progress seemed to be going into reverse: the regress of the Second World War and the Holocaust. Kant would also have been looking for periods of freedom, democracy and egalitarianism, cultural periods like the late 5th- and early 4th-century-BC Greek culture, aspects of the Renaissance (discounting the tyrannies), and the Enlightenment culture that created the Declaration of Independence in America and (shortly after 1784) the French Revolution, and he would have undoubtedly included the culture within the British Empire.

Kant's project of writing a Universal History that is philosophically serious and also empirical – history with progress and purpose that also refers to precise periods and dates – was initially taken up by Hegel. Hegel, seeing liberty, equality and fraternity as the ideals of the French Revolution and believing that they offered "the society with the greatest freedom" and that they would shape the society that followed the French Revolution, believed that the end-point of world history came in 1806 when revolutionary France under Napoleon beat the Prussians at Jena and ensured that the rights of man would triumph. Alexandre Kojève, the Russian-French philosopher, Hegel's interpreter, thought the same, as Francis Fukuyama points out in *The End of History*.[4]

The lesson of Hegel is that one should beware of believing that one's own time is the end-point of world history, a warning that applies to Fukuyama. Jacques Derrida complained that we have not reached the perfection of the ideal of liberal democracy as "never have violence, inequality, exclusion, famine and thus economic repression affected as many human beings in the history of the earth and of humanity".[5]

I find that the baton has passed to me, and that I am now grappling with Kant's idea of pinpointing the end-point of world history. In my Universalist history[6] I have traced the progress of each of 25 civilizations, covering the whole of the recorded history of the last 5,000 years, from their birth in response to a metaphysical idea, their growth and empires, and then their decline into secularisation when the idea is lost – but also into outer equality and democracy, Unions and federations.

Each of my 25 civilizations goes through 61 similar stages. In the past, when a civilization reaches its end, stage 61, it has passed into another civilization, just as the Mesopotamian and Egyptian civilizations passed into the Arab civilization in 642, when they adopted Islam and Allah. Most of my living civilizations are in stage 43 or 46, union or federalist stages. I see all my living civilizations as ultimately flowing into, or more accurately beneath, a supranational world-wide civilization for a while (see pp.216–217). It is a law in my Universalist history that in any conflict between civilizations, the younger is victorious over the older, and the youngest living civilization dominates all the rest.

Thus this world-wide civilization must necessarily be influenced by the youngest extant civilization, the North-American, which is in stage 15 of its 61 stages, the same stage that the Roman civilization was in during the Roman Empire. The world-wide civilization they will all pass into, or rather beneath, will not be a formal American Empire as the Declaration of Independence supports the freedom and equality of all peoples, and therefore opposes turning them into colonial dependants; but it will be strengthened by American encouragement and leadership.

It can therefore be said that although civilizations rise and fall, grow and decay, they will all reach a time when many are in Union or federalist stages and one is in a dominant, stage-15,

"Roman-Empire" stage, a time when all growing-decaying civilizations progress to an end-point which will be a world-wide civilization that espouses liberal democracy. The entry into this world-wide civilization and "civic constitution" will coincide with the requirements of the rise-and-fall patterns of all the living civilizations, most of which are looking for Unions and federations under a dominant younger civilization. The entry into a world-wide civilization will thus happen naturally – in the sense that the rise-and-fall patterns demand it at that particular period of time.[7]

However, it is important to recognise that until the beginning of the world-wide civilization actually happens, the rise-and-fall pattern of civilizations will continue. It is the norm, and the world-wide civilization will be superimposed on the norm, which will continue beneath it.

In Kant's Universal History, civilizations flow towards the open sea of universal freedom and liberal democracy forever. My scheme shows a similar flow. Many of my civilizations have just passed through stage 42, a period of egalitarianism, and I show several stage-43 and stage-46 civilizations passing under the influence of the stage-15 US. At some point all living civilizations will flow into, or under, the influence of a world-wide civilization for a while as if flowing into, and through, an intermediary great lake. I would say that they will resume as themselves with their original identities as civilizations, the other side of the lake.

For both of us, history is therefore a progressive and unitary history of mankind, even though I hold that the individual civilizations which carry forward this progressive evolutionary thrust rise and fall, decline and disintegrate on their way to historical unity. Kant would have recognised my Universalist history as Universal History.

The progress of history to an end-point therefore resembles the flow in the chart on pp.216–217, in which all civilizations ultimately flow into, or under, a world-wide civilization for a while and remain there in Hegel's sense for a while. Events continue, individual civilizations continue to go through their stages and die into other civilizations just as the currents from rivers continue when they have merged in a great lake, but history will have reached its end-point for a while in widespread liberal democracy. This end-point will be the goal of history, but it will not terminate the progress of history and last forever – no historical arrangement has ever lasted forever, not the Roman Empire, not the British Empire. That is the view as to what will happen of Universal History, which includes my Universalist history.

Despite this caveat the chart on pp.216–217, 'From One to One', reveals history to have a very satisfying symmetry – one that is in history's civilizations rather than in the eye and mind of the beholder.

The Collapse of the Old Order

The re-emergence of the federal idea after the Cold War and the formation of regions and Unions raised hopes that liberal democracy had triumphed over totalitarianism following the demise of the Soviet Union, and would last indefinitely. Events during the next two decades in the War on Terror in Afghanistan, Iraq and Syria suggested these hopes were illusory.

Old thinking sees the world in terms of nation-states and nationalism. New thinking sees the world in terms of supranationalism. Einstein had said (see p.xvii):

> A new type of thinking is essential if mankind is to survive and move toward higher levels. The fundamental problems we face cannot be solved at the same level of thinking with which we created them.

From the perspective of the new thinking, the old world with its old thinking in terms of nation-states and nationalism seemed on the verge of collapse.

According to universal history, history progresses towards a new order, which will last for a while but will not be permanent.

A world-wide civilization with liberal democracy for a while has been made more likely by the convulsive death-throes of the old order that have taken place in the 20th century and the first decade of the 21st century (as part of the financial crisis of 2008). All the old certainties – capitalism, socialism, totalitarianism, the nation-state, colonialism, nationalism, sovereignty, self-determination, internationalism, collective security, superpowerdom and religion – seemed to be tottering.

The new order has been brought into being by new supranationalist thinking. New thinking sees the ruin of the old world which is based on capitalism and nation-states, and looks ahead with visionary clarity to the new order's World State.

Capitalism

The existing world order has been underpinned by the capitalist system, the system of free enterprise, free trade and free competition under which the means of production are privately owned and production is guided, and income distributed, through the operation of markets.

The system began with the break-up of feudalism and gathered strength in the 16th century in the course of the growth of the English cloth industry. The excess of production over consumption, when ploughed back into the means of production, enlarged productive capacity and was not invested in unproductive projects such as cathedrals. Hard work and frugality were encouraged by the 16th-century Protestant Reformation. Prices rose faster than wages, and the capitalists benefited from the ensuing inflation. From c.1500 to c.1750 the early capitalists of the mercantilist era were supported by strong national states, nation-states which achieved uniform monetary systems and legal codes that aided economic development.

In 18th-century England during the Industrial Revolution, capitalism shifted from being based on commerce to being based on industry. Capitalists invested their profits in advancing technical knowledge that promoted industrial growth. Adam Smith, in *Inquiry into the Nature and Causes of the Wealth of Nations* (1776), advocated leaving economic decisions to market forces and not the state bureaucracy, which, he felt, should be disbanded. This was a theory of *laissez-faire*: the abstention of government from interfering in the workings of the market.

In the 19th century after the French Revolution and the Napoleonic Wars, capitalism became dominant. Political liberalism stood for free trade, sound money linked to the gold standard, balanced budgets and minimum poor relief. There was a good measure of economic freedom, although the free economy was in fact a system of warring national economies guided by political rather than economic considerations.

This form of capitalism collapsed with the First World War, when trade was disrupted by air attacks on ships. In the 1920s international markets shrank, the gold standard was abandoned during the Great Depression of the 1930s in favour of managed national currencies, and banking supremacy passed from Europe to the United States. There were revolts against European colonialism in Africa and Asia, and trade barriers multiplied. Protectionism replaced economic freedom. The Great Depression of the 1930s discouraged the State from interfering in economic decisions, but warring national economies undermined free trade.

The Second World War intensified protectionism. Air attacks on ships again disrupted sea trade. By the end of the war economies had become even more national and protected, currencies were not convertible and international trade continued to suffer. The Bretton Woods Conference of July 1944 had set up the International Bank for Reconstruction and Development to make capital available to states needing foreign aid, and the International Monetary Fund to finance short-term imbalances in international payments and to stabilise exchange rates. In Britain socialist measures attacked monopolies and inheritance and introduced social welfare, weakening capitalism. However, after the war US firms moved into Europe and the rest of the world, and US multinational corporations dominated the car, chemicals and computer industries. Capitalism revived. This was the beginning of global capitalism.

Global capitalism was a consequence of developed global financial markets and the growth of transnational corporations and their domination over national economies. It was strengthened through the offshore market in Eurodollars (deposits in US-dollar denominations held at banks outside the US) in the 1970s. It was reinforced around 1980, when Margaret Thatcher and Ronald Reagan removed the State from the economy and allowed market forces to thrive, including privatisation. Private enterprise proved better at creating wealth than the State. To attract and retain capital other countries had to follow their lead. There was strict monetary discipline, and as a result there was a recession and the international debt crisis of 1982 followed.

In 1989 the Berlin Wall fell, the Soviet Empire began to disintegrate and capitalism swept through the ex-Soviet Union, becoming truly global. The spread of communications, including television and the internet, reinforced it. Information and culture slowly became globalised through the widening use of telephones, faxes and computers. Air travel reached all parts of the globe more quickly. The technology for this information revolution was developed from the early, relatively unsophisticated computers that had directed NASA's landing on the moon in 1969. It was US technology.

New York and London were the world's financial centres. The global economy expanded until 1997. Then the removal of the currency peg in Thailand led to the Thai *baht*'s being floated and halved in value, and to financial markets ruining economies in the developing countries.

Globalisation offered individual freedom – free competition on a global scale – that could not be matched by national states. It probably accelerated global growth. However, globalisation hindered national states' taxation, which had traditionally raised revenues to fund their expenditure. For every nation-state's consumers bought goods from many different countries throughout the globe, which meant that they bought fewer domestic goods. Welfare states suffered from the reduction in taxation. Multinational corporations and international financial markets were in conflict with national politics, whose politicians endeavour to please their electorates in order to retain power.

Then came the financial crisis. The housing bubble in the subprime mortgage market burst following widespread 100-percent borrowing on inflated house prices without any need for the borrowers to place a deposit. This led to the collapse of the financial system. The theory that financial markets tend towards equilibrium was proved wrong. In August 2007 the crisis spread to other markets. Hedge funds collapsed, and some lightly regulated financial institutions such as Lehman Brothers, whose creditworthiness proved untrustworthy, crumbled. The financial system went into meltdown. A large money-market fund that had invested in commercial paper issued by Lehman Brothers found that its asset value was below the amount it had deposited. There was a run on money-market funds, which stopped buying commercial paper. The issuers of commercial paper drew down their credit lines, ending interbank lending. The Federal Reserve System injected $1,800 billion into the system. Soon outlays by the Federal Reserve and US government agencies staggeringly came to over $13.5 trillion.

The stock market slumped. Everywhere, consumers were late in settling their bills. Businesses had to pay their staff out of reduced cash flow, and the banks were not lending. Small and medium-sized businesses went into administration.

In the US, Britain, Europe and in many other countries the State bailed out banks and became a majority shareholder. The Thatcher-Reagan revolution went into reverse. A form of nationalisation replaced privatisation as taxpayers' money was injected into the financial system which it would take a generation for taxpayers to repay. Western governments adopted the policy of printing money – quantitative easing – advocated by Keynes in 1932. Expansionist monetary policies replaced tight monetary control to head off a new Great Depression. Levels of government debt rose. Countries looked as if they might go bankrupt: Iceland; Britain; China. In such countries the State, burdened with a massive bureaucracy and Welfare State, and in America's case trying to expand the State's provision of healthcare, was unable to create the wealth that private enterprise had created in the mid-1990s. Bankers were reviled for having created financial chaos and for being rewarded with inflated bonuses they did not deserve.

In 2016 protectionism returned with President Trump's victory in the US Presidential election and the UK's declared departure from the EU in 2019 ('Brexit') following the UK referendum on the EU. Both in the US and Europe so-called 'immigrants' – Mexicans in the US, and in Europe refugees from the Middle-Eastern wars, and indeed EU citizens exercising freedom of movement – were blamed for taking jobs and benefits and depressing wages. Deficits were a problem in the US, the UK and Southern Europe, especially Greece. There was instability and uncertainty. Trump's 'America First' policy in the US was designed to cut the American deficit, including healthcare. It was not certain how the UK would make up for losing its exports to the European single market, and both Scotland and Northern Ireland sought independence from the United Kingdom. Capitalism, which had performed so well under liberal democracy's freedom of movement for economic migrants, seemed to have stalled in the face of multinational protectionism. In all parts of the world there were problems and future prosperity seemed in doubt.

The future for global capitalism looked dismal. The old financial order seemed to have run its course, and to be waiting for a new model.

Socialism

If capitalism has played a large part in bringing history to an end-point in permanent liberal democracy by its collapse, socialism has also undermined the old order. It has promoted equality and fraternity – and has similarly underpinned the old order, modifying and weakening unbridled capitalism and in the process losing its own inspirational utopian drive and collapsing under etiolating compromises.

Socialism's roots can be traced back to Plato's *Republic* and More's *Utopia*, but as a movement it really began as a reaction to the harsh social and economic conditions created by the Industrial Revolution. In the early days of the Industrial Revolution, the injustice, inequalities and suffering were appalling. Employers exploited their workers, who produced the goods from which both made a living. Extreme socialists dreamed that the masses would wrest control of the means of production and of the government from capitalists. Some urged the complete nationalisation of all the means of production. Others advocated selective nationalisation with controlled private ownership permitted in some industries. Market socialists sought to control the market economy by socialist planning.

Socialism began in the early 19th century with utopian thinkers: in France, where François-Marie-Charles Fourier and Comte Henri de Saint-Simon dreamt of a new society in which all would have an equal opportunity to rise in relation to their talents regardless of capitalist competition; and in England, where Robert Owen, a capitalist employer in textile works, supported growing trade unionism. Pierre-Joseph Proudhon was more anarchistic and attacked private property. Karl Marx produced the Communist Manifesto in 1848, a year of European revolutions. This saw society in terms of class struggle and antithetical, antagonistic forces: out of the clash between the capitalists and labour would come a new synthesis, a socialist, communist society.

The Marxist movement came to dominate socialist thinking during the last third of the 19th century. Influenced by Marx, moderate German social democracy was born in 1869. It urged government to provide capital to emancipate labour from capitalist domination. There were Social Democratic Parties in France, Scandinavia and Central Europe, and there was a rise in anarchism. The Second International of 1889 provided a kind of international parliament of socialist movements, and under German leadership conveyed Marxist revolutionary ideas. British Fabianism, on the other hand, pursued a socialist, non-Marxist course: a "gradual", non-revolutionary reform of society to improve the conditions of the masses.

The rise of Russian socialism in the 1860s and 1870s incorporated Marxism, and under the Leninists led to the October Revolution of 1917 and a city-based communism. The Third International of 1919 strengthened communist parties and advocated world revolution. The masses did not in fact now own the means of production, and the communist state did not wither away, as promised, but became repressive. It soon became clear that the masses had not been liberated as a result of class struggle, but were being oppressed under a dictatorship, and that the revolution seemed more of a national Russian revolution than a socialist one. The Soviet Union turned violent under Stalin's Great Purge of the 1930s, and European socialists split from communists. Socialists achieved power in Germany, the United Kingdom, Italy, France and Sweden. Nazi Fascism was opposed by the Free World, including the Soviet Union, and this confrontation between left-of-centre and far-right gave socialism a temporary ideological boost that owed much to opposing Fascism.

After the Second World War, a new agrarian socialism spread among peasants in the backward, developing countries, notably China, and fuelled liberation struggles against colonialism. In Europe, socialism evolved from class struggle to concern for social welfare within free markets, and post-war socialist parties came to power in Germany, Britain, France and Italy. Meanwhile socialism swept Africa, the Arab world and South-East Asia. The British-Commonwealth countries Australia, New Zealand and Canada also saw a growth of socialism, as did Latin America, notably Chile. During these years, socialism seemed to be undergoing something of a revival.

The spread of socialism created egalitarian, democratic and fraternal societies of a moderate socialist nature. They were more concerned with social security and aspects of the welfare state than with class struggle and revolution. Their middle-of-the-road egalitarianism perfectly reflected stage 42 of my 61 rise-and-fall stages. Extreme Marxist socialism, which espoused revolutions to overthrow states in the name of the masses, who were then oppressed, largely collapsed when the Berlin Wall fell in 1989 and the Soviet Empire broke up in 1991. Communism lingered on in China, where it was mixed with capitalism and moderate socialism, and in extreme dictatorial states such as North Korea. But Communism looked finished. With the demise of extreme Marxism, socialism as a strong modifying force that would advance the masses could be deemed to have run its course and to have failed. It looked a pallid form of its previous self.

Most of the world's liberal democracies had a uniform, left-of-centre, watered-down socialism that paid lip-service to liberty, equality and fraternity. They governed from near the centre. Fairness and equality of opportunity were combined with some private ownership. In general, liberal democracies steered clear of class struggle and anti-capitalist measures. The EU encouraged this process and political posture: as Western Europe joined together with Eastern Europe, both could meet in the centre, and so Western-European liberal democracies tended to shift leftwards and East-European liberal democracies tended to shift rightwards. A similar process moved most parties onto common centre ground. There was soon little to choose between governments and opposition parties on this uniform, central ground.

The pervading uniformity of states' outlooks had the effect of watering down socialism. British New Labour had been created as a deliberate watering-down of socialism, mixing it with private enterprise and investment and abolishing the extreme-socialist Clause 4. Socialism seemed a pale imitation of the socialism that was known in earlier times.

The financial crisis seemed to reinstate socialism as in a number of countries the State poured huge amounts of funds into banks, taking stakes in them on behalf of taxpayers and using "quantitative easing" to print money, a measure that in the past has always resulted in inflation. Socialism seemed to revive when across the world, in the US, Europe and Far East, politicians acting on behalf of taxpayers handed $3 trillion in bail-outs to banks, whose leaders then carried on as if there had never been a crisis.

The revival of socialism was an illusion. For there was now less money available for public spending and welfare, and there would have to be cutbacks in most areas of government. In many ways the financial crisis had brought about the collapse of socialism just as it had brought about the collapse of capitalism. Only an uninspiring, watered-down socialism survived within the uniform, left-of-centre governments of many liberal democracies.

The upheaval of Brexit coincided in the UK with an extreme-left ex-Trotskyist socialist leader becoming Leader of the Opposition. The ex-Blairite MPs lost their positions, and the Labour Party was shunned by the British electorate, which wanted traditional certainties and practical solutions to the economy, health and education in a time when there might have to be more cuts as the UK's post-Brexit revenue in the years following 2019 might be reduced.

In truth, the socialism of the old order had passed, not with the dramatic suddenness of Soviet Marxism, but it had nevertheless unobtrusively fallen sick and quietly died.

Totalitarianism

Totalitarianism, another feature of the old order, has also run its course: a form of government that permits no individual freedom and subordinates individuals' lives, and all social life, to the totalitarian government's authority. Benito Mussolini coined the word *totalitario* (the Italian for "totalitarian") in the early 1920s and reflected its sense in his 1932 entry in the *Enciclopedia Italiana* which described the Italian Fascist state: "All within the State, none outside the State, none against the State." Totalitarianism soon came to mean single-party government.

By the Second World War, Germany's Hitler and the Soviet Union's Stalin had shown themselves to be totalitarians as had Spain's Franco and Japan's Tojo. They used central rule to coerce and repress after the manner of the Indian Mauryan dynasty and the Chinese Ch'in (now written Qin) dynasty of the 3rd and 2nd centuries BC. Under their totalitarianism all legal, social and political traditions were swept away. Their totalitarian nation-states pursued a special goal linked to conquest, and any dissent was branded evil and punished. Whole classes of people were liquidated: Jews in Germany, *kulaks* or wealthy peasant farmers in the Soviet Union. Their police operated without any regulation or constraint by law, and laws were made by one man, who behaved deliberately unpredictably to rule by terror and repress dissent. Conformity was enforced by propaganda, censorship, regulation and force.

Hannah Arendt, in *The Origins of Totalitarianism* (1951), tracked the origins of totalitarianism back to 19th-century anti-Semitism and imperialism, and saw its rise as a consequence of the disintegration of the nation-state. Thus, in Germany, the Weimar republic collapsed amid hyper-inflation and high unemployment, and Hitler rose out of its ruins.

Since the Second World War there have been numerous totalitarian regimes. Mao's China is an obvious example. Individuals were herded into communes and every aspect of their lives was controlled by the State. Any dissent or failure to conform was punished, often by execution. The 1966 Cultural Revolution imposed conformity in the form of the *Little Red Book* of Mao's sayings, which citizens had to wave. It identified unreliable citizens and locked them up or did away with them after a brief hearing in a local court. China is still totalitarian, but the harshness of the regime has eased.

Many other nation-states are totalitarian. In 2017 Freedom House's annual survey found that democracy scores had declined in many countries. The survey found that of 209 nation-states and related and disputed territories 88 nation-states were deemed to be free, 64 were deemed to be partly-free and 57 not free. (See Appendix D2.) 125 were deemed "electoral democracies" (see Appendix D1). There was thus a total of 152 (88 + 64) free/partly-free liberal democracies (of which 125 were considered to be "electoral democracies"), leaving 57 assessed as not free, that are considered not to be democracies. (See Appendix D3.)[8] These include: the Russian Federation and many ex-USSR states; Arab and African totalitarian states like Iran, Iraq, Libya and Zimbabwe; Asian totalitarian states like North Korea and Myanmar (Burma); and the Latin-American Cuba.

2016 was characterised by the erosion of democratic institutions, and although Colombia improved, 11 countries showed downward trends: China, Ethiopia, Hong Kong, Mozambique, Nicaragua, the Philippines, Poland, South Sudan, Turkey and Zambia. In 2017 Turkey slid back from parliamentary democracy to an authoritarian elected dictatorship which could remain in power until 2029. (I lived in Libya under Col. Gaddafi during the first year of the Libyan Revolution, and witnessed the dismantling of the monarchy and its parliamentary institutions and their replacement by a totalitarian government in which the threat of execution – one night dramatically exercised against me – asserted terror and repression and controlled dissent.[9])

Another organisation, using more stringent criteria, has come up with different findings. The UK-based Economist Intelligence Unit has measured the state of democracy in 167 countries since 2006 in terms of 60 indicators, and in 2016 found only 19 full democracies, 57 being flawed democracies (including the US and most of the European nation-states), 40 hybrid regimes and 51 authoritarian regimes, suggesting that world-wide democracy is less free than Freedom House's survey indicates.[10]

Declining democracy scores and conflicting criteria aside, by the outbreak of the financial crisis it seemed that totalitarianism had reached a dead end. China faced bankruptcy and under Deng took a capitalist direction while the totalitarian Mao's portrait remained in Tiananmen Square. North Korea, unable to feed its own people, claimed to have renounced weapons of mass destruction and in return received American cash and tons of food aid. It then became apparent that it had built a couple of nuclear bombs. After 40 years of totalitarianism, during which billions of dollars were squandered on terrorism and supporting anti-American and anti-British causes, Gaddafi renounced weapons of mass destruction and returned oil-rich Libya to the policies in operation under the monarchy. (Libya after Gaddafi has since collapsed into chaos.)

All round the world in our global time, repressive rule by autocrats is opposed by their subservient peoples. Strong rulers such as Iraq's Saddam Hussein, Iran's Supreme Leader Sayyid Ali Khameini and first Mahmoud Ahmadinejad, then Hassan Rouhani (the heirs of Ayatollah Khomeini), Syria's Bashar al-Assad and Zimbabwe's Robert Mugabe may all have believed they could control and repress public opinion in a globalised world, but their local peoples used the internet and Twitter to send messages to the outside world and their totalitarian regimes could not stop them.

Totalitarianism is now discredited in terms of all sound values, but there are still many dictators. The peoples of the last totalitarian regimes are ready to throw off the tyrants who have ruled them just as Romania threw off the Ceausescu regime. Totalitarianism belongs to the old order of the old world. It is among the flotsam and jetsam of history, and in our time the totalitarian tyrants (see Appendix D4 for the world's 59 dictators in not-free nation-states) inspire loathing and contempt for their colossal mistreatments of their peoples.

The nation-state

Capitalism, socialism and in some countries totalitarianism have all operated through the nation-state, another feature of the old order which now looks to be in decline.

A nation is a body of people who share a real (or imagined) common history, culture, language, religion, ethnic origin and common descent and who typically inhabit a particular country or territory.[11] Historically, the concept developed slowly. Cicero, in *Philippics Against Mark Antony* (44BC), contrasts external, inferior races of "people" (*nationes*) with the Roman "community" (*civitas*). St Jerome uses the term of non-Christians. Liutprand, Bishop of Cremona, uses it in conjunction with language and territory (in 968). Medieval universities used the term "nation" (*natio*) to refer to a subdivision of students who spoke the same language. This was the case in the University of Paris; also in the University of Prague, where subdivisions included Bohemian, Bavarian, Saxon and Polish "nations" (*nationes*).

The nation as a primary focus of political allegiance grew out of the Westphalian system that was created by the 1648 Treaty of Westphalia, which established the notion of territorial sovereignty as a doctrine of non-interference in the affairs of other nations. Until the 18th century the focus was on a smaller political unit: a feudal fiefdom, a religious group, a city or the immediate neighbourhood. The religious unit had revealed itself during the Crusades, when Crusaders had allegiance to the supranational Christian community as a whole, known as Christendom. Until the 18th century the state was therefore one of a number of focal points for political activity.

At the beginning of the 18th century Europe was dominated by multi-ethnic empires: the Austro-Hungarian Empire, the Russian Empire, the Ottoman Empire, the French Empire and the British Empire. They were all monarchies ruled by a king, emperor or sultan. Each empire was dominated by one ethnic group and its language was the language used in public administration. Some smaller European states were dynastic, ruled by a royal house (such as Savoy).

The rise of large centralised states ended the feudal structures and local city allegiances, and the national ruler came to be viewed as the state's head. The new nation-states were sovereign, territorial units. Nations as sociological, cultural units had a long historical narrative in their early phases but became nation-states when they developed modern industrial states and nationalist movements. This happened towards the end of the 18th century when formulations of political demands occurred after the American and French Revolutions, during the writing of the American Constitution of 1788 and of the French Constitutions of 1791 (in which sovereignty was held by parliament) and 1793 (when sovereignty was transferred to the people).

The state was a political and geopolitical entity. The nation was a cultural and often an ethnic entity. A nation-state was born when the social concept of a "nation" coincided with the political concept of a "state". The nation-state was thus a combination of the political, geopolitical, cultural and ethnic. Often its boundaries did not coincide with its ethnic and cultural boundaries, but it claimed sovereignty within its own territory.

The early nation-state, such as England and France, guarded its borders and considered itself an economic unity, as did Germany when its customs union, the Zollverein, was created in 1818. The United Kingdom was formed by the merger of two independent kingdoms (the Kingdom of England and the Kingdom of Scotland). Each state continued with its own distinct features, and the UK is now variously regarded as a nation-state and as a multinational state (including Wales and Northern Ireland), "countries within a country". Portugal and the Dutch Republic were early nation-states, and Italy was created during its 19th-century unification. More nation-states were created as the empires broke up: Austria, Hungary and Bosnia and Herzegovina grew out of the break-up of the Austro-Hungarian Empire. The Russian Empire broke up into the states of the Soviet Union. The ethnically-diverse Ottoman Empire broke up into the many nation-states extending from the Balkans through Turkey to Morocco.

Independent regions had their identities subordinated to national identity: Alsace-Lorraine to both France and Germany at different times; Catalonia to Spain; Brittany and Corsica to France; and Sicily and Sardinia to Italy. Some smaller states survived and became nation-states: Liechtenstein, Andorra, Monaco and San Marino. Switzerland began as a confederation of cantons with four official languages and became a federation when the cantons ceased to be sovereign, and in the process a Swiss national identity emerged.

Some nation-states had political boundaries that did not correspond to their ethnic and cultural boundaries, and disputes led to late transfers of peoples into nation-states: for example the Hatay Province was transferred from Syria to Turkey. The Kurds are a people without territory between northern Iraq, eastern Turkey and western Iran. Denmark has sovereignty of the Faroe Islands and Greenland. China includes the Han ethnic group and 55 ethnic minorities.

An anomaly of the nation-state system is that some members of nations live outside their nation-states' borders. These are thus ethnic minorities in another nation-state. The nation-states that have absentee members want to annex areas to include these populations. Irredentist claims (a concept based on the 19th-century Italian practice) have led to nations asserting that they have a "Greater" nation, one that restores their own ethnic absentees living in other territories. For example, Belgium seceded from the United Kingdom of the Netherlands in 1830 and its Flemish population in the north speaks Dutch and is often claimed by Dutch supporters of a Greater Netherlands ideal.

It is worth listing the many similar instances to underline the muddle that exists within the nation-state system: Greater Albania; Greater Balochistan; Greater China; Greater Croatia; Greater Finland; Greater Germany; Greater Hungary; Greater India; Greater Indonesia; Greater Israel; Greater Iran; United Macedonia; Greater Mongolia; Greater Morocco; Greater Netherlands; Greater Portugal; Greater Romania; Greater Serbia; Greater Somalia; Greater Syria; Greater Greece (*Megali Idea*); Pan-Turkism. All these claims may lead to attempts to recover areas and could lead to local wars.

It is clear that there is an arbitrariness about the borders of existing nation-states. Their boundaries often do not include all the ethnic, cultural and linguistic groups that properly belong with them. In the feudal time there were feudal fiefdoms that divided humankind into warring groups, each under different laws of medieval dukes, counts and barons. It is now being grasped that the new nation-states returned the multi-ethnic empires to the equivalent of feudal states, each with its own laws and with institutions replacing the king, emperor or sultan as instruments of government. Nation-states subdivide humankind into segregated groups and rule on their behalf while ignoring the rest of humankind.

There has been a growing realisation that conflicting nation-states led to the First and Second World Wars and have produced many wars during the 19th and 20th centuries. Nation-states have now become more interdependent, taking part in rounds of meetings like the G20, and in Europe the federalism of the European Union has placed a new tier over the nation-states and removed perhaps 80 per cent of their right to make laws. The German figure may be 84 per cent. The President of the European Union Parliament from 2007 to 2009, Hans-Gert Pöttering, said that once the Lisbon Treaty was fully implemented, the EU would be responsible for "nearly 100 per cent" of all laws made in Europe.[12]

In the Lisbon Treaty the EU state was given a legal entity which was above that of its component nation-states and signalled the subordination of the nation-state to a new federal structure. Devolution has weakened the nation-state, or multinational state, in the UK.

If nation-states did indeed have a social contract with their peoples under which they provided security and harmonious living in return for taxation and other duties, including military service in harm's way when demanded, some nation-states have forfeited adherence to this contract by breaking their side of the bargain. In the case of the UK, after Churchill cashed in the British Empire to fight for freedom and protect the British people from Nazi rule, the spivs of New Labour borrowed and pretended their brilliance had created a boom by letting 3 million immigrants in to share it, and when it went bust, carried on borrowing and saddled the British people with a deficit of over £800 billion which would take years for taxpayers to repay. A British taxpayer, called on to pay for nation-state recklessness in the face of war and financial crisis, could be forgiven for concluding that a deceptive Government had broken its side of the contract, and that there must be a better way of running everyday life to provide harmonious living. The nation-state has to earn its respect. It cannot take respect for granted.

Following the UK's decision to exit from the EU (which was

largely a reaction to the influx of EU migrants) there were calls for Scotland and Northern Ireland to become independent so they could retain links with the EU's single market, and the British nation-state looked as if it was beginning to break up. The British nation-state had been assembled over 500 years. In 1536 England and Wales united to create the Kingdom of England and Wales. In 1707 this Kingdom merged with Scotland to create the Kingdom of Great Britain. In 1800 this Kingdom merged with Ireland to create the United Kingdom of Great Britain and Ireland. In 1922 Eire (Southern Ireland) separated from Northern Ireland and exited the Union, leaving behind the United Kingdom of Great Britain and Northern Ireland. Now it seemed that the UK might collapse back to the 1536 borders of the Kingdom of England and Wales.

There was talk of a federal country, of the four constituent nations – England, Scotland, Wales and Northern Ireland – withdrawing from the Union and each being independent within a federation. But, however one looked at it, the British nation-state seemed about to fragment due to the strains created by Brexit. In my poetic works since 1958 I had observed and reflected the decline and dissolution of the British Empire, and now I might be witnessing and reflecting the break-up and dismantling of the United Kingdom and the British nation-state. I might be an eyewitness of the transience of the nation-state into which I had been born, which might not survive my lifetime.

There is a widespread feeling that the haphazard nation-state system no longer merits support as a receptacle for combining those who share a culture, history, common language, religion, ethnic origin, and common descent, and that in a regional time the concept of the nation-state has become discredited and has passed, although it still wields power structures over its peoples. The nation-state has run its course and is a remnant of the old order that has undergone a protracted collapse.

Colonialism

Colonialism was the building and maintaining of colonies in one territory by people from another territory, after the manner of the ancient Phoenicians, Greeks and Romans.

The era of European colonialism was from the 15th to the 20th centuries. It began with the emerging European nation-states – England, France, Portugal, Spain and the Low Countries – shortly before c.1500 and with the early voyages of discovery. Twelve European nation-states had empires: the British (who had two, one in America and then one in the rest of the world), French, Portuguese, Spanish, Italian, Dutch, German, Belgian (in the Congo), Danish, Swedish, Russian and Ottoman nation-states. At the same time the United States had an empire in the Philippines.

The colonial pattern was the same under all the empires. The mother country settled a colony, installed a garrison to hold it and sent out more settlers. The mother country then imported its resources, and as the colony became established exported its own goods. In due course it acted as a civilizing force, educating and training the locals. The amount of training settlers received varied between empires.

Colonialism had run its course by the middle of the 20th century. Decolonisation accelerated from 1945. Great Britain granted India and Pakistan their independence, and the greater part of the British Mediterranean, African, Asian, Pacific and West-Indian colonies received their independence in the ensuing decades. France, Belgium, Portugal and the Netherlands decolonised in most of their territories from the 1950s to the 1970s. Liberation movements sprang up in many colonies to press for independence.

The era of colonialism has now passed. It belonged to the old order: although a few small colonies still remain, history has swept the colonial system away.

Nationalism

Nationalism, the creed of those who believe that fidelity to one's state is more important than fidelity to international principles or individual interests, is inextricably linked to the nation-state. Nationalism grew out of the creation of the early nation-states, and loyalty to these nation-states was strengthened during wars. Since the Second World War, as we have seen, the European nation-states weakened as a result of interdependence and the growth of the EU. Nationalism in Europe similarly weakened, but has undergone a recent revival as in several European nation-states far-right political parties and groups have protested against the rise in immigration caused by the exodus of refugees of Middle-Eastern wars.

In some cases nationalism led to the creation of nation-states, particularly in post-war Asia and Africa where liberation movements, anti-colonialist movements, sprang up to press for independence. But as colonies were given independence, and became enmeshed in interdependent regional structures, nationalism weakened.

During the Second World War nationalism was associated with partisans and resistance-movement guerrillas, who sought to liberate their countries from Nazi rule. In the mid-1980s I played a part in calling for the liberation of the East-European states from the Soviet Union. I wrote a paper entitled *FREE* (Freedom for the Republics of Eastern Europe) and broadcast into Eastern Europe – not to stoke up their nationalism but to swell the regional Union, the European Community (which has since passed into the European Union).[13] In a world of regions and Unions, and very few remaining colonies, nationalism of this kind was to be found in the Middle East and Afghanistan, among guerrillas fighting Western dominance.

The main expression of nationalism today can be found at international sporting fixtures. Just as the nation-state and colonialism had passed as remnants of the old order, so nationalism, which was inextricably linked with them, increasingly looked outmoded.

Sovereignty

Sovereignty is the ultimate law-making authority over a territory or a state's decision-making process and maintenance of order. In the Middle Ages medieval monarchs shared power, and therefore sovereignty, with the feudal aristocracy.

In 16th-century France Jean Bodin, the French jurist and political philosopher, reacting to the chaos caused by the French wars of religion, used the new concept of sovereignty to strengthen the French king's power over rebellious feudal lords and effect the replacement of feudalism by nationalism. Influenced by the Roman jurist Ulpian (2nd–3rd century AD), who held that the Roman *imperium* of the people was transferred to the Emperor, who was not bound by the law and whose word was law, Bodin wrote in *Six Books of the Republic (Six livres de la république,* 1576) that "the sovereign who makes the laws cannot be bound by the laws he makes" ("*majestas est summa in cives ac subditos legibusque soluta potestas*"). However, to Bodin the sovereign was restricted by the constitutional law of the state, though possessing absolute and perpetual sovereignty. According to Bodin sovereignty was conferred by divine law as the divine right of kings.

The English philosopher Thomas Hobbes identified the sovereign with might rather than law. He held that the sovereign could not be limited by the law he commands, and that sovereign power was therefore absolute. This led to sovereigns imposing their will on other sovereigns and therefore to a perpetual state of war. Like Bodin, Hobbes called for a strong central authority.

In *Leviathan* (1651) he defined sovereignty as supreme legal coercive authority over a particular population and territory. In this work Hobbes argues for a social contract and rule by an absolute sovereign. He analyses the twelve principal rights of a sovereign and three types of commonwealth. He writes that chaos or civil war, situations of a state of nature, could only be averted by strong central government.

The book was written during the English Civil War, and published after its end, and it is clear that Hobbes was a supporter of the Royalist cause. The frontispiece of *Leviathan* by Abraham Bosse, who discussed it with Hobbes, shows a giant Charles I rising over hills, beneath a quotation from the *Book of Job, "Non est potestas super terram quae comparetur ei"* ("There is no power on Earth to be compared to him"). This links the figure of Charles

I to the monster leviathan in the *Book of Job*. However, Hobbes irritated both sides: the Royalists by his social contract theory, the Parliamentarians by his support for absolute monarchy. He fled to Paris where he taught the future Charles II mathematics. His thoughts on commonwealths were primarily linked to the situation in England.

Hobbes argued that although individuals surrender their liberties for protection, a plurality of sovereign states is not burdensome: "Because states uphold the Industry of their Subjects; there does not follow from the international state of nature, that misery, which accompanies the Liberty of particular men."[14]

In the 17th and 18th centuries, John Locke and Rousseau developed a theory of popular sovereignty: that a state is based on a compact of its citizens who entrust their powers to a government for common protection.

Rousseau, in the second book of *Du contrat social, ou Principes du droit politique* (1762), argues that sovereignty, or the general will, is inalienable and acts through laws. The legislator has no authority of his own; he is only a guide who drafts and proposes laws which the people alone (the sovereign or general will) has authority to pass and impose. In his *The Social Contract* (1762) Rousseau argues that "the more the Government has to use force to contain the people, the more force the Sovereign should have in order to contain the Government".

Rousseau's theory of popular sovereignty found expression in the American Declaration of Independence of 1776. Reflecting Rousseau's popular sovereignty, the French Constitution of 1791 stated: "Sovereignty is one, indivisible, unalienable and imprescriptible; it belongs to the Nation; no group can attribute sovereignty to itself nor can an individual arrogate it to himself."

In the ensuing years different views of sovereignty evolved. The 19th-century English jurist John Austin held that sovereignty was vested in a nation's parliament. The US Constitution was the fundamental law of the federal Union, not the legislature, a view that was reinforced by the Supreme Court's right to declare laws unconstitutional. Political scientists such as Léon Duguit, Hugo Krabbe and Harold J. Laski championed pluralistic sovereignty, locating sovereignty in various political, economic, social and religious groups.

For 200 years sovereign states had claimed the right to judge disputes with, and enforce war on, other sovereign states. In the 20th century the sovereignty of nation-states was restricted. The 1899 and 1907 Hague Conferences established rules about the conduct of war on land and at sea. The Covenant of the League of Nations restricted the right to go to war. The Briand-Kellogg Pact of 1928 condemned going to war to solve disputes. The Charter of the United Nations (Article 2) required member states to settle disputes "by peaceful means in such a manner that international peace and security, and justice, are not endangered" and to "refrain in their international relations from the threat or use of force". Somehow this injunction had to be reconciled with the UN's "principle of sovereign equality of all its Members".

States have now accepted a body of law limiting their sovereign right, by consent or autolimitation. States are sometimes considered bound even if acceptance has not been expressed or implied. There is thus a balance between states' sovereignty and the needs of international society. The principle of federalism established divided sovereignty (sovereignty divided between the federal Union and states). The growing interdependence of states has resulted in the pooling of sovereignty to establish Unions such as the European Union. States' national governments and organs of the world community are now exercising authority on behalf of peoples. Nation-states are often now considered the instruments of their sovereign peoples.

The spreading of divided sovereignty has undermined the investing of sovereignty in institutions, and to the extent that sovereignty has been invested in nation-states and nationalism, it has been further undermined by the decline of the nation-state as a result of the rise of regional Unions and interdependence. Austin held that British sovereignty was invested in parliaments. In 2009, around 80 per cent of European laws were jointly decided between the European Parliament and the Council of Ministers. The British Parliament, which used to make all Britain's laws, then enacted less than 20 per cent of laws as 80 per cent were enacted in Brussels by the European Union, which could therefore be regarded as having taken over 80 per cent of British sovereignty on a pooling basis.[15] As we have seen, after the ratification of the Lisbon Treaty the European Union was set to pass nearly 100 per cent of Europe's laws, leaving just over 0 per cent to national parliaments.

Following Brexit the UK will once again be in control of 100 per cent of its own laws, and sovereignty can therefore be said to have undergone a revival in the apparently crumbling British nation-state. The same can be said of the US. However, in the EU and the many regional organisations, sovereignty is pooled, and in the greater part of the world where there are federations and regional Unions the sovereignty of many nation-states has been shared.

The sovereignty of nation-states' institutions is not as strong as it used to be. The people are sovereign according to many constitutional experts, which means all the people in the world, and splitting them up and dividing them into nation-states' territories has failed to remove sovereignty from the people of the world. The sovereignties of the last 200 years that were located in monarchs or nation-states belong to the old order and have passed. Only a World State with a world government can reflect, in the areas over which it has authority, the sovereignty of the peoples of the world.

Self-determination

During the First and Second World Wars many peoples living under empires in occupied nations, and during the decolonising time many settlers, dreamed of self-determination: of founding an independent nation-state with the right to determine its own government and allegiance. The occupied and downtrodden settlers longed to do as they wished within their own frontiers, no matter how harmful it was to the rest of the world. The longing for a new nation-state led to interdependent aggregates of peoples within an empire splitting themselves into smaller, newly-sovereign units in the name of "ending the occupation", "ending imperialism", "abolishing colonialism" and "national independence from empire".

Those who fought for self-determination then found themselves living in newly-sovereign nation-states – and facing the problems sovereign nation-states have suffered: disputes with other sovereign nation-states and new local wars, then a time of interdependent regions when nation-states were scorned. Within two decades many of the new nation-states created after 1919, after the Second World War and during decolonisation were conquered and enslaved by other nation-states. Thus, the self-determination of Lithuania ended in its occupation by Poland, and Polish self-determination ended when Germany and later the USSR conquered Poland. Many East-European nation-states were swallowed by the Soviet Empire. Nationalism devoured its children.

Like the nation-state and sovereignty, in our regional world self-determination's time seems to have passed and increasingly appears to belong to the old order.

Internationalism

Internationalism is a political movement that advocates greater economic and political co-operation among nation-states for the prevention of wars. It means "inter-nationalism", a co-operation between nation-states.

Such co-operation failed during the first half of the 20th century. The Covenant of the League of Nations was based on the principles of national sovereignty, national self-determination and the right of every nation-state to do as it wished within its own boundaries. If Stalin wished to execute one million in his purge of 1934 and kill a further 10 million in the next few years, other nation-states should not interfere – the Westphalian approach to nation-states.

The League of Nations' replacement, the United Nations, was

in 2017 an aggregate of 193 sovereign nation-states. We have seen that nation-states are competitive units whose disputes can slide into wars. The UN deals with a world in which until the Second World War nationalism, though weakening, still dominated democracy, capitalism, socialism, liberalism, Christianity, politics, religion, economics, monarchies and republics. Nationalism suggests that conflicting nationalisms can be bridged; that the UN can reconcile disputes between sovereign nation-states, conflicting nationalisms.

As the UN's powerlessness to prevent the 2003 war in Iraq demonstrates, powerful nation-states can ride roughshod over the UN, which has had no power to prevent any of the 162 wars since 1945 (see Appendix C8).[16] Internationalism, being between conflicting nationalisms, looks outmoded and also belongs to the old order. There is a case for its being replaced by a better system.

Collective security

Collective security is a security arrangement in which nation-states co-operate collectively to provide security for all by taking action against any nation-states within groups (such as the Warsaw Pact) which challenged the existing order by using force. It marshals nation-states into achieving a balance of power, as NATO did during the Cold War when it counterbalanced the power of the Soviet bloc within Eastern Europe.

Collective security, then, amounts to some nation-states banding together to act against other nation-states which have also banded together. Both bands see their cause as the more just. There is as much potentiality for conflict in the opposition of two conflicting systems of collective security as there is among conflicting nation-states. The collective security just takes place on a group level now.

The collective security of the League of Nations failed when Japan occupied Manchuria, part of China, in 1932. The League called for Japan to withdraw. As a member of the League of Nations, Japan vetoed the resolution. After two years the League passed a resolution condemning the invasion without committing the League's members to act. The Japanese left the League of Nations, and the problem was not solved.

The League's collective security also failed when it allowed Mussolini to get away with invading Abyssinia in 1935 because Britain and France, seeing Mussolini as an ally who might block the rise of Hitler's Germany, did not condemn the Italian invasion.

During the inter-war years the League fell down because some major states such as the US did not join or give support, and because every state had a veto which some were quick to use to their own advantage.

The successor to the League of Nations, the United Nations, suffered from similar weaknesses. Dealing with sovereign nation-states, the United Nations was positioned between them all. It was originally stymied because the General Assembly was composed of all UN member states, each of which had one vote, no matter how large or small states were. This meant that it was cumbersome for the great powers to secure agreement. The Security Council was developed to circumvent a paralysed General Assembly. However, the five most powerful nation-states within the Security Council, including the Soviet Union, had the veto and used it whenever it suited them, paralysing the UN's ability to resolve disputes.

Consequently, member states of the United Nations frequently failed to condemn aggressors. When Argentina invaded the Falkland Islands, overseas territories of the UK, many UN members stayed out of the dispute and the arguments within the UN Security Council as it did not affect them. The US sat on the fence as it was a member of the Inter-American Treaty of Reciprocal Assistance (the Rio Pact). It adopted an even-handed, balancing posture which did nothing to head off war.

NATO is the best-known collective-defence organisation. Its Article 5 (see Appendix B2) calls on, but does not commit, member states to assist other members under attack. This article was invoked after the September-11 attacks in the US, after which

NATO members provided assistance to the US War on Terror in Afghanistan. In more recent times, NATO has supported Coalition troops in both Afghanistan and Iraq, defending the old order of sovereign nation-states against latter-day "barbarians": the Taliban and al-Qaeda, who would like to possess – and in al-Qaeda's case probably do possess – weapons of mass destruction and who have to be held in check by the West's military equivalent of the Roman legions.

During the Cold War the roles of the UN and NATO as a mediator between, and defender of, nation-states has not been without success. However, as we saw on p.89 there have been 162 wars since 1945 which the UN has failed to prevent, including 37 wars still being fought in 2017 (see Appendix C8). A fully comprehensive list of all the wars in 124 countries can be found in Appendix C6,[17] and there are 72 wars still being fought in 2017 despite the efforts of the UN according to this list (see asterisks in Appendix C6). This is a shocking statistic that cries out for the creation of a World State. The UN's and NATO's collective security has often not been effective in dealing with such situations as peacekeeping forces have been too small.

However, since the end of the Cold War in 1991, collective defence, which has to be against an enemy, has been turned against Islamic fundamentalism in Afghanistan, and specifically bin Laden's purchase of at least 20 nuclear-suitcase bombs from the Chechen Mafia from 1999 onwards (confirmed by Hans Blix of the IAEA in 2004). I have detailed the evidence for this in the Appendix[18] of my epic poem on the nightmare Armageddon threatening our generation: al-Qaeda's plan to detonate ten simultaneous nuclear explosions in ten American cities and bin Laden's attempt to revive the Caliphate – which was discontinued with the formal end of the Ottoman Empire in 1924 – in Baghdad, the seat of the Abbasid Caliphate. During my research for this work, I was able to confirm that this threat to the West is real and is reflected in the degree of the presence of Western troops in Afghanistan.

The fact remains, collective security amounts to one lot of

nation-states banding against another lot, and just as the nation-state itself is outmoded, so too is the system of collective defence. Collective security's time is passing, and it, too, belongs to the old order.

Superpowerdom

There is a strong feeling that the Bush Administration deliberately exploited the September-11 attacks to pursue a policy of American supremacy, a supremacist ideology based on the 1997 Statement of Principles and mission statement of the Project for the New American Century (see Appendix B3), a neo-conservative policy-advocacy group with a strong pro-Israeli outlook. It can be argued that, on the contrary, the Bush Administration saved America from the nuclear Armageddon of bin Laden's nuclear purchases, and that any exploitation of September 11 was perpetrated by the *élites* pursuing an industrial agenda.

Whatever the truth, American superpowerdom following the collapse of the Berlin Wall in 1989 and the fall of Communism in 1991 is tantamount to one nation-state lording it over all the others, either to promote US industrial oil-and-gas-pipeline interests, or to harry the al-Qaeda leadership so they could not carry out a nuclear plot against the US. Superpowerdom comes across to the rest of the world as one nation-state bossing all the other nation-states either to its own advantage or for the "collective security" of all nation-states against the threat of modern Armageddon.

At the time of the 2016 American Presidential election the American Administration had three choices. Either America can be isolationist; or it can pursue an American Empire; or it can build a World State, either out of industrial self-interest, or on the basis of philanthropy. President Trump's presidency began with what looked like a return to isolationism. There was talk of 'America First' and of a wall along the 1,954 miles of the US border with Mexico, and there were protectionist trade measures. The US seemed to be trying to save money, for example by getting other nations to increase their contributions to NATO to enable the US to bring the deficit under control.

The American policy of isolationism was reversed in 2017 by interventions in Syria – the firing of 59 cruise missiles in response to a sarin gas attack; in Afghanistan – the dropping of the largest-ever non-nuclear Massive Ordnance Air Blast (MOAB) GBU-43/B bomb, nicknamed "mother of all bombs" near IS-held caves; and off North Korea – a task force of many ships monitoring Kim Jong-un's missile tests.

Studies have suggested that although at present only the US fulfils the criteria to be considered a superpower, other nation-states are rising and may reach superpowerdom at some point in the 20th century, notably: China; India; the European Union; and the Russian Federation. If just one of these four succeeds in becoming a rival superpower to the United States, then once again a nation-state will be in competitive conflict with another.

Just as warring nation-states are of the old order, so conflicts between superpowers, which are inflated nation-states, also belong to the old order.

Religion

The organised religions command followings throughout the world. Christianity has the biggest following (about 2 billion), followed by Islam (1.1 billion), Hinduism (800 million) and Buddhism (350 million). There are many more faiths. In descending order of support they are: Sikhism, Judaism, the Bahá'i Faith, Confucianism, Jainism and Shinto.

Each organised religion has sects, which are subdivisions. Christianity includes: the Roman Catholic Church (1.05 billion); the Eastern Orthodox Church (240 million); the African Initiated Church; Pentecostalism; the Reformed/Presbyterian/Congregational/United Churches; Anglicanism/the Episcopal Church; the Baptist Church; Methodism; Lutheranism; the Jehovah's Witnesses; the Latter-day Saints; the Adventist Church; the Apostolic/New Apostolic Church; the Restoration Movement; New Thought/Unity/Christian Science; the Brethren (including Plymouth Brethren); the Mennonites; and the Friends/Quakers. Islam includes: Sunnis (940 million); Shias (120 million); Ahmadis; and Druzes. Hinduism includes: Vaisnavism; Saivism; Neo-Hindus and Reform Hindus; and Veerasaivas/Lingayats. Buddhism includes Mahayana, Theravada, and Vajrayana/Tibetan Buddhism.

Organised religions think of themselves as conveying universal truths. However, they segregate groups of people. Each organised religion cuts up and subdivides the whole of humanity into a part, and sects within an organised religion subdivide even more. Consequently universal truth is cut up, subdivided and replicated for a part of humankind, and its universality is thus compromised.

In the past, Christianity saw universal truth as Christianity-dominated, and this has evolved into national organisations. Thus the Catholic Church is based in Vatican City, which is not listed by the UN as one of its 193 member states. The Church of England is a national organisation and its head is the sovereign, the Queen. Its universal truth is compromised by its being enmeshed in the nation-state since the time of Henry VIII. Thus, today there are prayers for the Queen and the Government. The same is true of sects of Islam, which have become enmeshed with nation-states.

Originally Christianity taught a monotheism that was universalist. It taught that all human beings were created equal in the sight of God and are ruled by one God. The history of Christianity has been one of its evolution into a totalitarian hierarchy under an infallible Pope; and the reaction to it that led to schism and later to sectarianism. The universal has degenerated into centralised absolutism and separated, segregated sects and denominations.

The Christian churches have abandoned their initial universalism and their moral principles apply within their segregated groups of people within a nation-state. "Thou shalt not kill", originally a universal truth, now means "Thou shalt not kill a human being of one's own nation-state, but in times of war it is permissible to kill a human being of the same faith from another nation-state", which is what happened between English and German soldiers during the Second World War. In Islam, the universal teaching of Mohammed, the unity maintained by the *Koran* from Morocco to Pakistan, has been split up and subdivided into nationalist groups and became Pan-Turkism, Pan-Arabism or Pakistani Muslims (whose first allegiance was not to Islam but to Pakistan). There has been a split between the Wahhabism of Saudi Arabia and the Muslim Brotherhood based in Egypt. The return to the 7th-century Caliphate sought by the Islamic State (IS) or Daesh has introduced a new, backward-looking Muslim sect with its own fundamental slant that has brought further division to Islam.

Tom Paine, the American Founding Father, grasped that nation-states had corrupted the universality of religion and had had a segregating effect on the world when he wrote in *The Age of Reason* (1794): "I do not believe in the creed professed by the Jewish church, by the Roman church, by the Turkish church, by the Protestant church, nor by any church that I know of. My own mind is my own church. All national institutions of churches, whether Jewish, Christian or Turkish, appear to me no other than human inventions, set up to terrify and enslave mankind, and monopolise power and profits."[19]

A return to Universalist religion can be expected: to one world-wide religion of the Light which is common to all organised religions, the Divine Light called God by religious mystics in all cultures and civilizations, which can be known through the inner Light. A federal world religion would have this Universalist tier, and beneath it the many regional, segregated organised religions, all of which espouse the Light amid the nation-state-ised focus of their worship. I set out the common ground for such a Universalist religion in Part One of *The Fire and the Stones*.[20]

It is now widely grasped that nation-state-ised organised religions have failed to convey universalism. Nation-state-ised religions belong to the old order.

A Time of Transition: Ptolemaic Old Order, Copernican World State

The old order that seems to be passing is a bit like the Ptolemaic view of the universe, the geocentric theory laid down by Ptolemy in 2nd-century-AD Alexandria which lasted 1,400 years. In *Almagest*, the climax of Greek astronomy, Ptolemy explained that the Earth was the centre of the universe, and that the sun, moon and stars revolved around it. The coming order of a World State is a bit like the Copernican theory of the 16th century, the heliocentric theory. Copernicus proposed that the Earth itself rotated and was no longer a stable point, and that it and the planets revolved round the sun. (In fact, the Copernican hypothesis was anticipated by Pythagoras in the 6th century BC and by Aristarchus of Samos in the 3rd century BC.)

Copernicus set out his view in a work titled *Hypothesis*. He did not claim it was based on scientific fact for he knew the Church would oppose his thesis as heresy, just as it would later oppose Galileo.

Our world is already Copernican in shifting to structures that reflect the unity of humankind – regions and Unions – and towards a Universalist World State. But our political and social conceptions are still Ptolemaic and tied to the notions of nation-state, sovereignty and the concepts behind the other headings in this chapter. We are in a time of transition between the institutions of a collapsing old order and a coming World State.

We need to see where we are heading and understand the flow of history. History is teleological and approaches its goal, an end-point which will last for a while and not forever. A philosophical history challenges empirical history by showing that history has a plan and purpose. The purpose of history is to achieve a civic constitution that enshrines freedom. History progresses towards a republican liberal democracy, the institutionalisation of freedom. Human progress shows humankind evolving from barbarism to egalitarian unity in a World State while living in civilizations that rise and fall. All civilizations ultimately flow into a world-wide civilization within a World

State for a while.

We have seen that the system under which humankind has lived since c.1500 is outmoded and collapsing. Capitalism has weakened following the financial crisis. Socialism has weakened following the fall of Communism. What remains is a pale, watered-down mixture of capitalism and socialism. Totalitarianism is outmoded. The nation-state subdivides and segregates part of humankind from the whole of humankind, and has been weakened by interdependence and regional administration, as has nationalism (which is based on fidelity to the nation-state). Colonialism is defunct following the fall of empires and decolonisation. Self-determination (the birth of a new nation-state) has weakened with the weakening of the nation-state before interdependence and regional administration.

Internationalism is outmoded as it urges co-operation between weakened but defiant nation-states to preserve peace, and should be replaced by a better system. Collective security (which is based on the collective defence of nation-states) has weakened. Superpowerdom (the dominance of one nation-state) is discredited as belonging to the old order. Organised religions segregate parts of humankind from the whole. A Universalist religion which is universal to humankind is needed. We have seen that the World State involves a new Copernican perspective that will replace the Ptolemaic nation-state.

The collapse of the old order has left a heap of problems for the world which the nation-state system has been unable to solve: war, poverty, pandemics, climate change, famine and financial crash. As we survey the *débris* of the old order in which we now conduct our lives in our time of transition to an interdependent, regional world that is not yet complete, our conclusion can only be that the old order is passing, and that beyond the nation-state is a new order based on supranationalism, in which humankind will live under a democratic World State that can bring hope to the younger generation that has been dismayed by the dismal wars so many of the earth's regions have had to endure.

PART TWO

Supranationalism

Nation-states subdivide humankind into segregated groups and rule on their behalf while ignoring the rest of humankind.

Nicholas Hagger, *World State*, pp.79–80

5

Beyond Existing Models

I have made the case for moving beyond the nation-state and the old order to a new order's supranational federal authority. I have shown there is a need for a World State, that the forms of government including the nation-state are transient and that there is a drift towards regional organisations and a World State, for which there has always been a profound longing and which conquerors have long attempted to bring in by conquest. I have shown the failure of the old order and its expressions of capitalism, socialism, totalitarianism, the nation-state, colonialism, nationalism, sovereignty, self-determination, internationalism, collective security, superpowerdom and religion.

Now it is time to consider how international law can best create a supranational authority that can abolish war. The first thing to do is to recall all the constructive ideas that have been put forward in the past within the field of international law.

International Law in the Past

The idea that international law can create a supranational authority which can compel sovereign political units to avoid war through binding arbitration goes back to the Middle Ages.

It can be found in the work of Pierre Dubois, whose *De Recuperatione Terrae Sanctae (On the Recovery of the Holy Land,* 1306) asserted that peace in France depended on extending the royal authority of Philip IV in his struggle with Pope Boniface VIII, and that peace in Europe depended on Philip IV's assuming the power of the position of Holy Roman Emperor, an office then vacant. Universal and perpetual peace would then be established by the international arbitration of a council, a confederation of equal Christian states, based in a headquarters at Toulouse. The council would be directed by Christian princes, one for each existing monarchy, who would be supported by a court. This would be composed of three lay prudent men and three wise ecclesiastics, who would be mediators in conflicts. This council would have the power to impose sanctions on a disobedient kingdom, which would include the power to place an embargo on food imports.

Dubois' idea for international arbitration seems to have been transmitted to George of Podebrady, who was chosen King of Bohemia in 1458. A French adventurer, Antonio Marini, probably conveyed Dubois' ideas to him. Podebrady's supranational project, *Congregatio Concordiae,* was very similar to that of Dubois.

We have seen (on p.25) that Dante wrote *De Monarchia* in 1317–1318, ten years after Dubois' work. Did Dante know of Dubois? Books on Dante make no connection between the two, but Dante also sees his "Monarch" or "Emperor" who would rule humankind as arbitrating conflicts. He invested the power of arbitration in a council: he proposed that disputes between sovereign princes be settled by means of arbitration by a council of appointed clerics and laymen from each nation. So it is possible that Dante did know of Dubois' work, and that he did not arrive at international arbitration independently.

Desiderius Erasmus served the future Emperor Charles V as councillor in 1516, and the next year he composed *Querela Pacis (The Complaint of Peace*), condemning war as an instrument of tyranny. He warned temporal rulers to preserve Christian harmony. Erasmus kept the idea of international peace alive at a time when Europe was fragmenting as a result of Luther's Protestant Reformation, but he did not add anything to Dubois' international arbitration.

The Duc de Sully appeared to revive arbitration in 1595. In his *Economies royales* he credits Henry IV, whose minister he was, with organising a coalition of all the states of his empire against the Habsburgs of Vienna and Madrid, and with planning their downfall. Europe would be redivided into 15 states. Perpetual peace between the 15 would be guaranteed by congresses of perpetual peace. In fact, it has been proved that this idea was the product of Sully's imagination. Henry IV did not plan to keep international peace by congresses.[1]

The pioneer of international arbitration was Émeric Crucé, who in *Le nouveau Cynée (The New Cyneas*, 1623) imagined he was the peacemaker Cineas at the court of the 3rd-century-AD Pyrrhus, King of the Molossians of Epirus. He called for a permanent assembly of princes or their delegates to arbitrate international disputes. Crucé saw this assembly as exercising moral pressure rather than sanctions to enforce settlements. His scope was global for his day, and arbitration would take place between the nations of Europe, Asia and Africa.

The Dutch jurist Hugo Grotius was thinking about international law's ability to keep peace when he wrote *De Jure Belli Ac Pacis (On the Laws of War and Peace*, 1625). This is generally taken to be the starting-point of modern international law, based on natural law.

Living during the Eighty Years' War between Spain and the Netherlands (1568–1648) and the Thirty Years' War between Catholic and Protestant European nations (1618–1648), Grotius was preoccupied with the conflicts between nations and religions. He dedicated *De Jure Belli Act Pacis* to his patron, Louis XIII, and set out a system of principles of natural law which should bind all people and nations, regardless of local custom. In this work he writes:

> Throughout the Christian world I observed a lack of restraint in relation to war, such as even barbarous races should be ashamed of; I observed that men rush to arms for slight causes, or no cause at all, and that when arms have once been taken up there is no longer respect for law.[2]

Grotius saw international law as a means of maintaining peace.

Grotius, a many-sided man who published works of poetry, philology, history and theology and became Swedish ambassador in Paris, helped form a concept of an international society as a community sharing the idea that states and rulers have rules that apply to all. All in this international community (today called a "world" or "global" community) should be subject to international law.

The Quaker William Penn, founder of Pennsylvania, put forward a plan for peace in his essay *Towards the Present and Future Peace of Europe* (1693). It included settling disputes between nations by arbitration rather than war, and his plan is today considered to be a prototype of the United Nations. Significantly, United Nations Day is celebrated on Penn's birthday (24 October). I attended Penn's school, Chigwell School in Essex, England, and it is appropriate that I should be writing this book, having trodden in his footsteps.

We have seen (on p.30) that Abbé de Saint-Pierre, in *Project for Making Peace Perpetual in Europe* (1713), envisaged that European sovereigns would contract to form a perpetual alliance and establish a permanent Diet or Congress that would arbitrate all disputes between the federation of princes. Arbitrating decisions would be enforced by armed action. This proposal gave teeth to the idea of arbitrating under international law.

We have also seen (on p.30–31) that Rousseau was inspired by Abbé de Saint-Pierre but proposed a federation of morally-perfect states. In *The Social Contract* (1762) Rousseau does not advance the idea of arbitration in international law.

Jeremy Bentham, the English philosopher, took the idea up in *Plan for Universal and Perpetual Peace* (1789). His reconstructed skeleton, with a wax head that replaced his skull (which was mummified), dressed in his own clothes, can be seen sitting upright in a glass-fronted case in University College, London.

We have seen (on pp.32–33) that Kant, in *Perpetual Peace: A Philosophical Sketch* (1795), a title that echoes Bentham's as well as Abbé de Saint-Pierre's, called for a federation of free states as an interim stage to an "international state" (*civitas gentium*) or world government. The idea of arbitrating disputes lies behind Kant's proposal, but he adds little detail to his forerunners in thinking about international law.

To these proposals must be added the more practical attempts to create a supranational authority that can use international law to bring permanent peace: The Hague Conference conventions of 1899 and 1907, the League of Nations and the United Nations coupled with the International Court of Justice. Their relative lack of overall success in abolishing wars in the 20th and 21st centuries has led some to believe that establishing world peace through international law is an enduring illusion. Others point out that the UN has failed to resolve conflicts between superpowers because it has never been given the power to do so.

To sum up, there is a tradition of proposals that disputes should be solved by arbitration. The arbitrator should be a council (Dubois) or a Monarch/Emperor (Dante). In Crucé the council has become a permanent assembly of princes or their delegates, and in Penn the assembly has become a prototype of the United Nations.

However, all these attempts to bring universal peace by international law assume arbitration between nation-states. Only Kant envisages a World State, and then concedes that in the prevailing conditions of his time a World State had no immediate prospects of being established.

The lesson of the international law of the past is that international law *can* in theory bring universal peace, but only a World State with supranational authority can actually do this in practice.

The Goals of a Supranational Authority

The old order is collapsing as we have just seen, and in consequence the world is faced with urgent problems that have to be solved. The goals of the kind of supranational authority that emerges will have to solve these problems. They are:

1. bringing peace between nation-states, and disarmament;
2. sharing resources and energy so that all humankind can have a raised standard of living;
3. solving environmental problems such as global warming, which seem to be beyond self-interested nation-states;

4. where possible, ending disease;
5. where possible, ending famine;
6. solving the world's financial crisis; and
7. where possible, redistributing wealth to eliminate poverty.

For further details see pp.194–196.
The most desirable kind of supranational authority is the one that can best achieve all these goals.

So what is the most desirable kind of supranational authority?

I have to ask whether a loose, tightly federal or radically different model is best suited to achieving these goals. Are the world's problems best solved by continuing with a form of the existing system of nation-states and old order? By proceeding to a more federal arrangement with arbitration? Or by radically replacing the existing system with a new system?

Seven Models for a Supranational Authority

There are in fact different kinds of supranational authority. It is possible to take ideas from some of them to achieve the most desirable authority.

Proposals for abolishing war by international law envisage different kinds of supranational authority. Seven kinds of supranational arrangement can be identified:

1. developing a sense of world community through regional and functional international organisations that operate in assistance of world law;
2. sticking with the United Nations and the *status quo* and strengthening great-power agreement by using policy and non-constitutional sources of law such as international treaties, to resolve disputes;
3. a World Constitutional Convention to draft a world constitution that nation-states would accept;
4. revising the UN Charter to strengthen international law to give the UN the power to resolve disputes between super-

powers and outlaw war;

5. creating under treaty a new UN-related organisation that would exist alongside the UN and strengthen it in observing international law in areas not covered by the UN Charter;
6. advancing towards world government through *élites*' exclusive groups and deceptive New World Order; and
7. democratising the UN and making global governance accountable.

I have not included the option of abolishing the United Nations and returning the world to the potentially warring and disputatious nation-states: the world that existed at the end of the 19th century. This would invite new empires and a host of wars and would not advance international peace at all. In fact, it would be completely retrogressive and counter-productive. It would be like abolishing the referee in a football match. The United Nations is imperfect, but its resolutions do blow the whistle on the activities of nation-states which contravene the spirit of international law. Abolition of the UN is an intellectual option but in practical terms it is merely an academic option as it carries the world away from rather than towards peace.

Nor have I included the two models of a fully federal United States of the World, and the model of a New World Order's federal Union, detailed on pp.154–155, as these models involve a world government with total control of all global governance and not just the areas of the seven goals.

I now want to look at each of the seven models one by one. In each case I need to ask if a particular model is able to solve the world's problems and thus achieve the goals of a supranational authority.

1. World community through regional organisations

This model would spread a world community gradually through the planting and growth of international organisations: the regional organisations and functional organisations of global governance (see pp.10–16). This has been happening since the Second World War and has produced a partial world community and interrelatedness.

In 1985 the stockpile of global nuclear weapons reached its zenith, with the US and the Soviet Union having 60,589 between them: the US having 21,392 nuclear weapons and the Soviet Union 39,197, almost double the number (increased from 30,062 in 1980 whereas the US reduced its nuclear weapons from 23,368 in 1980). The *Guardian*'s figure for the total number of global nuclear weapons in 1985 was 69,401.[3] The consensus was that the only way of keeping the peace was through a "balance of terror". Neither side dared fire nuclear weapons at the other as if it did, it would bring about its own destruction. Peace was kept through "mutually assured destruction". It was against this background that seeds were planted to grow into a world community. The regional organisations have all grown out of relatively small beginnings.

The European Union is now a political rather than an economic union and has become a superstate. Its legal base is a succession of international treaties: the Treaty of Rome (1956), the Treaty of Maastricht (1992), the Treaty of Amsterdam (1999), the Treaty of Nice (signed 2001, came into operation 2003) and then the Treaty of Lisbon (2009). Its structure is the interconnection of social institutions: the European Commission; the Council of the European Union (or "Council of Ministers"), the central decision-making authority in the EU; and the European Parliament. This institutional triangle forms the decision-making centre of the EU system and is supported by the European Court of Justice, the European Court of Auditors and the European Council, which was established as a result of summit meetings involving heads of state and governments in 1969. The buildings housing these institutions are all within walking distance of each other in Brussels, though the Parliament also meets in Strasbourg. Related to these institutions are the European Central Bank and the European Investment Bank. (See Appendix E8.)

The European Union has been a noble endeavour that has brought peace to Europe for 70 years since 1946. For two thousand years there have been regular wars between European nation-states, most recently in 1870, 1914 and 1939 (as I said on p.xviii), and for all its faults and need to reform, the supranational European Union has managed to keep the peace within its borders. (The break-up of Yugoslavia saw war in Bosnia, Croatia and Serbia in the 1990s, but these latter-day nation-states were then outside the EU's borders and there has been peace since they joined the EU.)

To some the European Union would be a United States of Europe with redrawn European regions that would mix bits of nation-states to break down national Europe. To others the EU would be too undemocratic to be a United States of Europe and would border on the totalitarian.

The EU has become a superstate but within the European Union there is a tension between nation-states that want intergovernmentalism, such as the UK, Denmark and Sweden; and those that want supranationalism, which is strong in France, Germany, Italy and the Benelux countries.

The functional organisations (see pp.15–16) had supranational authority in as much as their remit was to cross the borders and boundaries of nation-states, which have had to comply with their requirements. The scope of all these organisations is transnational.

Supporters of this model say that these organisations are meeting the world's practical needs in a gradualist manner while establishing a sense of community that makes conflict across national and ideological borders less likely and peaceful resolution more likely. Nationalist opponents of this model say that these organisations should operate in ways that do not conflict with national self-interest as the fundamental psychological loyalty of each people should be to their nation-state.

Can this model guarantee perpetual peace? It represents the gradualist approach of the *status quo*, with nation-states grouping themselves, or being grouped, into membership of regions and membership of transnational organisations. The *status quo* has not prevented wars in our own time: wars in the Balkans, Iraq, Afghanistan and Syria. It has not prevented nuclear weapons from falling into the wrong hands, as seems to have happened when some of the ex-Soviet nuclear-suitcase bombs fell into the hands of the Chechen Mafia, who sold them on to bin Laden for use by al-Qaeda. Spreading world community through organisations has taken place under the umbrella of the US, which has acted as the world's policeman (Britain's role in the days of the British Empire).

This model cannot solve any of the world's problems which have so far proved insoluble under the *status quo*. Something more fundamental than the *status quo* is needed to solve the world's problems. This model does not give the kind of supranational authority that can achieve my stated goals.

2. Sticking with the UN and strengthening Great Power Agreement

The most significant apparently supranational authority embodying international law in our time has been the actually inter-national United Nations, which was established in June 1945 for 49 original member states to stop wars and provide a platform for dialogue.

Its stated aims are facilitating co-operation in international law, international security, economic development, social progress, human rights and the achieving of world peace. Its aims can be found at the beginning of its Charter:

> We the peoples of the United Nations determined
>
> to save succeeding generations from the scourge of war, which twice in our lifetime has brought untold sorrow to mankind, and
>
> to reaffirm faith in fundamental human rights, in the dignity and worth of the human person, in the equal rights of men and women and of nations large and small, and
>
> to establish conditions under which justice and respect for the obligations arising from treaties and other sources of international law can be maintained, and
>
> to promote social progress and better standards of life in larger freedom,

and for these ends

to practise tolerance and live together in peace with one another as good neighbours, and

to unite our strength to maintain international peace and security, and

to ensure, by the acceptance of principles and the institution of methods, that armed force shall not be used, save in the common interest, and

to employ international machinery for the promotion of the economic and social advancement of all peoples,

have resolved to combine our efforts to accomplish these aims.

The UN's purposes are stated in Article 1:

The Purposes of the United Nations are:

1. To maintain international peace and security, and to that end: to take effective collective measures for the prevention and removal of threats to the peace, and for the suppression of acts of aggression or breaches of the peace, and to bring about by peaceful means, and in conformity with the principles of justice and international law, adjustment or settlement of international disputes or situations which might lead to a breach of the peace;
2. To develop friendly relations among nations based on respect for the principle of equal rights and self-determination of peoples, and to take other appropriate measures to strengthen universal peace;
3. To achieve international co-operation in solving international problems of an economic, social, cultural, or humanitarian character, and in promoting and encouraging respect for human rights and for fundamental freedoms for all without distinction as to race, sex, language, or religion; and
4. To be a centre for harmonizing the actions of nations in the attainment of these common ends.

The principles of the United Nations are:

> The Organization and its Members, in pursuit of the Purposes stated in Article 1, shall act in accordance with the following Principles.
>
> 1. The Organization is based on the principle of the sovereign equality of all its Members.
> 2. All Members, in order to ensure to all of them the rights and benefits resulting from membership, shall fulfil in good faith the obligations assumed by them in accordance with the present Charter.
> 3. All Members shall settle their international disputes by peaceful means in such a manner that international peace and security, and justice, are not endangered.
> 4. All Members shall refrain in their international relations from the threat or use of force against the territorial integrity or political independence of any state, or in any other manner inconsistent with the Purposes of the United Nations.
> 5. All Members shall give the United Nations every assistance in any action it takes in accordance with the present Charter, and shall refrain from giving assistance to any state against which the United Nations is taking preventive or enforcement action.
> 6. The Organization shall ensure that states which are not Members of the United Nations act in accordance with these Principles so far as may be necessary for the maintenance of international peace and security.
> 7. Nothing contained in the present Charter shall authorize the United Nations to intervene in matters which are essentially within the domestic jurisdiction of any state or shall require the Members to submit such matters to settlement under the present Charter; but this principle shall not prejudice the application of enforcement measures under Chapter VII.

In 2017 the 193 member states of the UN (see Appendix C4) included most sovereign states in existence. The UN's administrative organs are: the General Assembly; the Security Council; the Economic and Social Council; the Trusteeship Council (already virtually abolished); the Secretariat; and the International Court of Justice. (See Appendix C1.) Additional bodies deal with the governance of other UN system agencies, such as the World Health Organization (WHO) and the United National Children's Fund (UNICEF). (See Appendix C2.) It functions in six languages: Arabic, Chinese, English, French, Russian and Spanish. It is financed from assessed and voluntary contributions from member states. There are many UN organisations (see Appendix C3).

The General Assembly is the main deliberative assembly of the UN. It is composed of all UN member states and meets yearly. Each state has a vote, and votes require a two-thirds majority. It was originally intended that the General Assembly would be the main UN chamber, but because every state, no matter how large or small, has one vote, getting business done became unwieldy, and in the early days ever more use was made of the Security Council. Over the years the focus shifted to the Security Council, which had fewer members and was less cumbersome.

The Security Council is charged with maintaining peace and security between nation-states. It consists of 15 members of the UN, 5 Permanent Members (China, France, the Russian Federation, the UK and the US) and 10 Non-Permanent Members (elected for two-year terms, currently Bolivia, Egypt, Ethiopia, Italy, Japan, Kazakhstan, Senegal, Sweden, Ukraine and Uruguay). The 5 Permanent Members have the power to veto substantive but not procedural resolutions. The Soviet Union overused the veto in the early days, paralysing the Security Council. The Security Council has the power to make binding decisions that member governments have agreed to carry out, under the terms of Article 25: "The Members of the United Nations agree to accept and carry out the decisions of the Security Council in accordance with the present Charter." Its decisions are the UN resolutions that maintain peace and security.

The Security Council arbitrates between nation-states as the jurists and philosophers of the past dreamt an assembly or council would. However, the members of the Security Council have little power to coerce, and their resolutions are subject to agreement by the member governments. Each member has one vote, and decisions on substantive matters require an affirmative vote of nine members, including the concurring votes of the Permanent Members (under Article 27).

The UN has well-known weaknesses. In Article 2(4) and elsewhere by implication the Charter allows sovereign nations to use force that they claim is for defence. Many of the local wars since 1945 have been conducted on the basis that they were in self-defence: the invasion of Afghanistan in 2001 was for the self-defence of the US following 9/11; Russia invaded Georgia in August 2008 for reasons of self-defence; and Israel invaded Gaza in early 2009 for reasons of self-defence.

Another example of the UN Charter's weakness concerns sanctions. The Charter itself does not mention the word "sanctions". They are justified by Article 41, which states: "The Security Council may decide what measures not involving the use of armed force are to be employed to give effect to its decisions, and it may call upon the Members of the United Nations to apply such measures. These may include complete or partial interruption of economic relations and of rail, sea, air, postal, telegraphic, radio and other means of communication, and the severance of diplomatic relations." However, it can be argued that sanctions violate Article 2(3) and (4): that Members "shall settle their international disputes by peaceful means in such a manner that international peace and security, and justice, are not endangered", and that Members "shall refrain in their international relations from the threat or use of force against the territorial integrity or political independence of any state, or in any other manner inconsistent with the Purposes of the United Nations". Any violation hinges on the interpretation of "peaceful means" and "political independence".

Since 1966 the UN Security Council has established 26 sanctions regimes in Southern Rhodesia, South Africa, the former Yugoslavia, Haiti, Iraq, Angola, Sierra Leone, Somalia, Eritrea, Liberia, Democratic Republic of the Congo, Côte d'Ivoire, Sudan (twice), Lebanon, Democratic People's Republic of Korea (North Korea), Iran, Libya (twice), Guinea-Bissau, Central African Republic, Yemen and South Sudan, as well as against ISIL (Daesh), al-Qaeda and the Taliban (twice). Sanctions were only used twice during the Cold War, between 1945 and 1990: against Southern Rhodesia (1968) and South Africa (1977).

In 2017 there were UN sanctions regimes in the following eleven countries: Somalia/Eritrea, Iraq, Liberia, Democratic Republic of the Congo, Côte d'Ivoire, Sudan, Lebanon, Democratic People's Republic of Korea (North Korea), Iran, Libya and Guinea-Bissau. There were also UN sanctions regimes against al-Qaeda, ISIL (Daesh) and the Taliban.[4]

In April 2000 the Security Council set up a working group on sanctions to consider whether the Security Council should change its practice when imposing new sanctions, and make them more humanitarian. The working group considered enlargement, questions of regional representation, criteria for membership, the relationship between the General Assembly and Security Council, accountability and the use of the veto. It took stock of these areas rather than made any fundamental changes.

Article 42 provides for the use of armed force by the UN if other measures are considered to be unworkable: "Should the Security Council consider that measures provided for in Article 41 would be inadequate or have proved to be inadequate, it may take such action by air, sea or land forces as may be necessary to maintain or restore international peace and security. Such action may include demonstrations, blockade, and other operations by air, sea, or land forces of Members of the United Nations."

An example of non-constitutional sources of law that might strengthen great-power agreement have been international treaties, conventions, covenants and precedents, all of which can be found in the growth of regions and Unions. We have seen that the growth of the EU went through the treaties of Rome, Maastricht, Amsterdam, Nice and Lisbon. There was a constitutional convention to draft the European Constitution. Other regions have used such European measures as precedents.

Supporters of this model argue that when the great powers – notably the permanent five on the Security Council – agree (and therefore do not use their veto), international law is expressed in the form of UN resolutions and sanctions. They claim that the Charter threatens enough force to make the UN work as an international power that can as a last resort use armed force to restrain a warring nation-state. They claim that it is thus not the UN structure that needs changing, for which public support would have to be won before changes could be pushed through, but great powers' agreements.

Does this model guarantee perpetual peace? Although the UN has promoted agreement between the great powers it has fallen short of preventing wars between nation-states such as the 2003 war in Iraq or the 2011 war in Syria. (In March 2011, at the time of the Arab Spring, protests demanding greater freedom and an end to corruption began in Deraa. The regime began arresting and torturing the demonstrators.) Since 1945 the UN has failed to prevent 162 wars.[5] Because it is between nation-states and is only above them when the member states agree, the UN is part of the *status quo* and of the old Cold-War order which is outmoded.

This model does not go far enough in creating supranational authority, for the UN is only supranational when its member states agree. It is relatively powerless when they disagree. This model does not give the kind of supranational authority that can achieve my stated goals.

3. World Constitutional Convention

A supranational authority or world government can be formed by a World Constitutional Convention. A constitutional convention is a gathering for the purpose of writing a new constitution or revising an existing constitution.

Supporters of a World Constitutional Convention argue that nation-states and their national governments hinder the expression of a world community. Nation-states will not voluntarily give up a part of their sovereignty or accept international decisions that conflict with their national self-interest. They claim that as the UN is composed of representatives of nation-states and their national governments, there is no point in working through the UN.

For example, until recently the UN had not implemented the UN's provisions for reorganisation. In 1997 Kofi Annan began a reform program: an attempt to change the Permanent Membership of the Security Council, which reflects the power relations of 1945; making the bureaucracy more transparent, accountable and efficient; making the UN more democratic; and imposing an international tariff on arms manufacturers. In 2005 the UN convened a World Summit "to take bold decisions in the areas of development, security, human rights and reform of the United Nations". But it has to be said that the reforms proposed were procedural and cosmetic rather than fundamental and substantive. And the issue of the Permanent Membership of the Security Council was not resolved.

The UN has failed to reform itself in other ways as well. The US adopted the Connally Reservation, which limits the jurisdiction of the International Court of Justice to those cases the US agrees it should hear. The USSR and other powers refused to grant any degree of compulsory jurisdiction to the International Court of Justice.

Supporters of this model believe that what is needed is a new world institution, not strengthened international institutions. They see world law being enforced through a World Constitutional Convention which would draft a constitution for the world and present it to the nation-states. The governments of nation-states would be called upon to send delegates to the World Constitutional Convention. If necessary, world constitutionalists would operate independently of nation-states and their governments, for they would represent the nation-states' peoples, not the nation-states. Just as the US Constitution began "We the people", not "We the states", so the World Constitutional Convention's world constitution would begin "We the assembled peoples of the World".

There have been a number of constitutional conventions over the years which can act as precedents for a World Constitutional Convention. The United States was first. The Annapolis Convention (1786) proposed the Philadelphia Convention (1787), which drafted the United States Constitution for the states to ratify. In France, the National Convention (20 September 1792) convened to write a Republican Constitution after the French monarchy was suspended. The Convention abolished the monarchy the next day. During the American Civil War, the Missouri Constitutional Convention (1861–1863) established Missouri's provisional government. In Canada, the Quebec Conference met in 1864 and the London Conference of 1866 followed soon after. In Australia, there were four constitutional conventions: in 1891, 1897, 1973 and 1998. In the Philippines, a Philippine Constitutional Convention met in 1935 to create the autonomous Commonwealth of the Philippines under the US Tydings-McDuffie Act, and in 1971 to draft a revised constitution that replaced the US-organised constitution of 1935. In Germany the Parliamentary Council (*Parlamentarischer Rat*, 1948) drafted the Basic Law of the Federal Republic to be ratified by the *Länder*.

In Northern Ireland, a Constitutional Convention (1975–1976) failed to find a solution to the status of Northern Ireland. In Scotland, a Scottish Constitutional Convention (1989) produced a plan for Scottish devolution. The European Convention (2001) drafted the Constitution for Europe, for it to be approved by the European Council and ratified by member states. Constitutional conventions have also been used by states of federations, including individual states of the United States, to create, replace or amend their own constitutions.

The American Constitutional Convention of May 1787 consisted of 55 delegates, who met in the Pennsylvania State House, Philadelphia (now called Independence Hall). The Convention's aim was "to render the Constitution of the Federal Government adequate to the exigencies of the Union".

The main reason for the 1787 Convention was that the articles of Confederation (1781) required the unanimous consent of all 13 states before the US Government could take action. The system was cumbersome and unworkable. George Washington was elected president of the Convention. The Convention established the principle of a national authority with a bicameral Congress, equal representation in the Senate and proportional representation in the House of Representatives. This plan was sent to a committee of detail, which listed 18 specific powers of Congress, including the power "to make all laws". In ten days it achieved a charter of government. The plan was returned to the Convention, which approved the draft constitution and sent it to a committee of style. The convention approved the final draft and adopted it on 17 September.[6] Article 5 established that further conventions could be called for proposing amendments to the Constitution. Amendments could also be made on a vote by two-thirds of each house of Congress.

Just as the American Constitutional Convention approved the principle of a national authority, so a World Constitutional Convention could approve the principle of a supranational authority. Every state except Hawaii has made applications for an Article-V convention, mostly in the 20th century. There is no official record of how many applications have been made, but one count suggests there have been 567.[7]

The European Convention had its origin in the European Council conference for Heads of State held in Nice in December 2000. It was agreed that there should be a "broader and deeper debate" on the future of the EU before the European Council met in Laeken the following year. In Laeken the European Council made a declaration committing the EU to greater democracy, transparency and efficiency, and setting out the process by which a constitution could be written. There was to be a convention which would produce a draft constitution that would be handed over to the Intergovernmental Conference expected to be held in 2004.

The European Convention was established with 105 members drawn from the national parliaments of member states and candidate countries, the European Parliament, the European Commission and representatives of heads of state and governments. It was chaired by former French president Valéry Giscard d'Estaing. The Convention met for the first time in February 2002, and there was a plenary session once or twice a month. It deliberated in public in the European-Parliament building in Brussels. The draft was unveiled on 28 October 2002. In a speech in Bruges on 2 October 2002 Giscard d'Estaing, the President of the Convention, had said: "I see [the Union] as being a Union of European States closely co-ordinating their policies and administering certain competences, along federal lines."

The word "federal" originally appeared in Article I-1. It was swiftly removed and replaced by the word "Community", but it was clear that greater integration would be achieved by the Treaty establishing a Constitution for Europe. The opening words of the Constitution are: "Reflecting the will of the citizens and States of Europe to build a common future, this Constitution establishes the European Union, on which the Member States confer competences to attain objectives they have in common. The Union shall co-ordinate the policies by which the Member States aim to achieve these objectives, and shall exercise on a Community basis the competences they confer on it."[8] In other words, there was to be a union of European States which, while retaining their national identities, would closely co-ordinate their policies at a European level and administer certain common competences on a federal basis.

Just as the European Convention established the European Union, so a World Constitutional Convention could establish a World State.

Supporters of this model say that a World Constitutional Conference could draft a world constitution. A World Constitutional Conference may, indeed, be a good method of bringing a World State into being. However, it is only a method. To follow a similar procedure to the one that took the European Convention from the Treaty of Nice to Laeken and thence to the draft Constitution would require the nation-states to accept it, just as the European states had to accept the European Convention. UN member governments have always put their "overriding vital interests" first. We are left with a (for now) unanswered question: How could the nation-states be induced to accept a World Constitutional Conference?

Nevertheless, convening a World Constitutional Convention is a valid method of creating a World State, and as we shall see on pp.156 and 160 it could be used to present the Constitution for a supranational authority I have drawn up (The Constitution for the United Federation of the World, see p.xi) to the UN General Assembly as part of the process of creating a World State. In other words, this approach can be used for the kind of supranational authority that can achieve my stated goals but in itself it is not a supranational authority, just a method for getting a supranational authority established.

4. Revising the UN Charter to strengthen international law

The first three models were all relatively close to the *status quo*. The next two attempt to reform the UN, each in a quite different way.

We have noted some of the weaknesses of the UN. Its Charter has proved itself unable to prevent wars, as we saw when we considered model 2, whose supporters prefer to work within the existing system.

Reforming the UN Charter, a (perhaps deliberately) vague document in places whose loose wording allows room for interpretation and inclusiveness and broadens the chances of international agreement, is an arduous task. This task was undertaken in the 1950s when Grenville Clark, a Harvard-educated lawyer and Harvard friend of Roosevelt, and Louis Sohn, a Harvard Professor in international law and friend of Dean Rusk, co-authored *World Peace Through World Law* (1958).

The book was reprinted in 1960 and amended to include provisions for an Outer Space Agency. This second edition of the book set out detailed proposals for revision of the UN Charter. Its call for disarmament must be understood within the historical context of its time. The British Foreign Secretary Selwyn Lloyd had proposed "comprehensive disarmament" in the UN on 17 September 1959, and the Soviet leader Nikita Khrushchev had called for "general and complete disarmament" in the UN the next day, 18 September 1959. On 1 December 1959 the US and Soviet Union, and ten other major countries, agreed to the Antarctic Treaty, which banned all weapons and military activities from Antarctica.

President Kennedy created the US Arms Control and Disarmament Agency, with the aid of Republican John McCloy. On 20 September 1961, the Soviet Union and US issued a "Joint Statement of Agreed Principles for Disarmament Negotiations", which came to be known as the McCloy-Zorin Agreement, which aimed to negotiate a "general and complete disarmament". Kennedy spoke on 25 September 1961 before the UN General Assembly and said: "Mankind must put an end to war – or war will put an end to mankind."[9] The Cuban crisis of 1961, when the Soviet Union, still ruled by Khrushchev, was caught on film sending missiles by ship to Cuba and President Kennedy successfully ordered Khrushchev to remove them from Cuba, put an end to all talk of disarmament.

A third edition in 1966 included a proposed Treaty Establishing a World Disarmament and World Development Organization (see model 5). In 1973, *Introduction to World Peace Through World Law* appeared after Clark's death, with an updating essay 'Two Alternative Plans' by Sohn, and essays by others.

These various editions and versions are all important, and in what follows I regard the evolving work as a whole.

The fundamental premise of the Clark-Sohn book is President Eisenhower's statement on 31 October 1956, the first day of the Suez crisis during which Britain, France and Israel invaded Egypt, a sovereign nation-state, and a week before the Hungarian uprising against the USSR, which was crushed by Soviet tanks: "There can be no peace without law." He meant the "law" of a World Authority that could be uniformly applied to all nations – Britain, France, Israel and the Soviet Union – and forbid violence.

The principles behind the book were:

1. that only enforceable world law can preserve peace, which meant that all nations must completely disarm, and adopt and uphold a law against violence on a worldwide basis;
2. the world law against international violence must be stated in statutory form and forbid the use of force by any nation against any other for any cause except self-defence;
3. world judicial tribunals should interpret and apply the world law, and there should be organs of mediation and conciliation to set up peaceful means of adjudication and adjustment in place of violence;
4. there should be a permanent world police force which should suppress any violation of the world law against international violence;
5. the complete disarmament of all nations (rather than mere "reduction" or "limitation" of armaments) is essential for lasting peace, and should be conducted in a simultaneous and proportionate manner, with verified stages and inspections;
6. the vastly different economic condition of differing regions should be equalised, to remove a major cause of instability of conflict; and
7. common resources, such as outer space and the oceans, should be managed equitably.

There were supplementary principles:

1. all nations must actively participate in the world peace authority, which should be universal, and any nations

that for whatever reason opt out must abolish their armed forces, so that the constitutional document creating the world peace organisation will have a majority of all nations and peoples of the world;

2. the world law should apply to all individuals as well as nations;
3. the basic rights and duties of all nations to maintain peace should be stated in the constitutional document, which should also set out the powers of the new world organisation;
4. the powers of the world organisation should be restricted to the maintenance of peace, and all other power should be with the nations and their peoples;
5. to be acceptable, the peace plan must demonstrably be seen to be capable of preventing war while safeguarding the powers of nation-states.

The main features of the revision of the UN Charter are:

1. virtually all nation-states of the world (193 within the UN in 2017 and various related and disputed territories) should have Permanent Membership of the new world organisation before the revision of the UN Charter takes effect, and the revised Charter would require ratification by five-sixths of all nation-states;
2. the General Assembly should have its powers, composition and method of voting revised, with (to ensure wise decisions) the four largest nations having 30 representatives, the 10 next largest 12, the 15 next largest 8, the 20 next largest 6, the 30 next largest 4, the 40 next largest 3 and the smallest nations 1, making a total in 1970 of 744 representatives from 143 nations;
3. the Security Council would be abolished and replaced by an Executive Council, composed of 17 Representatives elected by the General Assembly (the four largest nations having Permanent Representation, five of the 10

next largest having seats in rotation, and the eight chosen by the General Assembly from the representatives of other nation-states), and this veto-less Executive Council would decide whether each stage of the disarmament process was satisfactorily completed;

4. the Economic and Social Council (and the Trusteeship Council, recently recommended for abolition) would be continued, but with larger and different composition;
5. the disarmament process would involve a step-by-step elimination of armaments over a six-year period, and the UN Peace Force would take possession of arms handed over;
6. military forces would be completely eliminated, and breaches of the enforced peace would be suppressed by a World Police Force, which would have a strength of 200,000–400,000, as determined from year to year by the General Assembly, and a Peace Force Reserve would have a standing strength of 300,000–600,000 as determined by the General Assembly;
7. the adjudication or settlement of international disputes should be conducted by the Judicial and Conciliation System, under which the International Court of Justice would have the authority to decide on the interpretation of the revised Charter and the regional UN courts would introduce enforceable world law regarding world peace, while a World Conciliation Board would mediate and conciliate in disputes, which could then be placed before the International Court of Justice or the World Equity Tribunal;
8. enforcement would involve prosecution in UN regional courts of individuals who have violated disarmament provisions, following investigation by a UN civil police force of 10,000 working under the UN Attorney-General, and there should be penalties for violation of Charter regulations;
9. a World Development Authority would grant interest-

free loans to assist the economic and social development of underdeveloped areas, and the World Development Commission would be supervised by the Economic and Social Council;

10. a UN Ocean Authority should be established, with a structure similar to that of the Outer Space Authority;
11. the United Nations Environment Protection Authority would be set up with an intergovernmental Council representing developed and developing nations, and a five-member Environment Commission to co-ordinate national and international environment programs;
12. a United Nations Revision System would raise funds to pay for the new world institutions (UN Peace Force, the Inspection Service, the World Development Authority, the Nuclear Energy Authority, the Outer Space Authority, the Ocean Authority, the Environment Protection Authority, the World Equity Tribunal and the World Conciliation Board), especially for the UN Peace Force which was expected to cost $12 billion annually in 1970, while the World Development Authority was then expected to need $75 billion to even out economic disparities between nations and regions;
13. the privileges and immunities of UN personnel should be set out in the constitutional document, and safeguards against abuse of privileges and immunities should be in the Treaty;
14. the limitation of the authority of the new UN organisations should be defined with great precision, and guarantees should be given against violation by the UN and included in the constitutional document of individual rights;
15. ratification of the revised Charter should be by five-sixths of the world's nations, including all the four nations with the largest populations and at least six of the ten next largest nations, the aggregate of the populations of the ratifying nations equalling at least five-sixths of the total

world population, and each nation's ratification should be by its own constitutional processes;

16. amendments to the revised Charter should be by a vote of two-thirds of all General Assembly Representatives or of a General Conference held for the purpose of amendment, and ratification should be by four-fifths of the member nations, including 10 of the 14 member nations entitled to 12 or more Representatives in the assembly;
17. the existing UN organs and agencies should be strengthened, and thus the Executive Council which should replace the Security Council would be veto-less; and the International Court of Justice should have enlarged jurisdiction and greater authority.

It must be stressed that the above scheme was last updated in the early 1970s. Since then the composition of the four largest nations in the world has changed. In 1970 they were the People's Republic of China, India, the Soviet Union and the United States. The break-up of the Soviet Union means that Indonesia is now the fourth-largest nation in the world in terms of population, and the Russian Federation is therefore outside the top four. This anomaly will have to be addressed. It would be bizarre to give non-nuclear Indonesia Permanent Representation on the Executive Council and to bar the nuclear Russian Federation, which holds over half the nuclear warheads in existence, from having Permanent Representation, and the same applies to barring the Russian Federation from being among the four Permanent Members in ratification. The Clark-Sohn plan states that the UN Trusteeship Council should continue, but this was recommended for abolition as part of UN Secretary-General Kofi Annan's reform plan as the newly independent 11 trust territories had been dissolved.

The two co-authors, Clark and Sohn, print the existing UN Charter down the left-hand side of each page and their proposed text for the revised Charter alongside each Article and Chapter on the right-hand side, with "comment" beneath each Article.

The detail fills more than 367 pages.

To taste the flavour of their amendments, it is worth giving their proposed text for the areas I picked out on p.111. Their version of point 1 of the purposes of the United Nations is:

> To maintain international peace and security, and to that end: to abolish all national military forces and, through a United Nations system of inspection and a United Nations military force, to take effective measures for the enforcement of disarmament, for the prevention and removal of threats to the peace, for the suppression of acts of aggression or other breaches of the peace, and for ensuring compliance with this revised Charter and the laws and regulations enacted thereunder; and through United Nations agencies and tribunals, to bring about by peaceful means, and in conformity with the principles of justice and international law, adjustment or settlement of international disputes or situations which might lead to a breach of the peace.

The proposed text of point 1 of the principles of the United Nations (see p.112) is:

> All nations shall be equally entitled to the protection guaranteed by this revised Charter, irrespective of size, population or any other factor; and there are reserved to all nations or their peoples all powers inherent in their sovereignty, except such as are delegated to the United Nations by this revised Charter, either by express language or clear implication, and are not prohibited by this revised Charter to the nations.

In other words, all nation-states would retain their sovereignty under the revised UN Charter.

The proposed text for the revised Article 41, which is cited as justifying sanctions (see p.114), omits "and it may call upon the Members of the United Nations to apply such measures". The revised UN Charter has strengthened this Article, which no longer depends on a "call" to UN Members. The revised UN Charter would be stronger in enforcement and penalties, and so it would not be necessary to "call" on Members to take measures. These would be mandatory.

The proposed text for the revised UN Charter's Article 42, which provides for the use of armed force by the UN (see p.115), is:

> Should the General Assembly or the Executive Council in the circumstances defined in paragraph 2 of Article 39 consider that measures provided for in Article 41 would be inadequate or have proved to be inadequate, it shall direct such action by air, sea, or land elements of the United Nations Peace Force as may be necessary to maintain or restore international peace and security or to ensure compliance with this revised Charter and the laws and regulations enacted thereunder. Such action may include demonstrations, blockade, and other operations; but any such action shall be taken pursuant to the procedures and subject to the limitations contained in Annex II.

Annex II (several pages long) is about the United Nations Peace Force.

This model removes the right to violence (except in the case of self-defence) from nation-states but leaves all their other powers intact. The proposed text for the revised UN Charter has been in the public domain since 1960.

I can legitimately ask, why has it not been taken up? Undoubtedly the US-Soviet arms reduction programs owe much to its call for disarmament, but the Cold War continued for 30 years after the Clark-Sohn plan first appeared, and fear of the nuclear Soviet Union, and security considerations, no doubt prevented the implementation of the plan during those years.

It could be that its legalistic approach has not captured the imagination. Its law-based proposal was both conservative and radical: law and order in the world is a conservative theme, yet giving up national sovereignty to world institutions is a radical change. The mixture of conservative and radical outlook may have proved confusing. Lawyers offering side-by-side charters can split hairs in their wording, inviting a contrast between a shade of emphasis in the UN Charter and a slightly different shade of emphasis in their proposed text. The result may appear over-legalistic, like the text of the European Constitution, which is in places unreadable and therefore has not inspired the European people. The simplicity and directness of the Declaration of Independence, on the other hand, is still inspiring.

Be that as it may, the fact remains that a very full plan for this model has been on the table since 1960 and could easily be brought up to date. It would reassure nation-states that their power would continue, even though they were giving up deciding disputes by resorting to war.

Does this model guarantee perpetual peace? We are back to my conclusion regarding model 2 (see p.116). Except for the one area of abolishing violence, the *status quo* is preserved. And the UN remains an essentially inter-national body attempting to fulfil a supranational role. Does the supranational authority of this model go far enough? Quite simply, no. Should there be a supranational authority that is external to the inter-national UN? Yes.

5. A treaty for a new organisation to exist alongside, and strengthen, the UN

In the 1966 3rd edition of their *World Peace Through World Law*, Clark and Sohn offered an alternative to reforming the UN Charter: a Draft Treaty that would create a new organisation that would exist alongside the UN and strengthen it – the World Disarmament and World Development Organization.

In this alternative plan, the UN – with the Security Council still intact – would continue to exercise the limited powers under the existing Charter and would receive additional powers under the proposed Treaty. The Treaty would supplement the existing machinery of the UN. Much of the proposed text in the revised UN Charter could be shifted into the Treaty, giving the same disarmament plan and abolition of violence we encountered in model 4. Features 1–17 of model 4 therefore also apply to this model. Thus, all nations would be members of the new organisation.

The Draft Treaty is some 120 pages long with 114 Articles. Article 1 states:

> The purposes of the World Disarmament and World Development Organization are:
>
> 1. To bring about and maintain a permanent state of universal and complete national disarmament under effective international control;
> 2. To establish effective institutions for the maintenance of peace and to provide reliable procedures for the settlement of all international disputes by peaceful means; and
> 3. To provide adequate machinery and resources to mitigate the immense disparities in the economic condition of various regions of the world which endanger international peace.

The relationship between the UN and the new organisation would be a close one, for the Treaty provides:

1. that all the new organisations should consult with the United Nations' organs and agencies on all matters of mutual interest;
2. that annual and special reports on the Organization should be made to the UN;
3. that persons authorised by the General Assembly should have the right to take part, without vote, in the deliberations of the General Conference of the Organization, and that persons authorised by the Security Council and the Economic and Social Council of the UN should take part, without voting, in the deliberations of the Executive Council and the World Development Authority;
4. the General Assembly and other organs of the UN may make recommendations to the Organization; and
5. all sanctions should be initiated by the UN through its Gen-

> eral Assembly or Security Council, or by the General Conference of the Organization, which would support the UN in such measures.

The new Organization's institutions would have the words "United Nations" before them. Thus the Peace Force would be called the "United Nations Peace Force". The United Nations would remain as a world forum for debate, but the World Disarmament and World Development Organization would have financial, judicial and military powers which the United Nations now lacks – which the framers of the UN Charter did not give it.

This model recognises that the United Nations has always lacked a standing world police force; a judicial system with compulsory jurisdiction over international disputes; and a revenue system. Supporters of this model claim that the UN has done useful work to keep world peace, that it should not be abolished, but that it should be supplemented so it can maintain peace more effectively.

Supporters of this model claim that although the World Disarmament and World Development Organization's living alongside the existing UN would be an awkward arrangement, it would be worth putting up with some awkwardness if it was effective in enforcing and keeping world peace.

This model has the same features as model 4, from which it differs in one respect: instead of revising the UN Charter, it creates a new organisation to exist alongside it, and the 17 features would therefore be within the new organisation rather than within a revised UN Charter.

This model is therefore as much a part of the *status quo* as model 4, and the same doubts apply. Why has it not been taken up when it has been on the table since 1960? The same answers apply as on p.130. As with model 4, the *status quo* is preserved except for the one area of abolishing violence. Again, the UN remains an essentially inter-national body attempting to fulfil a supranational role. Again, does the supranational authority of this model go far enough? No. Should there be a supranational authority that is elsewhere than alongside the inter-national UN? Yes.

6. Élites*' secretive world government through exclusive groups*
This model involves the New World Order and is more radical as it would subsume nation-states and absorb them into a world government. The New World Order was made possible by *élite*s who have operated for nearly 250 years.

To understand the *élite*s we need to look at who controls the wealth in the world. In 2017 0.1% of humankind were worth as much as the bottom 90%.[10] The dynastic families of the past such as the Rothschilds and Rockefellers have inherited wealth that has been distributed among the branches of their descendants. Having been hugely influential in the past these dynastic families now existed among the up-and-coming computer-related and trading 'nuclear' families ('nuclear' in the sense of a couple and their children, the basic social unit). According to the American business magazine *Forbes*,[11] most of the 10 wealthiest American families in 2016 were computer-related: Microsoft (Bill Gates, who owns $81 billion[12]) was the top company, above (in descending order) Amazon, Facebook, Oracle, Bloomberg LP, Google and its parent company Alphabet. The wealthiest trading families were the Walton, Koch and Mars families (in retailing, industries and confectionery respectively).

Banking families were very influential: Barclays, JP Morgan, Citibank and particularly Goldman Sachs. The official records of the ownership of Goldman Sachs allegedly show that the chief owner is Lord Jacob Rothschild,[13] and Goldman Sachs may be a relatively new front for Rothschilds' policies. Nine of President Trump's administration have been drawn from Goldman Sachs: chief strategist Steve Bannon, who was worth $48 million, used to work for Goldman Sachs, as did Trump's former communications director Anthony Scaramucci and Steven Mnuchin, Gary Cohn, Jay Clayton, Alexander Blankfein, Dina Powell, Erin Walsh, Harry Markopolos, and Henry Poulson.[14]

(Also, Mark Carney, the Governor of the Bank of England,

worked for Goldman Sachs for 13 years. The prevalence of ex-employees of Goldman Sachs in public office within the West has led some to speculate whether the advent of Trump's 'America First', urged by Bannon, and of the UK's Brexit may be fronts for a financial manoeuvre by the Rothschild banking dynasty. Some speculate whether the plan is to create an off-shore low-corporation-tax haven, profit from the movement of funds, bring the pound, dollar and euro to parity and establish a *de facto* global currency. Some speculate whether Trump's administration and Brexit are both transient, and can be allowed to collapse once the financial killing has been made. Some even wonder if the UK could become an unofficial 51st state of the USA.)

Four US banks (The Bank of America, JP Morgan Chase, Citigroup and Wells Fargo) own the four main oil companies (Exxon Mobil, Royal Dutch Shell, BP and Chevron Texaco) in tandem with Deutsche Bank, BNP, Barclays and other European old-money corporations. It has been reported that 80% of the New York Federal Reserve Bank is owned by eight families: four residing in the US (Goldman Sachs, Rockefellers, Lehmans and Kuhn, Loebs of New York) and four residing in Europe (the Rothschilds of Paris, Berlin and London, the Warburgs of Hamburg, the Lazards of Paris, and the Israel Moses Seifs of Rome).[15]

The French economist Thomas Piketty in *Capital in the Twenty-First Century* focuses on the inequality of wealth and income in Europe and the US since the 18th century. He shows that the return on capital is greater than the rate of economic growth, and that the consequent concentration and unequal distribution of wealth causes social and economic instability. He proposes a global system of progressive wealth taxes to reduce inequality and prevent the vast majority of the world's wealth from being controlled by a tiny minority, and this progressive tax can be taken up by the World State.

Within this concentration of wealth the dynastic élitist families are thought to have amassed inherited wealth that dwarfs the wealth of the richest computer-related, trading and banking families. The Rothschilds' banking dynasty which began in 1740 allegedly amassed $350 billion, some say $400 billion,[16] and the Rockefellers' oil monopoly from 1839 to 1937 is thought to have amassed $340 billion.[17] These two dynastic families worked together from the 1860s to control the world's resources for the benefit of their families, in conjunction with other élitist families. In our time they have organised secretive meetings to dominate world policy to their business advantage.

In 1954 Rothschilds and Rockefellers co-founded the secretive Bilderberg Group, which was named after the Hotel de Bilderberg in Oosterbeek, Holland, where the Group first met. The Group worked for the unification of Europe, which began to happen with the 1956 Treaty of Rome. The annual meeting of the Bilderberg Group still takes place, and the most prominent attender of the Group since 1954 has been David Rockefeller, who died aged 101 in 2017. The meetings are attended by the most powerful people in the world, all handpicked: the Presidents of the IMF, World Bank and Federal Reserve, chairmen of a hundred of the most powerful corporations in the world, Vice-Presidents of the US, directors of the CIA and FBI, Secretaries-General of NATO, US Senators and members of Congress, European Prime Ministers and leaders of opposition parties, pro-world politicians, top editors and CEOs of leading newspapers. They meet to establish a consensus between America and Europe on which forthcoming policy can be based. Bilderberg recommendations have a habit of being implemented during the following year: the 1989 fall of Thatcher and the 2003 invasion of Iraq are two of many such recommendations.[18]

They meet under the Chatham House Rule under which participants are free to use the information received so long as the identity of the speakers and the location of the forum in which it was conveyed is not revealed. Future presidents and prime ministers turn out to have been attenders of the Bilderberg Group's meetings. The agenda of the Bilderberg Group is confidential, and an aura of secrecy and deception surrounds their discussions. The hotel is taken over, the delegates arrive secretly, troops surround the hotel, helicopters hover and a security cordon prevents parking within half a mile. An open body having a straightforward meeting does not resort to such secretive practices.

In the early 1970s David Rockefeller created the Trilateral Commission to bring together about 250 members from the US, Europe and Pacific nations (particularly Japan). This group meets annually, and the G7 industrial powers are represented.[19]

It has been reckoned that these *élite*s have around 6,000 sympathisers, who covertly run a world of more than 7.5 billion people by undertaking advance planning and active discussions of population reduction programs. These are all Rockefellerite in inspiration. In 1952 John D. Rockefeller established a Population Council to urge "zero population growth". In 1971 the secretive Rockefellerite Club of Rome, which first met on David Rockefeller's private estate in Bellagio, Italy in 1968, published a report, *Limits to Growth*. In 1972 Laurance Rockefeller issued a report on population growth. The 1980 *Global 2000 Report to the President* was built on Rockefellerite policies. Its accompanying *Global Future: Time to Act* made recommendations and declared "that global population would eventually stabilise at 8 billion". There was some ambiguity. If read in one way, the Report seemed to be implying that humankind should be reduced by 2 billion people.[20] The Rockefellerite 1974 Kissinger Report had referred to "useless eaters"[21] of the Third World: Africans and Asians who are not productive, do no work and consume the Earth's food. The *Global 2000 Report* implies that they are the ones who should be reduced, and that reduction will take place by contrived wars, diseases (like AIDS) and famine.

In defence of the élitist view of population control, it must be said that the world's population is at present growing at a colossal rate and the world's food is not growing at the same rate. The world's population in 2017 was 7.520 billion and is forecast to be 9.725 billion by 2050.[22] A comparison between the population figures of individual nation-states in 2009 (in Appendix D3 on pp.245–255 of *The World Government*) and in 2017 (in Appendix E3 on p.316) is revealing and shocking. The nation-states least able to afford population growth are those that have grown the most, for example Nigeria (from 154m in 2009 to 191m in 2017, with a growth to 400m forecast by 2050), Ethiopia (from 79m in 2009 to 104m in 2017, with a growth to 278m forecast by 2050) and Pakistan (from 167m in 2009 to 196m in 2017, with a growth to 309m forecast by 2050).[23] A coming democratic World State will have to address this problem openly and limit population growth in the environmentally challenging areas in Africa and Asia to prevent mass migrations of future refugees. There will have to be more active educational birth-control programs in these areas, and some countries with the greatest growth families will have to be limited to one child per family – a decision that will have to be taken by the wise decision-makers of the supranational federal authority.

The Western population has remained relatively stable as can be seen from the same Worldometers source, the US having grown from 307m to 324m from 2009 to 2017 with a growth to 388m forecast by 2050, and the European Union from 502m to 511m from 2009 to 2017, with a growth to 526m in 2050 (or, without the UK's 75m in 2050 and if no further additions, 450m in 2050). Interestingly the population of Europe as opposed to the EU decreased from 740m in 2010 to 739m in 2017, with a decrease to 706m forecast by 2050 (hence Europe's willingness to accept refugees). (European population is normally measured within standard boundaries rather than the continental divisions of the Caucasus and Ural mountains and the Bosphorus.) Between 2009/2010 and 2017 the growth of the population of Nigeria (37m) alone exceeded double the growth of the US (17m) and Europe (-1m) put together. In short, the world desperately needs centralised planning to counteract accelerating birth rates.

Meanwhile the US military and arms industry, given the go-ahead by Congress and financed by borrowings from *élites*' banks, dominated American life. In 1961 Eisenhower gave this warning at the end of his presidency: "We have been compelled to create a permanent armaments industry of vast proportions. Added to this, three and a half million men and women are directly engaged in the defense establishment. We annually spend on military security more than the next income of all the United States corporations. This conjunction of an immense military establishment and a large arms industry is new in the American experience. The total influence – economic, political, even spiritual – is felt in every city, every State house, every office of the Federal Government.... We must guard against the acquisition of unwarranted influence, whether sought or unsought, by the military-industrial complex. The potential for the disastrous rise of misplaced power exists and will persist."[24] In an earlier draft he referred to the "military-industrial-congressional complex".[25] Eisenhower was referring to the *élite*s (see pp.133–136) and expressing fears first uttered by the Founding Fathers that the republic's values could be corrupted.

During the Cold War, the *élite*s sold arms to both sides – both the Soviet and US Governments – and made a fortune out of funding the production of stockpiles of nuclear weapons. From a high of 69,401 nuclear weapons in 1985, in 2009 there were about 8,200 active nuclear warheads. In total there were 23,574 nuclear warheads in the world. In 2009 Russia had about 12,987 nuclear weapons, the US 9,552, France 300, Israel 200, the UK 192, China 176, Pakistan 90, India 75, and North Korea 2.[26] During the course of 2016 the world's nuclear weapons shrank to 15,375. The Federation of American Scientists estimated that the total number of nuclear weapons was 15,350 (Russia 7.300 and the US 6,970) by the end of 2016 and 14,900 in early 2017[27] (see p.45 and Appendix C9). Many of these weapons of mass destruction were bought with money borrowed from these *élite*s, who increased their wealth at the expense of taxpayers saddled with paying for their governments' borrowing.

Out of this view of the world grew the New World Order. The concept of a "new world" was first used in this sense in modern times by the US President Woodrow Wilson in an address to Congress outlining Fourteen Points on 8 January 1918: "We wish her [Germany] only to accept a place of equality among the peoples of the world – the new world in which we now live – instead of a place of mastery".[28] The term grew from the Latin tag *Novus Ordo Seclorum* (*Seculorum*), "New Secular Order" or "New Order of the Ages", which was placed on the US one-dollar bill by Henry A. Wallace, the US Secretary of Agriculture from 1933 to 1940 who was in charge of presenting the New Deal. In 1933 or 1934 Wallace drew President Roosevelt's attention to the tag, which he translated as "the New Deal of the Ages".[29] *Novus Ordo Seclorum* echoes a phrase of the epic poet Virgil, adapted from lines 5–8 of the 'Fourth Eclogue': "*Magnus ab integro saeclorum nascitur ordo*", "The great order of the ages is born afresh". (Virgil, an epic poet who wrote of war, nobly longed for and dreamed of a new era of peace that would benefit humankind, just as I, who have written two epic poems about war, long for and dream of a new era of peace that will benefit humankind in this work.)

The phrase "New World Order" was taken up by Hitler who was quoted as saying during the Second World War: "National socialism will use its own revolution for the establishing of a new world order."[30] He told Hermann Rauschning, the President of the Danzig Senate: "Yes, we are barbarians. We want to be barbarians. It is an honourable title. *We* shall rejuvenate the world. This world (or the present world) is near its end. It is our mission to sack it (or cause unrest)."[31] He saw himself as standing for a new world order.

Nelson Rockefeller called for a World Federation – what I call a World State – in *The Future of Federalism* (1962), claiming that events demanded "a new world order" as the old order was crumbling. In October 1967 Richard Nixon echoed this call in *Foreign Affairs,* the Council on Foreign Relations Journal (October 1967 issue). Nixon wrote of nations' evolving regional approaches and of the evolution of a "new world order".

New York Governor Nelson Rockefeller was quoted by AP (on 26 July 1968) as pledging that "as President he would work toward international creation of a 'new world order'".

On 30 January 1976 a new Rockefellerite document, *The Declaration of Interdependence,* signed by 32 Senators and 92 Representatives, stated: "We must join with others to bring forth a New World Order.... To establish a New World Order of compassion, peace, justice, and security, it is essential that mankind free itself from the limitations of national prejudice, and acknowledge that... all people are part of one global community".[32]

Much was made of the New World Order during the First Iraq War. On 11 September 1990, Bush Sr said that "a New World Order can emerge" that could "shape the future for generations to come". Secretary of State James Baker said that "it would set an extremely unfortunate precedent for the New World Order" if aggression were rewarded and that "if we really believe that there's an opportunity here for a New World Order... we can't start out by appeasing aggression". President Bush made a number of references to the New World Order in January 1991. In an interview he said on 7 January, "I think what's at stake here is the New World Order. What's at stake here is whether we can have disputes peacefully resolved in the future by a reinvigorated United Nations." On 9 January he said: "[The Gulf crisis] has to do with a New World Order. And that New World Order is only going to be enhanced if this newly activated peace-keeping function of the United Nations proves to be effective." On 16 January he said: "When we are successful, and we will be, we have a real chance at this New World Order, an Order in which a credible United Nations can use its peace-keeping role to fulfil the promise and vision of the UN's founders."

On 6 February 1991 Bush was asked by a reporter: "Can you give us a definition of a New World Order, and if it depends on the collaboration between the Soviet Union and the United States?" Bush replied: "Well, it doesn't depend entirely on it, but it would be greatly enhanced by a Soviet Union that goes down the line with its commitment to market reform, to private ownership of land, to a free economic system, to a system that resists, and does not use force to assure order amongst the republics, that goes farther down the road with elections, and all the openness that I give President Gorbachev credit for.... Now, my vision of a New World Order foresees a United Nations with a revitalised peace-keeping function." It is clear that Bush envisaged the New World Order as a world democracy that would include the ex-Soviet Union.

In August 1991 he wrote: "In the Gulf we saw the United Nations playing the role dreamed of by its founders.... I hope history will record that the Gulf crisis was the crucible of the New World Order."[33]

The term "New World Order" at present has two meanings: American superpowerdom after the Cold War, when the world became unipolar rather than bipolar and there was no more balance of power, just one superpower; and a conspiracy among megabillionaires' families, led by Rothschilds and Rockefellers, under which their Syndicate – in its dictionary sense of "a combination of individuals or commercial firms to promote some common interest"[34] – corner all the world's resources including gas and oil, convey them to ports through pipelines and sell them to increase their profits in the post-arms-race world. I am in favour of the first, or good, New World Order and not the second, or bad, New World Order, which seeks to seize the world's resources for its own, not humankind's, use.

There is evidence that the commercial *élite*s were involved in engineering both the US invasion of Afghanistan in 2001 and the US invasion of Iraq in 2003. In both countries pipelines were involved: the Trans-Afghan pipeline and the abortive attempt to reconstruct the Mosul(Kirkuk)–Haifa pipeline (built between 1932 and 1934 and decommissioned in 1948), which has not been implemented due to the instability in Iraq. Both Rothschilds and Rockefellers professed to be aghast at George W. Bush's American-supremacist role which cut across their plans for a New World Order. Rothschilds' associate George Soros called Bush's pre-emptive military action "pernicious", and Senator Jay Rockefeller called for an inquiry into the poor quality of American intelligence.[35]

In Syria the US has supported a pipeline from Qatar to Turkey (via Saudi Arabia, Jordan and Syria). This was blocked by President Assad of Syria, who favoured a pipeline from Iran to

Syria (via North Iraq) supported by Russia.

Elsewhere[36] I have described in some detail how Freemasonry may have reached America with the 1607 voyage to Jamestown; how Freemasonry gave the Founding Fathers the idea of federalism through Anderson's *Constitutions* (1723); and how Freemasonry came to be enmeshed in the American State, and eventually in the 'bad' New World Order (the second meaning).

The banking *élite*s are behind moves to shift to a global currency. On 7 September 2009 the Geneva-based UN Conference on Trade and Development called for a global currency. To progress towards it, the organisation wants to eliminate all national currencies and have three regional currencies, the euro for the European Union, the "amero" for a similar American Union and a new currency not yet given a name for an Asian-Pacific Union. The world would be split into three giant regions, each with its regional currency. This would signal progress towards a democratic World State.

The 2008 banking crisis confused the progress to a World State. On 11 September 2008, the seventh anniversary of 9/11, there was a massive withdrawal from the American banking system. Between 9 a.m. and 11 a.m. $550 billion was withdrawn, and the Treasury spent another $105 billion in propping the currency up, making a total loss of $655 billion. Then the Treasury stopped trading for the day.[37] If it had not done so, there would have been a cascade and $5.5 trillion would have haemorrhaged by close of business. The US economy would have collapsed that same evening and the world economy the next day. The Treasury, Federal Reserve and President Bush agreed that the raid should be kept secret to avoid panicking Americans.

A massive hole had to be plugged as swiftly as possible, and on 23 September 2008 Congress agreed to make available $700 billion "to buy toxic assets from many banks". European and Asian governments also had to make funds available for banks. In all, $3 trillion was transmitted from the Western (American and European) and Eastern governments to banking *élites*' banks, which shored them up in preparation for going over to the three currencies.

Who was responsible for the withdrawal, which involved multiple central banks? One can only study the facts. Of 192 UN nations at the time (there are now 193), it is alleged that the Rothschilds' dynasty and its branches of inherited wealth owned or controlled 187 central banks. The only central banks in the world they did not then control were those in Iran, Sudan, Cuba, Libya and North Korea. In 2001 they did not own the central banks of Afghanistan and Iraq, but following the Anglo-US invasions of those two nation-states in 2001 and 2003, they do now.[38] This view may elevate the Rothschilds' banking dynasty's inherited wealth well above that of Goldman Sachs (which Lord Jacob Rothschild owns), JP Morgan, Citibank and the other banks that are heavily involved in world banking and the wealth of American families made from computers, trading and banking.

There seems little doubt that the *élite*s have planned to reshape the world and reduce its population to a "sustainable" figure by encouraging local wars, spreading disease and exploiting famine so that it can control the world and loot the Earth's resources for the benefit of its own select band of relatively few oligarchs – not for the benefit of the many people of the world. The world crises of the early 21st century have advanced their cause. The 2007–2009 financial crisis has strengthened world calls for a World Treasury[39] (or proper World Bank), and the possibly engineered outbreak of swine flu and fear of an ensuing pandemic has strengthened calls for a World Health department. All these calls are good so long as the *élite*s do not extend their control.

The *élite*s have manipulated Western political life and have delivered the regional and Union structure we encountered in model 1. The *élite*s have operated in great secrecy and with lack of openness. All European nation-states have lost at least 80 per cent – and once the Lisbon Treaty was fully implemented, were set to lose 100 per cent – of their law-making power to the EU without their peoples having a true say. A referendum in the

UK they did not want to happen resulted in Brexit, to their intense dismay. The methods of the *élite*s may be effective in the long run, but using secrecy, deviousness and deception to advance their ends has tarnished their work. Many feel that they have intrigued a world which will be dictatorial rather than democratic.

Is this model a desirable model? No, it is insufficiently open and too controlled by *élite*s. One way to circumvent self-interested *élite*s is to give the regions more power by strengthening democracy. International politics have gone wrong, with secret bodies and self-interested *élite*s exploiting world resources and energy, and a reform of global governance is now pressing. A Universalist initiative is needed to refocus on the interests of humankind. This model does not give the kind of supranational authority that can achieve my stated goals.

7. Democratising the UN and making global governance accountable

In 1995 the Commission on Global Governance released its recommendations for the strengthening of global governance, which "does not imply world government or world federation". It has been said that the difference between "world government" and "global governance" is the difference between "rape" and "date-rape".

Global governance is founded on the belief that the world is run on "a set of core values that can unite people of all cultural, political, religious or philosophical backgrounds". These core values are: "respect for life, liberty, justice and equity, mutual respect, caring and integrity". The machinery of global governance would be a General Assembly of the People and a Forum of Civil Society. Global revenue would be raised by taxation on the global commons, especially taxes on airline tickets, ocean maritime transport, ocean fishing, Antarctica, geostationary satellites and use of the electromagnetic spectrum.

This perspective on global governance was taken up by *The Charter for Global Democracy* (also known as Charter 99),[40] a grassroots movement with initial support from 60 countries that aimed to place democratic reform of global governance at the top of the international political agenda prior to the Special General Assembly of the UN in 2000, also known as the UN Millennium Assembly. The Charter was addressed in the form of a letter to Representatives of the Millennium Assembly. It said:

> There have been well-meaning and sometimes eloquent calls for world government; calls which pointed to the unfairness, inequality and injustice of the present distributions of wealth, power and policy-making – which mean that today one in five of us lives in absolute poverty; calls which emphasised the dangers to peace and even to human survival. If only we could work as one world, then we could solve the world's problems together.... But during the 1990s, demands for international government have taken on a new energy and precision.

Initiatives in the 1990s included: the Commission on Global Governance to draw up a framework for global politics; the Earth Summit in Rio, Agenda 21, The Earth Charter, the Real World Coalition, Earth Action's Call for a Safer World, the One Planet Initiative, Citizens' Public Trust Treaty, Global Coalition World Democracy 2010, which aimed to bring in global democracy and sustainable development; the Hague Agenda for Peace which sought to replace the causes of war with a culture of peace; the campaign against landmines, which changed international law; international conferences at New York, Vienna, Cairo, Copenhagen, Beijing and Istanbul on gender, family and social rights; the Inter-Parliamentary Union's 1997 Universal Declaration on Democracy, which has been endorsed by most parliaments in the world; Jubilee 2000, which sought to cancel the poorest countries' unpayable debts; the International Commission on Rights and Responsibilities, which attempted to codify human duties and responsibilities; the International Criminal Court, which was created at Rome in 1998 to reinforce international criminal law; and the Human Development Report 1999 called for more democratic global governance.

The Charter continues:

In addition, a growing scholarly literature on all aspects of globalisation has begun to explore how governments can regulate and democratise international affairs. There are now detailed, practical measures which set out an ambitious agenda for democracy in international decision-making, now increasingly known as 'global governance'. We believe that there is a profound and important reason for this historic shift. It is that in many ways we now have world government.

It is not to be found at the United Nations. Rather, the UN has been sidelined, while the real business of world government is done elsewhere. Global policies are discussed and decided behind closed doors by exclusive groups, such as the G8, OECD, the Bank for International Settlements, the World Bank, the International Monetary Fund, the World Trade Organization and others. These agencies are reinforced by informal networks of high officials and powerful alliances. Together they have created what can be seen as dominant and exclusive institutions of world government. All too often they are influenced by transnational corporations which pursue their own world strategies.

These agencies of actual world government must be made accountable. If there are to be global policies, let them be answerable to the peoples of the world.

We call on you, therefore, to start the new century by initiating the process of democratic global governance following three fundamental principles: openness and accountability; environmental sustainability; and equality and justice.

The Charter goes on:

The first aim is to make the already existing processes of world administration and governance accountable. We want to know what decisions are being taken and why. We want the decision-takers to know they are answerable to the public in every country which feels the breath of international bodies. Then we want all decisions to be compatible with public criteria of environmental sustainability.

Finally, if most ambitiously, we want them to be compatible with the principles of equality, human rights and justice, including social and economic justice.

What we want from the Millennium Assembly and Member States is decisive action to put these principles into practice. We do not think they will be easy to achieve. We do not have all the answers. But we believe the difficulties can and must be overcome. In our era everyone is linked through our shared environment, trade and communications. We live together as neighbours, and as neighbours we must respect the rights of all persons to address common problems. A joint effort of learning and negotiation, of trial and error, will be needed.

Many vital issues can best be tackled effectively at a global level, such as the environment, biodiversity and climate change; international security and disarmament; international trade, finance and labor rights; epidemics; communications; and international crime.

The first question is where should we start? We believe that the answer has to be at the United Nations. The inadequacy of the UN is well known. All around we see the principles of the UN subverted, sidelined and suppressed. Since the UN Charter was signed, more than 30 million people have been killed in war, most of them unarmed civilians; millions more people have been slaughtered in genocide and ethnic conflict; over 100 million people have fled their homes due to conflict or persecution, with over 20 million remaining as refugees today; Permanent Members of the Security Council have armed belligerents and engaged in war; governments have invested more in preparing for war than in strengthening peace; human rights have been violated with little redress.

Nevertheless the United Nations as an institution can hardly be blamed for the appalling behaviour of its member states. Without the UN, wars would have been even more frequent; they would have gone on longer; there would have been a greater number of victims, and many more refugees living without hope. The UN is the only arena in which all countries sit side by side. For all its weakness, it retains an unmatched legitimacy in world affairs.

The UN's founding Charter mandates you to achieve international co-operation in solving international problems of an economic, social, cultural or humanitarian character and to be a centre for harmonising the actions of nations (Article 1).

We therefore call on you to create effective mechanisms to hold every agency of actual world government to account. These include international economic alliances, military alliances, the central banking system and agencies for environmental, financial, social, sporting or other activity. All should have to answer regularly for what they have done and intend to do, for their impact on the world community and for their adherence to the UN Charter and international law. We want action to start the process now.

The creation of democratic global governance may be complicated. But the need for it is simple and urgent. Global problems will only get worse if international decision-making is left in the hands of the present undemocratic, exclusive institutions. Therefore we will continue to press for action and public support around the world.

World-wide campaigns have led to the end of *apartheid* in South Africa, to the Statute for an International Criminal Court, to the ban on landmines and some debt-reduction for the world's poorest countries. The time has come to make democratic reform of international affairs our priority, both as an end in itself and as a means of solving many serious social and economic problems. Many reforms are needed.

The Charter then becomes more specific:

The following 12 points are a summary of the many demands and proposals being made across the world for better international governance. As an urgent first step we call on you to set in motion a rigorous process to hold all agencies of global governance to account and democratise international decision-making according to the principles set out in this letter.

Strengthen democratic accountability and participation in international decision-making:

1. Give the UN General Assembly powers to scrutinise the work of UN agencies and other agencies of global governance; create a UN Parliamentary Assembly and an annual Forum of Civil Society; open international institutions to increased participation by civil society and elected representatives from member countries; bring the WTO (World Trade Organization) into the UN system and strengthen the co-operation between all international groupings under the UN system.
2. Create within the UN system an accountable, equitable and effective mechanism to monitor, supervise and regulate transnational corporations and financial institutions; and require transnational companies to adhere to an international code of conduct covering agreed principles concerning human rights, the environment and core labour standards.
3. Give UN institutions an additional and independent source of revenue such as taxation of foreign exchange transactions, aircraft and shipping fuels, arms sales and licensing use of the global commons.

Maintain international peace and security:

4. Reform the UN Security Council to open all decision-making to public scrutiny; phase out the single country veto and Permanent Membership; establish equitable representation from each region of the world; set up a high-level early-warning system; and provide effective authority to mediate and intervene in disputes at an early stage, within national boundaries where necessary.
5. Establish a permanent, directly recruited UN Rapid Reaction Force to hold the peace in a crisis, police gross violations of human rights and support multilateral defence against aggression and genocide.

6. Make the UN register of arms mandatory; ratify and implement the Landmine Ban Treaty; outlaw all weapons of mass destruction; initiate programs to control the arms trade, convert the arms industry to peaceful production and cut military spending world-wide; strengthen accountability to the UN of all international military action; and reduce the size of national armies as part of a multilateral global security system.

Uphold fundamental human rights:

7. Strengthen world citizenship based on compliance with and respect for the Universal Declaration of Human Rights and all international instruments on Human Rights, including the six core treaties on economic, social and cultural rights; civil and political rights; racial discrimination; discrimination against women, children's rights, torture, and the Conventions on genocide, refugees and labour standards.

Strengthen justice under international law:

8. Ratify the Statute of the International Criminal Court; accept compulsory jurisdiction of the International Court of Justice, the International Criminal Court and the UN Human Rights Committee; increase the Courts' powers of enforcement; open the ICJ to individual petition and protect the judicial independence of the ICC.

Promote social progress and better standards of life:

9. Establish a strong UN institution for Economic and Environmental security to promote international prosperity, protect the global commons and secure reasonable development.
10. Establish an International Environmental Court to enforce international treaties on the environment and protect the global commons.
11. Declare climate change to be an essential global security interest and establish a high-level international urgent action team to assist the UN Conference of the Parties on Climate Change to set up a scientifically based global ceiling on greenhouse gas emission, to allocate national shares of permissible emissions based on convergence to equal *per capita* rights, and to work with governments, companies, international agencies and

NGOs (non-governmental organizations) to cut emissions of greenhouse gases to a sustainable level.

12. Make poverty reduction a global priority: secure universal access to safe drinking-water, health care, housing, education, family planning, gender equality, sustainable development and economic opportunities, and strengthen the capacity of development agencies to eliminate malnutrition, preventable diseases and absolute poverty through conservation and equitable sharing of global resources. Cancel the unpayable debts of the poorest nations and institute measures to prevent severe debt burdens from ever building up again.

The Charter proposes a directly elected UN. We have already seen that the UN has weaknesses. The world is run by megabillionaires and power-brokers, allegedly in the interests of economic growth and progress. The borderless Earth seen by astronauts has no elected law-makers, no compulsory judging or mediation, no enforceable revenue source, and no penal, rehabilitating or incentive system other than superpower-sponsored trade bans (sanctions) or war. Article 2 and other Articles of the UN Charter allow sovereign nations to use force if they claim it is for self-defence. The UN spends less than a cent for each dollar (one per cent) spent on war industries. A directly-elected UN has been long overdue. If *The Charter for Global Democracy* were implemented, the UN General Assembly would become the "UN Parliamentary Assembly".

The Charter for Global Democracy calls not just for the democratising of the UN, but also for the accountability and openness of all the institutions of global governance: the G8, OECD, the Bank for International Settlements, the World Bank, the International Monetary Fund and the World Trade Organization and all the agencies of the UN. By implication, it would include the institutions of the New World Order, that I have dealt with earlier in this chapter, which have been so surrounded by secrecy and deception.

So does this model remove the right to violence of nation-states? No. Democratising the UN is a step forward, but directly elected representatives of nation-states in a UN Parliamentary Assembly operating under the existing UN Charter can still go to war too readily, and making the G8, the trade and banking organisations and institutions of the New World Order accountable will not by itself remove their secrecy, if they are minded to continue to act by stealth. Under this model there is no supranational authority except directly elected public opinion. We encountered electing a UN General Assembly in models 4 and 5.

Does this model guarantee perpetual peace? No, for apart from direct elections and scrutiny the *status quo* is preserved.

So none of the seven models we have just considered give the kind of supranational authority that can achieve my stated goals. We have looked at global governance in our time, and have concluded that democratising the UN and making global governance accountable, while steps in the right direction, are simply not enough. The UN would remain an essentially international body attempting to fulfil a supranational role. A more radical approach needs to be adopted. There must be a supranational authority with the legal clout to enforce peace and disarmament.

6

The Ideal Form of the World State: The United Federation of the World

We have been looking for a supranational authority capable of preventing war by enforceable means and of maintaining world peace. On pp.105–106 I established a World State's goals:

1. bringing peace between nation-states, and disarmament;
2. sharing resources among, and solving energy supply to, all humankind;
3. solving environmental problems such as global warming;
4. ending disease;
5. ending famine;
6. solving the financial crisis;
7. redistributing wealth to eliminate poverty.

Of these we have been particularly concerned with bringing peace between nation-states.

Tinkering with the *status quo*, reforming the UN and pursuing existing models of global governance with loose associations of nation-states and federal regional Unions are all, for various reasons, unsatisfactory. They do not abolish war, they leave nation-states in charge of war, and where organs of global governance have evolved they have a disturbing lack of openness and incline to downright deception. The federal arrangements for regional government are an intermediate stage to a more radical model.

And so I am compelled to turn to a more radical alternative: an eighth kind of supranational arrangement:

8. Creating a tier of government of international law above the UN that would bring in a world government and abolish war

This model would take us a little further towards supranationalism, but not so far towards it that the nation-state system is completely abolished for a fundamentally new system; and it would offer a supranational authority with as little surrender of sovereignty on the part of nation-states as possible. I need to draw on what statecraft I can muster to offer a blueprint for a World State that will achieve the seven goals I have set.

I am devising a supranational authority with as little surrender of sovereignty on the part of nation-states as possible. I want to be clear on what I am not distilling or proposing. I am not proposing:

- A United States of the World as a reflection of the United States of America, in which a federal world government is in charge and all nation-states, perhaps grouped into 50 regions, are reclassified as states, like the states of the US. The nation-state may be in decline and of the old order, but this would be a drastic change, in which everything would be fundamentally new, both at the federal level and at the local/regional level. Such a system could not be brought in abruptly without unsettling all the world's citizens. Such a United States of the World would not involve "as little surrender of sovereignty on the part of nation-states as possible". It is more extreme – more a "fundamentally new system" – than the model I have set out to propose.
- A United States of the World in the sense of Lenin's phrase in his writings,[1] a "dictatorship of the proletariat" with all nation-states grouped into regions as "Soviets" (Lenin's totalitarian conception). Following the fall of the Berlin Wall, Communism has died in the West, and although it lingers on in the East in China and in the nation-states surrounding it, to group regions into Soviets would be both anachronistic and undesirable. This concept is no longer an option.
- The New World Order of the *élites* in which the regions and

> Unions of global governance – the 13 listed on p.185 – would be linked, and their leaders would control the world's resources on behalf of the *élites*, who would only allow a veneer of democracy to co-exist with its multinational corporations. I rejected this as undesirable when I considered model 6.

So I am steering clear of the above impractical (or impracticable) or unsuitable possibilities. I am also steering clear of other attempts to devise a supranational authority, which have deficiencies: the World Constitution and Parliament Association's Constitution for the Federation of Earth, which took from 1968 to 1991 to come into being, which seeks a democratic world government but lacks detail regarding human rights and world constituencies; and the World Philosophical Forum's Universal State of the Earth, which I brought in while chairing the Constitutional Convention (see pp.xxiv and 43), which is insufficiently democratic.

The model of a supranational authority I am proposing and recommending should have a *partial* federal level that can be effective in a limited way in implementing the seven goals, including the enforcing of peace and disarmament by international law; while preserving the local/regional level in all other respects, so world citizens can experience continuity despite the structural change.

I will focus on key points, and the following 17 points offer a model of a supranational authority and World State that achieves the seven goals. I should point out that in contrast the 17 features of the revision of the UN Charter on pp.124–127 focused on nation-states. All of the following 17 points have emerged from our investigation in ch.5, and implement a tier of government above the existing UN in a blueprint for a partly-federal World State that will achieve the goals I have set.

A World Commission, World Parliamentary Assembly, World Senate, World Judicial Tribunals, World Armed Force, World Council of Ministers, World President, World Leaders' Guidance Council, World

Bank and World Court of Justice, all above the UN

1. A supranational authority above the UN should form a partial federation of all humankind, a partial federal association of all nation-states. The authority should be called 'The United Federation of the World', or UF (United Federation). This would be set up by a World Constitutional Convention on a US initiative that would be supported by the UN.
2. The authority would be given power to use international law to make peace and create a borderless Earth.
3. The authority would form a world government that would enforce peace and complete disarmament, which would be achieved in a phased process over a period of time. Its remit would be to focus on the seven goals. At the supranational level it would consist of an administration or World Commission that would propose laws (like the EU Commission); a directly-elected World Parliamentary Assembly (a General Assembly of the People) operating within the UN as a lower house (like the House of Representatives) and a World Senate operating at a supranational level as an upper house, that would together pass the laws; and a World Armed Force (or Rapid Reaction Force) of 200,000–400,000 and a reserve of 300,000–600,000, that would enforce laws. A World Leaders' Guidance Council of elders would give guidance, and a World Court of Justice would arbitrate on disputes and enforce supranational law.
4. At the inter-national level the UN General Assembly would be turned into a World Parliamentary Assembly (or General Assembly of the People) that would be largely chosen on the basis of population percentages. The four largest countries – China, India, the EU (following ratification of the Lisbon Treaty and excluding the UK and France, both Permanent Members of the UN Security Council), and the US (which will eventually be grouped with Canada and Mexico as North America) – should each have 30 members, the three Permanent Members of the UN Security Council not includ-

ed in these four (the Russian Federation, the UK and France) should each have 15 members, the 10 largest countries in the world after the four largest 12, the 15 next largest 8, the 20 next largest 6, the 30 next largest 4, the 40 next largest 3, the 49 smallest nations 1. Two seats would be allocated to Puerto Rico and Palestine, the non-UN-member states with the largest populations, which would have associate status until they become independent. There would be a total of 815 representatives (with the prospect of 850 when all dependent and disputed territories become independent and are allowed 1 member in their own right). All these members would be directly elected, from 193 UN member nations and (when they become independent) non-UN-member dependent and disputed territories.

At the supranational level the World Senate would be chosen on a regional basis. The largest and most populated continents and nation-states would be zoned (north, south, east, west). There would be 46 electoral zones or constituencies in all, each of which would elect two senators. As in the American system, both the lower house and the Senate would pass the laws, and the smaller membership of the Senate would permit more extended debate than could be expected in the Assembly. There would be less party control in the Senate. (See ch.8 for details.)

Universal democracy would be implemented in the directly-elected World Parliamentary Assembly when it has replaced the UN General Assembly, and in the upper-house directly-elected World Senate.

5. The weakened nation-state system would continue, and would continue to use the UN in the same way as at present. The UN would refer intractable conflicts up to the new authority, the World Commission, and a supranational Universal Declaration of Human Rights would be passed by the World Parliamentary Assembly and World Senate to protect the perpetuation of the freedom of all individuals at the supranational level.

6. The directly-elected UN General Assembly would be phased in. The Security Council would become a veto-less World Executive Council of 17. Five representatives would represent each of the Permanent Members, 5 of the next 10 largest nation-states would have rotational representation (so that all 10 are represented, but only 5 at any one time), and the other 8 would be chosen by the World Parliamentary Assembly from representatives of other nation-states. The activities of the World Executive Council would be scrutinised by directly-elected UN Assembly members.
7. The authority's world laws would be enforceable by World Judicial Tribunals, which would be under the World Court of Justice, following investigation by a civil police force of 10,000 working for the World Commission.
8. The authority would carry out work to achieve all its goals: besides bringing peace and complete disarmament, it would begin a phased redistribution of humankind's resources and energy supply to even up the disparities between regions, work to ease environmental problems such as global warming and manage common resources including outer space and oceans; end disease and famine; and solve the world's financial crisis. A minimum standard of living would be guaranteed to all humankind on a phased basis, and a World Development Authority would grant interest-free loans to assist the economic and social development of under-developed areas.
9. The authority would be funded by phased taxation from all nation-states and would be accountable.
10. All nation-states and individuals should participate in, and be bound by, the world law of the authority set up by a World Constitutional Convention at US and UN instigation.
11. The laws proposed by the World Commission and passed by the World Parliamentary Assembly and World Senate would be binding, and the arbitration of disputes and enforcement carried out by World Judicial Tribunals would be supported by armed action carried out by the World Armed Force (or

Rapid Reaction Force).

12. Nation-states represented at the UN General Assembly before its transformation into the World Parliamentary Assembly should be persuaded to agree to a World Constitutional Convention on a five-sixths' vote: five-sixths of the world's nations, including the four largest countries listed in point 4, the three Permanent Members of the UN Security Council separate from these four listed in point 4 (the Russian Federation, the UK and France), and at least six of the ten next largest countries in the world, the aggregate of the populations of the voting nations equalling at least five-sixths of the total world population.
13. To ratify the authority once the World Constitutional Convention has set it up, the UN General Assembly should vote by five-sixths of the world's nations on the same basis as in point 12 above. Further amendments should be by four-fifths of the directly-elected World Parliamentary Assembly and two-thirds of the World Senate.
14. The secretive *élite*s should be democratised; some delegates to the Bilderberg Group and Trilateral Commission meetings, and to those of other agencies, should be directly elected and these two *élite* organisations should submit their agendas and decisions to a World Openness Committee.
15. There would be no population reduction by devious means (contrived wars, diseases and famines) although there would be programs to educate regarding birth control in countries such as Nigeria, Ethiopia and Pakistan where there has been a population explosion since 2009. The authority would conduct a phased redistribution of the Earth's resources and energy supply so that they are spread among all humankind.
16. There should be a World Council of Ministers drawn from the directly-elected World Parliamentary Assembly. These Ministers, working under the chairmanship of their World President, or World-Lord, who should be directly elected like the US president, should undertake the government of the world government's departments. The organs of global

governance should be restructured to be under the control of the authority. There should be a World Treasury with one global currency, and a World Health department under the World Council.

17. Life within the weakened nation-states would continue, and the UN would be an intermediary body charged with resolving conflicts. Initially the supranational authority will share the UN buildings one day, and later two days, a week and an appropriate number of UN administrative staff will be seconded to a supranational level to get the new authority up and running. It is anticipated that the volume of the work of the UN, an association of nation-states, will be reduced once the supranational authority is established and more and more UN administrative personnel are seconded to fill supranational positions. The UN will refer upwards to the World Commission all disputes it could not resolve by peaceful discussion in the World Parliamentary Assembly, and the upper tier of world government, consisting of the World Commission, the World Senate, World Judicial Tribunals, the World Armed Force, the World Council of Ministers and their World President or World-Lord, will come into force and enforce peace and complete disarmament.

I have included the World Constitutional Convention of model 3 in point 1, and democratising the UN from model 7. I have drawn on all the models in different ways to create a tier of government above the UN that will be strong enough to abolish war.

Before we look at the 17-point supranational authority in greater detail, a few general observations are in order. For a start, it must be conceded that although President Obama of the sole superpower since 1989 has said that the world has ceased to be unipolar and has become multipolar with potentially several centres of power including China and India, the United States is still so powerful (and recently quasi-imperial) that the supranational authority could not come into being without American instigation. The authority can therefore be seen as the expression of a stage of the North-American civilization, which I have shown elsewhere[2] to be in stage 15 out of 61 stages, the stage the Roman civilization was in when it had a Roman Empire. Although Obama's US did not claim to be imperialistic it would in fact have been behind such a supranational authority and World State. It remains to be seen what the situation will be after Trump's 'America-First' presidency.

Secondly, the membership of the World Parliamentary Assembly cannot be based solely on population percentages. Otherwise, the nuclear Russian Federation, which in 2009 had 12,987 nuclear warheads and in 2016 still had 7,000, would have less membership than non-nuclear Indonesia, which has replaced it in the top four most-populated nations following the break-up of the USSR. However, Indonesia slides down to fifth when the EU is included as one nation-state following the ratification of the Lisbon Treaty. (See p.167 and Appendix E3.) Permanent Membership of the existing UN Security Council must be taken into account in the voting described in point 4, and in establishing the basis of the membership of the World Commission. For complete disarmament is the new authority's priority, and all nuclear powers must be represented at the highest level so that they fully participate in nuclear disarmament.

The importance of the UN General Assembly votes referred to in points 12 and 13 demands that a five-sixths majority should include the four largest countries (China, India, the EU and US) and the three Permanent Members of the UN Security Council not among these, whose status as original nuclear powers should continue to be recognised. Those nation-states with nuclear weapons must be heavily involved in setting up a World Constitutional Convention and ratifying it so that they disarm themselves.

For the basis of membership of the World Commission and World Senate, see ch.7.

Thirdly, it is of crucial importance that those in the World State's supranational institutions should have the wisdom and authority to make wise decisions. Much thought has been given to the allocation of representation within the democratic structure to ensure that wise decisions are made: decisions that will benefit all humankind as a whole and not one region that wishes to behave irresponsibly. For example, it would be completely wrong for Africans to encourage breeding when they are faced with droughts and food shortages. In times of starvation and drought within Africa it would be wrong to allocate funds without linking them to a birth-control program. At all times those dealing with the federal tier of the World State must consider the implementation of the seven goals set out on pp.105–106 and 153. The structure of the World State, with its checks and balances, is designed to attract the most able, best qualified and most humane minds in the world who will tirelessly rid the world of corruption and selflessly create a better world for all humankind.

Fourthly, the cost of a world government might seem to be prohibitive in the short and medium terms. The American economy is in debt with financial problems. The dollar has not been strong during the financial crisis, and the Chinese have proposed that the international currency should be BIS (Bank for International Settlements) credits. It has, however, been suggested that China could go bust. There are massive economic and social divisions between world citizens. Like America, Europe has no savings and is in debt. Some ex-Soviet nation-states had little or no pension provision, and were offered financial inducements to join the EU. These have been paid for by Germany, France and the UK. A quarter of the Indian population do not have electricity and therefore do not use light bulbs. There is a similar imbalance in China. Money has to be pumped into India and China to improve standards of living. All world citizens cannot be brought up to a minimum standard of living in one go. The process can be started in principle, and can only be phased. It may take decades before parity in the standard of living of world citizens is achieved.

In view of the financial crisis the world government should be established within the UN in an interim capacity, and staffed by UN personnel who would be seconded to the supranational authority. Initially, therefore, setting-up costs of the new authority would be kept to a minimum.

Without financial inducements many leaders of sovereign nation-states may not agree to vote for the UN to set up a World Constitutional Convention to establish a federal World State without financial inducements. How can such inducements be afforded in the early-21st-century's financial climate?

There may have to be a massive devaluation, whereby a new global currency is created, a new Earth dollar that is worth, say, 10 old dollars, a move linked to "quantitative easing" (or printing money) that at a stroke would write off nine-tenths of the previous global debt. This would mean that the entire foreign currency market would vanish overnight. The average daily turnover in global foreign exchange markets is estimated at £3.98 trillion[3] (against a daily stock-market turnover of about $100 billion). A new global currency would therefore involve a massive loss of business in the financial sector. I am not suggesting that this is a good way of proceeding. I am merely pointing out how the system of global governance could escape from the legacy of debt if such a scheme were applied to the whole world on the same day, and start afresh. Meanwhile, the dollar, euro and pound have been drawing together following the UK currency's 20-per-cent devaluation in the wake of Brexit.

Finally, the supranational authority would be Universalist. It would embody a form of political Universalism. The aim of political Universalism is to construct a World State, a federal association of all nation-states under a supranational world government. This is what this model would achieve.

I must emphasise that this model of the World State will not bring perpetual peace and harmony any more than did the Roman Empire or the British Empire. As I have said on p.20, history has a rise-and-fall pattern of civilizations that pass through similar stages which I set out in *The Rise and Fall of Civilizations*, and when civilizations leave stage 43 (union) for stage 46 (federation) they pass into federations. It so happens that most of the living civilizations are in this transition and (as I said on p.20) can flow like rivers into the lake of a World State and in due course flow out the other side to resume their progress as civilizations, just as the Nile flows from Tanzania into Lake Victoria to emerge the other side in Uganda. The World State will not last forever but it will bring universal peace and harmony for a while, and that – in the long term, transient – unification will be good for the progress of all civilizations and for all humankind.

Would this model achieve the goals a supranational authority would need to achieve in order to solve the old order's problems, the goals listed on pp.105–106 and 153 including bringing peace between nation-states and complete disarmament? Yes, it would. Model 8, the UF (or United Federation), escapes the difficulties associated with all the other models, which were too *status-quo* and insufficiently radical, and its regime of international law does offer the prospect of world peace. Let us see in greater detail how.

7

The Structure of a World State

I now come to the structure of the United Federation of the World, the 17-point supranational authority that can achieve my 7 goals in accordance with the concept Wendt urged (see pp.17–18). The actual structure of a World State will of course be determined by the World Constitutional Convention.

The proposals which I shall now set out really amount to one model for such a structure, a model that the World Constitutional Convention can either implement or vary depending on the thinking of the experts on the Convention. In making these proposals I am pointing a way forward, proposing a direction. It will be for the rank and file of Convention members to consider my proposal, flesh out the details and come up with the best-possible structure that will achieve the seven goals listed on pp.105–106 and 153.

It is best to begin with an overview, with the diagram/flow chart on p.173. This shows three different levels. The existing levels, the national and inter-national levels, are the levels of nation-states and of the UN, which is an association of nation-states. The supranational level is a level above nation-states and the UN.

I shall start with the existing inter-national level.

The Inter-national Level

Inter-national affairs are at present conducted by the UN General Assembly and Security Council, and a number of inter-national agencies which are offshoots from the General Assembly.

World Parliamentary Assembly

I have said that the UN General Assembly should become a lower house, the directly-elected World Parliamentary Assembly which would be involved in passing supranational laws proposed by the World Authority. The Assembly should be chosen on the basis of an initial allocation of 815 seats, along criteria stated by Clark and Sohn in *World Peace Through World Law* and modified to take account of, and adjust for, nuclear influence and Permanent Membership of the Security Council, as proposed in point 4 on pp.156–157.

I can now set out the structure of the representation on the World Parliamentary Assembly. The mathematics looks like this:

Countries	Multiplied by	Members	Equals	Seats
4	x	30	=	120
3	x	15	=	45
10	x	12	=	120
15	x	8	=	120
20	x	6	=	120
30	x	4	=	120
40	x	3	=	120
48	x	1	=	48
+2	x	1	=	2
		Initial total		815
In future				
+26	x	1	=	26
+8	x	1	=	9
		Eventual total		850

I can now flesh out these figures, using the UN-sourced world population percentages in Appendices E1, E2 and E3. These are based on 1 July 2017 estimates by the UN Department of Economic and Social Affairs – Population Division.[1] The alphabetical letter at the beginning of each line below corresponds to the alphabetical letters against the relevant countries in the Appendix. The "largest" and "next-largest" countries mean "most populated". The representation in the World Parliamentary Assembly (initially calculated on the 2009 data and criteria and now comprehensively updated to 2017) looks as follows:

Letter in Appendix E3	**Countries**	**No. each**	**Seats**
A.	The 4 largest countries: China, India, the EU (on the basis of 26 members all marked A, excluding the UK and France, see B), the US	30 each	120
B.	3 Permanent Members of the Security Council: The Russian Federation, France, the UK	15 each	45
C.	The 10 largest countries after the 4: Indonesia, Brazil, Pakistan, Nigeria, Bangladesh, Japan, Mexico, Ethiopia, Philippines, Egypt	12 each	120
D.	The 15 next-largest countries: Vietnam, Democratic Republic of Congo, Iran, Turkey, Thailand, Tanzania, South Africa, Myanmar (Burma), South Korea, Colombia, Kenya, Argentina, Ukraine, Sudan, Uganda	8 each	120
E.	The 20 next-largest countries: Algeria, Iraq, Canada, Morocco, Saudi Arabia, Uzbekistan, Malaysia, Peru, Venezuela, Nepal, Angola, Ghana, Yemen, Afghanistan, Mozambique, Australia, North Korea, Taiwan, Cameroon, Côte d'Ivoire	6 each	120
F.	The 30 next-largest countries:	4 each	120

	Madagascar, Niger, Sri Lanka, Burkina Faso (formerly the Republic of Upper Volta), Syria, Mali, Malawi, Chile, Kazakhstan, Ecuador, Guatemala, Zambia, Cambodia, Senegal, Chad, Zimbabwe, Guinea, Republic of South Sudan (separated from Sudan in 2011), Rwanda, Tunisia, Cuba, Bolivia, Somalia, Haiti, Benin, Burundi, Dominican Republic, United Arab Emirates, Jordan, Azerbaijan		
G.	The 40 next-largest countries: Belarus, Honduras, Tajikistan, Israel, Switzerland, Papua New Guinea, Togo, Serbia, Sierra Leone, Paraguay, El Salvador, Laos, Libya, Nicaragua, Kyrgyzstan, Lebanon, Singapore, Eritrea, Norway, Central African Republic, Costa Rica, New Zealand, Turkmenistan, Republic of the Congo, Oman, Kuwait, Liberia, Panama, Mauritania, Georgia, Moldova, Bosnia and Herzegovina, Uruguay, Mongolia, Armenia, Albania, Jamaica, Qatar, Namibia, Botswana	3 each	120
H.	The 48 next-largest countries: Republic of Macedonia, Lesotho, Gambia, Gabon, Guinea-Bissau, Bahrain, Trinidad and Tobago, Mauritius, Equatorial Guinea, East Timor, Swaziland, Djibouti, Fiji, Comoros (an island nation in the Indian Ocean), Bhutan, Guyana, Solomon Islands, Montenegro, Suriname, Cape Verde, Brunei, Belize, Bahamas, Maldives, Iceland, Northern Cyprus, Barbados,	1 each	48

	Vanuatu (an island nation in the South Pacific), Samoa, São Tomé and Principe (an island nation in the Gulf of Guinea), Saint Lucia, Kiribati (formerly known as the Gilbert Islands, in the Pacific Ocean), Saint Vincent and the Grenadines, Grenada, Tonga, Federated States of Micronesia, Seychelles, Antigua and Barbuda, Andorra, Dominica, Marshall Islands, Saint Kitts and Nevis, Liechtenstein, Monaco, San Marino, Palau (an island nation in the Pacific Ocean), Tuvalu (formerly known as the Ellice Islands, in the Pacific Ocean), Nauru (formerly known as Pleasant Island, in the South Pacific)		
I.	2 non-UN-members with largest populations: Palestine, Puerto Rico	1 each	2
	Initial total		815
J.	26 dependent territories outside the UN and not yet independent with associate status until they become independent, seats held in reserve for when they become independent: Macau, Western Sahara, French Polynesia, New Caledonia, Guam, Curaçao (an autonomous region of the Netherlands in the Caribbean), Aruba (an autonomous region of the Netherlands in the Caribbean), US Virgin Islands, Jersey (UK), Isle of Man (UK), Guernsey (UK), Bermuda (UK), Cayman Islands (UK), American Samoa, Northern Mariana Islands (a	1 each	26

	commonwealth in political union with the US, in the Western Pacific), Greenland (Denmark), Faroe Islands (Denmark), St Maarten (Netherlands), Saint-Martin (France), Gibraltar (UK), Turks and Caicos Islands (UK), British Virgin Islands (UK), Bonaire (an autonomous region of the Netherlands in the Caribbean), Cook Islands (New Zealand), Anguilla (UK), Vatican City (in view of its diplomatic importance)		
K.	9 disputed territories not on the UN-based list: Indian Kashmir (Jammu and Kashmir), Tibet, Pakistani Kashmir (Azad Kashmir), Kosovo, Chechnya, Transnistria, Abkhazia, Nagorno-Karabakh, South Ossetia	1 each	9
L.	13 island groups with populations under 12,000 to be represented by colonial power: Wallis and Futuna (France), St Barthélemy (France), Saint Pierre and Miquelon (France), Saint Helena, Ascension and Tristan da Cunha (UK), Montserrat (UK), Sint Eustatius (Netherlands), Falkland Islands (UK), Norfolk Island (Australia), Christmas Island (Australia), Saba (Netherlands), Niue (New Zealand), Tokelau (New Zealand), Cocos (Keeling) Islands (Australia), Pitcairn Islands (UK)		0
	Eventual total		850

It must be stressed that this is a flexible list. There would be movement within it. For example, as more nation-states enter the EU, those that enter would lose their individual representation, leaving a vacancy in their group for a country in the group below it to be promoted. Associate dependent territories in J. and K. obtaining independence will have one member each and those passing within another nation (as Hong Kong did when it became a part of China) would lose their independent representation. The 850 seats are a maximum that would not be reached immediately. There is scope for future developments within the designation of an eventual tally of 850 seats, and there is no reason why there should not in due course be 850 seats or more – up to 1,000 – if changes to national arrangements in the coming years require such an increase. The above list is therefore a transitional list to cope immediately with an ever-changing scenario.

Offshoots

All the offshoots from the UN General Assembly would continue to operate: the Economic and Social Council, the International Criminal Court, the International Court of Justice and the UN organs (UNDP, UNHCR, UNICEF and UNEP) and specialised agencies (FAO, UNESCO, WHO and WTO). (See Appendices C2 and C3.)

Of these, the International Court of Justice, based in the Peace Palace at The Hague, Netherlands, the primary judicial organ of the UN, would continue to settle legal disputes submitted to it by nation-states and give advisory opinions on legal questions placed before it by the replacement for the UN General Assembly, the World Parliamentary Assembly. Like the tripartite Assembly/Executive Council/Secretary-General, the International Court of Justice would continue to resolve legal problems arising from conflicts in the first instance.

World political parties

All members of the World Parliamentary Assembly would belong to one of the world political parties. There would be a World Centre/Right Party, a World Socialist Party and a Liberal

Centrist Party. In addition, no doubt, there would be a World Green Party, a Far-Left Party, a Far-Right Party and a Party for World Sceptics. Different world parties would have different views on the management of world resources and energy supply, and on the level of world taxation and redistribution.

World Executive Council

The UN Security Council would continue to operate as a veto-less World Executive Council. It would continue to have 5 Permanent Members and 12 Non-Permanent Members elected for two-year terms. The World Parliamentary Assembly would make recommendations as does the UN General Assembly, and the World Executive Council would decide as does the Security Council. The UN Secretary-General and his Secretariat would continue to implement decisions.

This tripartite UN structure would continue to field all conflicts requiring resolution in the first instance. Only the intractable problems on which the World Executive Council could not reach agreement would be passed up to the supranational level. The UN Peacekeeping Forces would continue to operate under the World Executive Council as under the Security Council in containable conflicts that do not require the involvement of the supranational level.

The World Executive Council's (ex-Security Council's) 17 representatives would be elected by the World Parliamentary Assembly. Five representatives would represent each of the Permanent Members, 5 of the next 10 largest nation-states would have rotational representation (so that all 10 are represented, but only 5 at any one time), and the other 8 would be chosen by the World Parliamentary Assembly from representatives of other nation-states. This veto-less World Executive Council would decide whether each stage of the disarmament process was satisfactorily completed.

It is important to stress that, from the point of view of the nation-states, life under the UN, and their experience of the UN

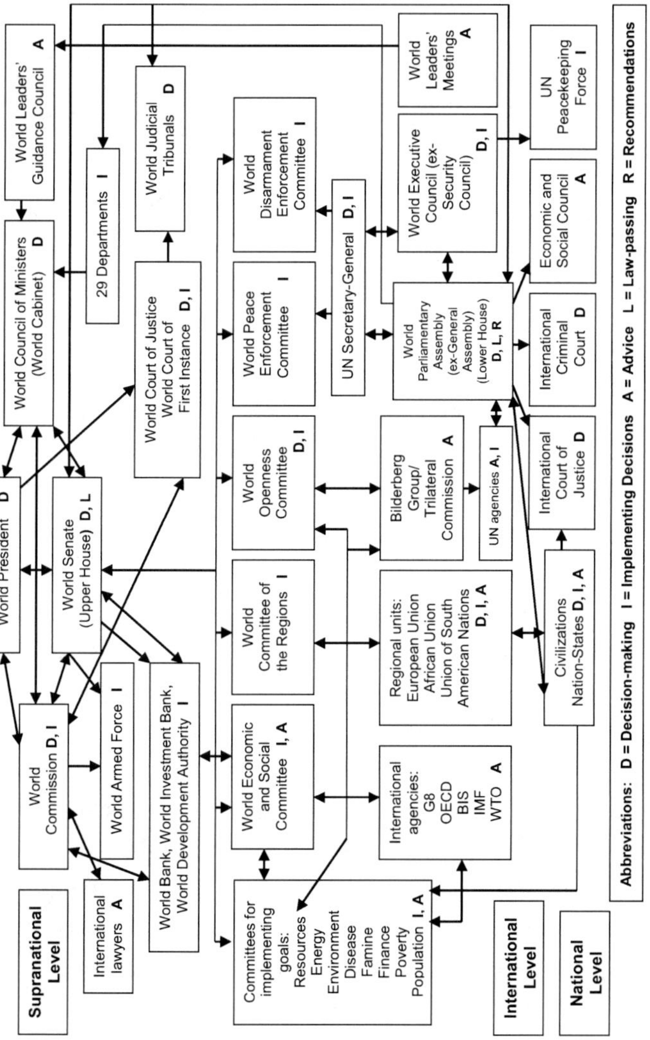

Diagram/Flow Chart of the Supranational Authority: The Structure of the World State

Diagram/Flow Chart of the Supranational Authority: The Structure of the World State

and the inter-national level, would go on pretty much as before except that the UN General Assembly would operate as a directly-elected Parliament. Life within each nation-state or regional grouping, whether loose, or tight (like the EU following the ratification of the Lisbon Treaty), would go on just the same, and nation-states would continue to pursue their self-interest within their implementing of the supranational authority's seven goals. Civilizations would carry on progressing through their various stages. At the inter-national level, the life of civilizations would continue.

There would be just one fundamental change, that from time to time the supranational tier would come into play. When a nation-state or civilization had a conflict that the UN could not deal with and might lead to war, as has happened in the case of conflicts involving 124 countries since 1945 according to one selection (see Appendix C6), and 162 conflicts since 1945[2] according to another (see Appendix C8), the conflict would be referred to the supranational level whose higher tier would enforce peace and impose a settlement just as if two American states had had a disagreement and had gone to court and been bound by the court's legal ruling.

The Supranational Level

The supranational level would provide the context within which the nation-states and their civilizations operate.

The executive, the World Commission – the supranational authority's equivalent of the European Commission – would propose laws, monitor the implementation of all directives and world policies, and represent the World Authority in the international institutions of global governance (the G8, OECD, the Bank for International Settlements, the World Bank, the International Monetary Fund, the World Trade Organization and all the agencies of the UN). The World Commission's proposals would all relate to the achievement of the goals listed on pp.105–106 and 153, including the enforcement of peace and disarmament, while guaranteeing the security of nation-states.

World Commission

The World Commission should be composed of 27 members, about the maximum number that can comfortably sit round a table and take part in world-authority meetings to enforce peace and conduct a world government. The 27 World-Commission representatives should be appointed on the basis of taking into account: regional representation; population percentages; topographical extent; Permanent Membership of the UN; and possession of nuclear warheads to be disarmed.

The data for these criteria can be found in the Appendix. The world population percentages for each nation-state are in Appendix E3, and historical movements of percentages are in Appendix E2. A fundamental approach to regions is in Appendix E1: Asia has 59.6 per cent of world population; Europe 9.8 per cent; North America 4.8 per cent; Latin America and the Caribbean 8.6 per cent; Africa 16.6 per cent; the Middle East and North Africa 3 per cent; and Oceania/Australia 0.5 per cent. As we shall shortly see, I have broken these regions up into smaller representational denominations. (I have done likewise in arriving at different representational regional zones or constituencies for the World Senate below.)

There are different schools of thought regarding regions. Sometimes Central America is linked to the Caribbean to form a region, and this region is distinguished from South America. The Rockefellerite Club of Rome, one of the undemocratic international agencies, put forward 10 regions in 1973.[3] (See Appendix E6.) These 10 zones, identified during the Cold War, included "centrally-planned Asia", meaning Communist Asia (Mongolia, North Korea, North Vietnam and China).

China's emergence as the most populated nation with industrial and nuclear power has required a rethinking of regional zones. It must not be forgotten that the main object of the World Commission is to deliver world peace through international law, and so it must include representation from all the nation-states that have been party to recent wars and conflicts. A balance has to be struck between representing the entire population of the world (as in the World Parliamentary Assembly) and representing the most powerful nation-states that need to sit round a table in order to deliver world peace and disarmament with the greatest degree of effectiveness.

The principle should be that members of the World Commission should be nominated by the governments or organisations of the countries/regions on the basis of no more than one member per region (as distinct from nation-state). I am basing my regions on the regions in the list in Appendix E4, but have varied some regions to achieve a scheme that works in relation to delivery of the seven goals (taking into account the list in Appendix E5).

I propose that the 27 members of the World Commission should be drawn up on the basis below. I have given reasons for my proposal in brackets. The abbreviation R means that there are regional considerations for the nomination; PM means Permanent Member of the UN; and N means that there are nuclear/disarmament considerations behind the nomination; wpp means world population percentage. The number 1 means one member to be nominated by a particular nation-state. Thus 1 China means one member nominated by China. My proposed members are as follows:

1 China (PM, N, wpp 18.5%)
1 Communist Asia (Mongolia, North Korea, N, Laos, Vietnam)
1 Russian Federation (PM, N, largest country in world)
1 Central Asia (ex-USSR)
1 Canada (topographical size) and Greenland
1 USA (PM, N)
1 UK (PM, N)
1 France (PM, N)
1 Western Europe including Germany (R)
1 Eastern Europe (R)
1 Central America and Caribbean (R)
1 North-East South America (including Brazil, N, R)

1 South-West South America (including Argentina, R)
1 Northern Africa (R)
1 Southern Africa (R)
1 Arab Middle East (R)
1 Israel (N)
1 Iran (N?)
1 Pakistan (N)/Afghanistan (R)
1 India (N, wpp 17.9%)
1 West-Central and South-East Asia (Bangladesh to Cambodia, R)
1 East Asia (Japan, South/North Korea, Philippines, R)
1 Indonesia (wpp 3.5%)/Malaysia
1 Australia/Oceania (R, wpp 0.5%)
1 UN (secondment of executive expert)
1 World Bank (secondment of expert)
1 Agencies of global government (secondment of expert)
27 Total

The allocation of governments'/agencies' nominations is a balance between regional representation, population percentages and world influence. It can be criticised from a number of angles.

Have I been too generous to the Russian Federation? I would say that the territory covered by the Russian Federation and the ex-USSR states east of the Caspian Sea and in Eastern Europe is perhaps four times as large as India.

Have I been too ungenerous to the US, the sole superpower? I would say that the principle has been one member per region, and there are certainly two regions (East/West) within the US. However, Canada only has one member and has larger territory. Australia is nearly as large as the US and has to share one member with Oceania (including New Zealand).

Have I given too much weight to nation-states with nuclear weapons? I would say that a World Commission committed to complete disarmament cannot have under-representation from the powers that produced 69,401 nuclear warheads by 1985, and reduced them to nearly 24,000 in 2009 and 15,375 by autumn 2016, and according to the Federation of American Scientists to 15,350 in the course of 2016 and to 14,900 in 2017 (see p.138),[4] which are still in storage throughout the world, whose co-operation it needs.

Is it right to include Israel, the Middle East and Iran and thus allocate three members to the Middle-Eastern region, the same number as Central and South America? I would say that the greatest threat to world peace is in the Middle East, where the World Commission needs to influence Islamists in Iraq, Palestine, Israel, Iran, and of course in Central Asia (Afghanistan and Pakistan).

Is it right to subordinate North Korea to one of three Communist-Asian nation-states? I would say that North Korea needs steadying, and that it would be wrong to allocate one seat to it for breaking rules but equally wrong to ignore it and isolate it.

Similar "cons" can be raised about each nation-state listed as nominating a member to the World Commission and I would say that for each "con" there is a "pro" that gives each listed nation-state a better right to nomination than the right of any other nation-state or region I have not included on the list.

There may be arguments about the detail of my list, which can easily be corrected, but the important thing is: the principle behind the choice of nominating countries/regions/agencies is right. In principle, I have put forward a workable list. In the interests of administrative efficiency, the representation on the World Commission should not be increased beyond 27.

World Senate

The World Senate would be a directly-elected upper house, like the American Senate. The relationship between the World Commission and the World Senate would be like that of the European Commission and the European Parliament – only there would be a bicameral system, one chamber (the World Parliamentary Assembly) being at inter-national level and the higher chamber (the World Senate) being at supranational level and dedicated to implementing the seven goals of the supranational authority by passing the appropriate laws to bring in and enforce a peaceful world.

The World Senate would be elected on a basis of regional zones, with weight being given to more scrupulously defined regions than the ones that would nominate the World Commission. The criteria would include regional representation, population percentages, topographical area, possession of nuclear weapons to be disarmed, political clout and environmental considerations.

I propose that there should be in the first instance 46 zonal constituencies, each of which would elect 2 Senators, making a total of 92 seats. I have based these regional zones on the lists of regions in Appendices E4 and E5, which include countries in each region. The numbers in what follows refer to the number of zonal regions or constituencies, each of which would have 2 Senators.

4 China: East, West, North (including Mongolia), South (PM, N,
wpp 18.5%)
3 Russian Federation: East, Central, West (PM, N)
2 Central Asia: North-Central (including Kazakhstan), South-Central (including Pakistan)
3 Canada: East, West, North (including Greenland and Arctic)
4 USA: East, West, North, South, including dependent territories (PM, N)
1 UK (PM, N)
1 France (PM, N)
4 Europe: 2 North-Western (including Scandinavia, Germany),
1 Eastern, 1 Southern (i.e. Northern Mediterranean – Spain,
Italy, Greece/Aegean)
1 Central America, including Mexico

1 Caribbean
3 South America: North-East (Brazil, Bolivia, Paraguay), South (Argentina, Chile, Uruguay and Antarctica), North-West (Peru, Ecuador, Colombia, Venezuela, North Coast)
4 Africa: North, East, West (including Atlantic Ocean), South (NB Middle Africa distributed among these 4)
2 Middle East: Northern (including Turkey, Iraq), Southern (including Egypt, Saudi Arabia)
1 Israel
1 Iran
3 India, North (including Nepal), Central, South (including Sri Lanka, Maldives and Indian Ocean)
2 East-Central Asia (Bangladesh, Myanmar/Burma, Thailand, Laos, Vietnam, Cambodia)
1 South-East Asia (Malaysia, Indonesia, wpp 3.9%)
2 East Asia (Japan, North/South Korea, Philippines)
2 Australia: East, West
1 Oceania (New Zealand, islands and dependent territories)
46 Total

Again, there may be disagreements regarding the detail and the number of seats allocated to a particular region, bearing in mind its population or topographical size. But I have done enough to demonstrate that 92 Senators can fairly represent all the nation-states and regions in the world. If this scheme were implemented there would be scope for 4 more zones to even up unfair allocations where regions feel hard-done-by, which would eventually give a Senate of 50 zones and 100 Senators.

The Senators would work closely with the World Commission, and with the World Parliamentary Assembly. The Assembly would send up to the World Commission matters beyond its competence, conflicts which would require enforcement, and the Commission would pass its proposals to the World Senate for them to become law. It is envisaged that some Senators would be experts in international law.

As in the case of the American system, each party would select a Senate leader who would appoint members of his or her party to Senate committees. These would include a World Committee of the Regions, a World Economic and Social Committee, a World Peace Enforcement Committee and a World Disarmament Enforcement Committee which would liaise with the World Commission, the World Court of Justice and the Assembly.

There would also be World Committees to implement the remaining six of the seven goals: a World Resources Committee, a World Energy Committee, a World Environmental Committee, a World Disease Committee, a World Famine Committee, a World Finance Committee, a World Poverty Committee and a World Population Committee.

World Openness Committee

The Senate Committees would include the very important World Openness Committee, which would review the position of the agencies and scrutinise all world personnel for any relationship with Rockefellers and Rothschilds dynasties and their self-interested world agendas. In view of the enmeshing of the New World Order, the Syndicate of the *élite*s and Freemasonry, this Openness Committee would be alert to undue Freemasonic influence and would particularly look for any hidden links to élitist agencies which might suggest that a candidate for world officialdom would be linked to their known wish to control the Earth's resources and energy supply, and effect population reduction by violent means, which would be a crime under World Authority international law.

Working in conjunction with the World Resources Committee, this Openness Committee would co-control the return of all privately-owned energy to the people of the Earth, including all Russia's oil and gas which was acquired by the Rockefellers dynasty in the early 1990s for about one-tenth of its market value.[5] Multinational corporations would be permitted to continue conveying energy, but would have to surrender private ownership to the World Authority.

Under this scrutinising regime the *élite*s would continue to operate and the Rothschilds dynasty would be free to continue to control 187 world central banks (if they do), but any manipulation of candidates, officials or policies would be identified and exposed as a breach of international law for which there would be severe penalties. The World Openness Committee would also receive advance copies of all agendas of meetings of agencies such as the Bilderberg Group and the Trilateral Commission, and all minutes made of their meetings. It would be a legal requirement that two representatives of the Senatorial World Openness Committee should attend all meetings of these groups and report back to the World Commission, to ensure that the work of all agencies was transparent.

The Syndicate of the *élite*s would be allowed to go on functioning but its activities would be controlled and members would be excluded from secret decision-making and would be subject to investigation by the civil police and law enforcement.

World Council of Ministers

Vetting by the World Openness Committee would also apply to the World Council of Ministers, the world Cabinet, which would be drawn from the directly-elected World Parliamentary Assembly.

There would be 29 Departments, and therefore 29 World Ministers, the absolute maximum number that can comfortably sit round a Cabinet table and take part in high-level World-Authority meetings.

Unlike the EU, where the Council of Ministers is an assembly of national Ministers, the World Council of Ministers would comprise ministers of World Departments:

- World Finance;
- World Treasury;
- World Peace;
- World Disarmament;

- World Resources;
- World Environment;
- World Climate Change;
- World Health (ending disease);
- World Food (ending famine, implementing crop-growing programs);
- World Regions, Communities and Families;
- World Work and Pensions;
- World Housing;
- World Economic Development;
- World Regional Aid and International Development (ending financial crises);
- World Poverty (eliminating poverty);
- World Population Containment (not reduction);
- World Energy Regulation;
- World Transport (world aviation, shipping, roads and rail);
- World Law;
- World Oceans;
- World Space;
- World Education;
- World Citizenship (law and order);
- World Culture and History;
- World Sport;
- World Unity in Diversity;
- World Dependent Territories;
- World Foreign Policies (liaising with nation-states' Foreign Ministers); and
- World Human Rights and Freedom (guaranteeing individual freedoms, including freedom from population reduction under the new system).

All these Departments would work closely with Senatorial Committees operating within their field.

World President

The World Council of Ministers would meet as the World Cabinet under the leadership of the World President, who would be elected every four years like the President of the United States.

The World President would be nominated by one of the world parties. There would be several candidates, one for each party, and each would be vetted by the World Commission and the Senatorial World Openness Committee for any links to élitist agencies that might suggest that a candidate would be likely to pursue élitists' agenda regarding world resources, energy supply and population reduction rather than a philanthropic agenda.

There would be a world election campaign involving visits to the main regions and television coverage of speeches that would go out to the whole world. There would be a world ballot involving polling stations in key cities and rural areas, postal voting and online voting.

The successful World President would be sworn in by the World Commission and a judge from the World Court of Justice. The President would lead the world Cabinet to achieve the seven goals, paying attention to the democratic sway of the electorate. He could stand for a second term and serve if elected.

World Guidance Council

A World Guidance Council of elder statesmen and distinguished world figures would assemble every three months, or more frequently if a crisis demanded, to give advice to relevant members of the World Commission, World Senators and World Council of Ministers. These wise elders would be chosen on merit and expertise, with consideration being paid to regional representation, population percentages and political clout, on the recommendation of the World Commission, World Senate and World Council of Ministers.

World Leaders' meetings

In addition to these guidance meetings, sometimes there would be a business meeting involving World Leaders of nation-states in key regions or their foreign ministers.

There would in particular be a Regional Leaders' meeting for the leaders of the 13 main regions: North America; Europe; Japan; Oceania; China; Tibet; the Russian Federation; South America; Islam; Africa; India; South-East Asia and Central Asia. There would be regular live link-ups between the World President and the Regional Leaders. There would be smaller groups of Regional Leaders, on the lines of the G4 and G8.

An appropriate member of the World Commission would be present at all meetings of World Leaders, along with the Minister of the appropriate department and a Senator. These meetings of World Leaders would be like the European-Council meetings.

World banking

The World Bank would be overhauled to operate at a supranational level. It would continue to make loans to poorer countries for capital programs to reduce poverty. The World Investment Bank would also be overhauled to streamline a new supranational role.

Through these world banking institutions the supranational authority/World Commission would carry out work to achieve all its goals. Besides bringing peace and complete disarmament, it would begin a phased redistribution of humankind's resources and energy supply to even up the disparities between regions; work to ease environmental problems such as global warming and manage common resources including outer space and oceans; end disease and famine; and solve the world's financial crisis. A minimum standard of living would be guaranteed to all humankind on a phased basis, and a World Development Authority would grant interest-free loans to assist the economic and social development of under-developed areas.

International lawyers

An executive of international lawyers would help the World Commission, World Senate and World Parliamentary Assembly turn the Commission's proposals into international laws. This executive would liaise with the World Peace Enforcement Committee and the World Court of Justice.

World Court of Justice

The World Court of Justice would have 25 judges. These would be chosen on the same basis as the World Commission excluding representation from the World Bank and agencies of global governance.

The Court's primary function would be to hear actions brought by the World Commission against a nation-state for breaking a directive. One of its briefs would be to rule against self-interested *élite*s' use of the world's resources and energy supply. It would also rule on conflicts, fulfilling a role of conflict resolution by ordering a nation-state to desist from actions that could result in war. It would hear cases regarding conflicts between nation-states referred up to the Assembly and brought by the World Commission before the Court.

It would rule on legal disputes between member states and between the World Commission and institutions and agencies. It would further disarmament. It would hear complaints against actions taken by a world institution. It would interpret world law at the request of national courts, and respond to direct petitions. It would establish rules and world law for all world citizens without having to resort to their nation-states. It would be responsible for making sure that all world law was upheld.

World Court of First Instance

A World Court of First Instance would exist alongside the World Court of Justice to ease the World Court of Justice's workload. This Court would hear actions brought by citizens and companies against the World Commission for its deeds or failure to act, and would hear actions for damages against the World Commission.

World Judicial Tribunals

There would be a substructure of World Judicial Tribunals under the World Court of Justice, which would further take pressure off the World Court of Justice. These Tribunals would hear cases in which world laws needed to be enforced.

The supranational authority's world laws would be enforceable by these World Judicial Tribunals, following investigation by a civil police force of 10,000 working for the World Commission.

World Armed Force

The World Armed Force or Rapid Reaction Force of 200,000–400,000 would be at the service of the World Commission, the World President, the World Senate and the World Court of Justice. The World Armed Force would be used to enforce laws for the World Commission just as the UN's Peacekeeping Force has been used to enforce laws for the Security Council. There would be a reserve force of 300,000–600,000.

The supranational tier, then, is above the inter-national tier in which associations of nation-states try to keep the peace between nation-states. From the perspective of nation-states, life under the UN, which would in turn be under the supranational institutions, would be little different from now. Civilizations would go on rising and falling, nation-states would continue with their progress.

Civilizations would all flow into one world-wide civilization in the sense that they would all be under the technical rule of the World Commission, World Senate and World Parliamentary Assembly, World President and World Council of Ministers, but the supranational structure would be sufficiently remote to allow civilizations to continue as before at the lower inter-national level.

Practical Consequences

The above scheme would have practical consequences:

1. Implementation and Constitution

The US President would propose the above scheme to the UN General Assembly, which would hold a vote for a World Constitutional Convention to draw up a world constitution that would establish these new institutions.

To help a World Constitutional Convention, I have drafted a Constitution for a United Federation of the World (see p.xi). This is ready to be laid before a World Constitutional Convention, and after amendments this should be presented to the delegates of the UN General Assembly for their adoption. This adoption would be a first step towards turning the UN General Assembly into a lower house of a World State which will have the supranational authority to end wars.

All nation-states would vote to grant federal powers in the areas of the seven goals to a new World Commission and the other supranational bodies. Nation-states would voluntarily opt to create a supranational authority that would abolish war and release funds thus saved, a 'peace dividend'.

2. Sovereignty

At the inter-national level nation-states would accept the authority of the World Commission and the new supranational structure. They would give up a small amount of sovereignty in the areas of the seven federal, supranational goals together with their right to fight wars and stockpile nuclear warheads. Otherwise, civilizations and nation-states would continue as before with a great amount of sovereignty intact.

By nominating representatives to the World Commission and electing members of the World Senate and its lower house, the Assembly, at the inter-national level, nation-states would be accepting the authority of the Commission and the new supranational structure and would all be giving up some sovereignty together with giving up their right to fight wars and stockpile nuclear warheads. But it must be emphasised that it would only be a relatively small amount of sovereignty that would be given up: just enough to secure the achievement of the seven supranational goals.

The structure I have described does not envisage a world government with total sovereignty and control over all our lives. It merely envisages a world government that would operate at a supranational level and permit the inter-national level to continue pretty much as before except for the seven areas relating to the seven goals – only there would now be more democracy and an end to some of the élitist abuses of global governance. My structure assumes that all nation-states would participate in world elections, no matter whether they are democracies or dictatorships. There is thus no need to exclude those listed in Appendix D2 and Appendix D3 as "Partly Free" and "Not Free". The dictatorships would soon be under pressure as their oppressed peoples would experience voting in world elections and would acquire a taste for democracy. To embark on such a scheme can only be good for the spreading of world democracy.

3. Political Universalism

A political Universalism would now have come into being. Having renounced the right to fight wars and stockpile nuclear weapons, nation-states opting for the new supranational structure would in effect unite humankind – provided that the vote in the UN General Assembly had backing from the majority of nation-states.

I am proposing a structure that would have no adverse impact on individual liberty outside the achievement of the seven goals, and which would bind all humankind together in an awareness of its unity. I have proposed a structure for a political Universalism that would unite humankind as all-embracingly as did the vision of St Augustine's *City of God*. The upper tier guarantees that life can continue in the two lower tiers without the upper tier's impacting on it except in the areas of the seven goals listed on pp.105–106 and 153, progress in each of which would benefit humankind. Conversely, the upper tier would only be federal in respect of the areas of the seven goals.

4. Location of the Supranational Assembly

The location of the supranational tier of government will initially be in the UN, on a rotational basis. Thus the UN General Assembly will continue to meet while the World Parliamentary Assembly is being set up and elected. And once elected, the World Parliamentary Assembly will then meet in the same UN chamber as the UN General Assembly but on different days. For a while there will be an overlap of the two bodies until the World Parliamentary Assembly is ready to succeed the UN General Assembly. The UN chamber in which the UN General Assembly meets can accommodate 1,898 persons in all[6] and so could easily accommodate the 850 seats of the World Parliamentary Assembly and attendant staff.

A chamber could be found somewhere within the UN where the 92-seat World Senate could meet. Conference Room Two on the fourth floor of the UN building in Vienna could be adapted to provide temporary accommodation. Office accommodation within or near the UN in New York would initially be provided for the World Commission of 27 Commissioners. In due course the World Commission could be more centrally located between East and West. It could be located in London, which is on the 0 meridian, perhaps eventually making use of the 2012 Olympic site.

London would make a good venue as English is the world's administrative language and Great Britain governed a quarter of the world in the early 20th century. The UK has acted as a bridge between the US and Brussels/Europe; it can continue to do so after Brexit.

Eventually a purpose-built site could be found to house all the buildings of the world government. Such a site might be found on the fringe of Docklands, London's Manhattan, where a cluster of high-rise buildings could be located.

If the world government is to be accommodated outside the US and not in London, then Hamburg may provide a venue. It should not be accommodated in Brussels, which is already too crowded from hosting the complex of EU buildings.

5. Funding

The funding of the supranational authority would partly be afforded out of the existing budget of the UN. Funding for the UN

General Assembly would be switched to the World Parliamentary Assembly that would replace it. At the same time the 18 separate budgets of the 18 agencies under the UN Economic and Social Council would be converted into a centralised UN budget that would cover the entire UN. This would be funded from nation-states' taxation revenues, which would no longer have to go towards military expenditure.

In other words, the change-over from the UN General Assembly to a World Parliamentary Assembly would be accompanied by another long overdue reform. All the agencies listed in Appendices C2 and C3 would be streamlined and the 18 separate budgets of the 18 agencies under the Economic and Social Council would be converted into one centralised UN budget.

There would be one budget for the entire UN and all its committees, agencies and operations. This budget would be funded from the nation-states' governments' taxation revenues. The budget would be reduced to take into account that the upper tier would be taking over work previously attempted by the UN, and this reduction would allow existing UN funds to be diverted to the supranational level's higher tier.

The funding of the setting-up of the supranational level would therefore be partly covered by these diverted UN funds and partly by (initially) new money made available on a cost-conscious basis by nation-states' governments' taxation revenues. Eventually this new money would be recouped from, and offset against, and more than covered by, the peace dividend, savings from reductions in military expenditure. The amounts contributed from these taxation revenues would reflect each nation-state's involvement in the world government, and would be *pro rata* in relation to the number of seats in the World Parliamentary Assembly and World Senate, and the extent of the representation within the World Commission and World Council of Ministers, that the nation-state had been allocated. The bigger the involvement, the more money to be contributed; the smaller the involvement, the less funding.

It must be emphasised that all nation-states would be able to cut their defence budgets dramatically as the World Commission would have abolished war and the need for expenditure on arms. The amount saved would be nearly $1.676 trillion a year (see below) and additional savings from the cost of renewing deteriorating nuclear weapons. Most nation-states would therefore be able to divert some of this saved military expenditure into funding for the supranational tier – and still be in surplus as savings on military expenditure would far outweigh contributions to the funding of the World Commission and the new world structure.

6. Peace dividend

The 'peace dividend' would be colossal. There would be a phasing out of the global military spending by nation-states which totalled $1,472.7 billion ($1.4727 trillion) in 2008 and $1,745 billion ($1.745 trillion) in 2012,[7] and $1.676 trillion in 2015 (see pp.199–200); of which $1,049.8 billion ($1.049 trillion) was spent by NATO alone in 2008 and $1,020 billion ($1.02 trillion) in 2013.[8] There would also be a massive saving from not having to replace deteriorating nuclear weapons following a world disarmament agreement.

Nearly $1.7 trillion per annum, minus the cost of financing the World Armed Force but plus the saving from not having to replace nuclear weapons, would be available to raise the standard of living for the benefit of all humankind, and there would be further savings which would fund the supranational authority's structure and seven goals.

The immediate creation of a supranational authority would make savings that would release funds for all nation-states and would arrest some nation-states' economic decline.

7. Timescale for introduction of World State

As to the timescale of the introduction of the world government, this could begin immediately on the cost-conscious basis of sharing the UN building in New York. Two sets of world elections could be organised as soon as world parties have come into being and candidates have come forward.

That will only happen when there is a Declaration of Intent regarding a forthcoming world government. The US President should go to the UN General Assembly and make a declaration of such an intent, and of his intention to organise a World Constitutional Convention if the UN General Assembly approves it. Such an announcement would be followed by a mobilising of democratic activity throughout the world, during which new political parties would be thrown up.

The point I am making is that the new structure could be implemented relatively quickly on a cost-conscious short-term basis. There is no question of having to wait a decade or a generation to start. There may not be a truly fair redistribution of wealth for more than a hundred years, long after the lifetime of all reading these words when they first appear. But the point is, that goal can only be achieved after a lengthy process, and a start can be made before the exact details are known as to how world poverty can be eliminated.

The structure I have proposed draws on, and blends, aspects of the US, British and European systems to create a new and distinct model that can assume its own legal personality and distinctive characteristics. It would be looser than a United States of the World and would not seek to control every facet of life within the nation-state. It would allow civilizations to continue within a new Era of Peace. Billions of dollars spent on armaments and war could be diverted to advance the progress of all humankind.

My new, moderately radical and distinct model offers the prospect of a realisation of the dream of a politically-unified known world that has fascinated thinkers since Western philosophy began with the Presocratic Greeks.

The supranational level can influence the inter-national fate of the world until the 22nd or 23rd century.

8

Manifesto for a World State

A manifesto is "a public declaration of policy and aims, especially issued before an election by a political party, candidate, government" (*Concise Oxford Dictionary*); and "a public declaration... making known past actions and explaining the motives for actions announced as forthcoming" (*Shorter Oxford English Dictionary*). In the last chapter I presented the kind of supranational authority that can achieve my seven goals – a World State I have named a United Federation – and its structure. I now turn to what the World State will do when it has been brought in, and how and why it will do it; its policy and aims in relation to the seven goals.

Manifesto

The World State will not be based on a fully federal United States of the World or on the model of the New World Order's federal Union (see pp.154–155) as these models involve a world government with total control of all global governance and not just the areas of the seven goals.

Implementing the seven goals

The World Parliamentary Assembly will operate at inter-national level and will cope with the world's problems through its 850 Representatives at that level of competence. It will pass up to the World Commission matters beyond its competence, conflicts which would require enforcement.

The World Senate will operate at supranational level and will be dedicated to implementing the seven goals of the supranational authority by passing the appropriate laws to bring in and enforce a peaceful world. It will make decisions and pass laws. It will deal with proposals from the World Commission, whose main object is to deliver world peace through international law.

The World Senate will deliver world peace by delivering laws which will turn the World Commission's proposals into law. In this it will be assisted by the World Court of Justice and the World Judicial Tribunals.

It will bring the seven goals into international law:

1. The World Senate will bring peace between nation-states by passing laws to abolish war and enforce peace through the World Armed Force or Rapid Reaction Force. The UN has failed to prevent 162 wars since 1945 (see Appendix C8), but the World Senate will prevent all wars, and there will be no wars it fails to prevent. After abolishing war the World Senate will enforce disarmament by passing laws to disarm all nation-states. The 14,900 nuclear weapons in existence in early 2017 will be surrendered, impounded and dismantled as a consequence of the political settlement that will set up the World Parliamentary Assembly and World Senate and abolish the need for war. The World Armed Force will assist in enforcing disarmament.
2. Working in conjunction with the 13 regional Unions (see p.185), which will be converted into elected democracies, and with the World Commission and the World Parliamentary Assembly, the World Senate will pass laws to share natural resources and energy so that all humankind can have a raised standing of living. The existing gas and oil pipelines will be extended to bring energy to all across the world's peaceful territories. Water will be piped to the drought-threatened areas of Africa to head off a flow of refugees in search of water.
3. The World Senate will pass laws to solve environmental problems such as global warming. Carbon emissions, atmospheric pollution, pollution of rivers and seas and many other environmentally damaging issues will be solved.
4. The World Senate will pass laws to facilitate the ending of disease. There will be extensive new programs of research into all medical conditions, and drives to eliminate diseases

such as malaria so humankind everywhere can live free from disease.

5. The World Senate will pass laws to facilitate the ending of famine. There will be extensive planting and crop-growing programs to make victims of famine self-sufficient and able to live without aid.
6. The World Senate will pass laws to reform and stabilise the world's financial institutions and to deliver a system of sound finance that can assist all humankind.
7. The World Senate will pass laws to redistribute wealth so as to eliminate poverty. All adult members of humankind will receive a basic income and will make contributions to the global society.

Globalisation

Globalisation is a process in which regional economies, societies and cultures have become integrated in a network that stretches round the globe. This process has gathered pace since the US became the sole superpower, and the US has left its stamp on globalisation.

In an economic context globalisation "refers to the reduction and removal of barriers between national borders in order to facilitate the flow of goods, capital, services and labour" (The United Nations Economic and Social Commission for Western Asia, or UN ESCWA).[1]

Globalisation has impacted on the world in a number of different ways:

- Industrially, world-wide production markets have emerged, giving consumers and companies access to foreign companies so that material and goods can move between national boundaries. The American-developed internet has led the world in such industrial globalisation.
- Financially, world-wide financial markets have emerged that give borrowers better access to financing. Again, the American-developed internet has led to a global financial

infrastructure which is outside transnational regulation. It has proved unstable, as the 2008 financial crisis has shown.

- Economically, a world-wide common market has emerged. It is based on the freedom of exchange of goods and capital between national markets. Again, the US-developed internet has led to such interconnected markets. There has been deregulation of banks and markets. However, economic collapse in one market or country cannot be contained within that market or country, but affects the whole, as the 2008 financial crisis illustrated.
- Politically, a potential world government has emerged which regulates the relationships between governments through institutions of global governance, and guarantees rights between governments. The United States has led such political globalisation because of its strong and wealthy economy. It is the world's fourth-biggest exporter (behind the EU, Germany, and China).[2] The United States has helped the rapid growth of the People's Republic of China to extend its influence among world powers, and America can be seen as being behind the rise of China.
- Informationally, an increase in information flow has emerged between geographically remote locations. The United States has led this with technological innovation, much of which came from America's NASA-driven space program. The new technology includes fibre-optic communications, satellites, and increased availability of cellphones and the internet.
  Linguistically, a global language has emerged. It is English, which first emerged as a result of the British Empire. The role of English as a global language has been extended by American superpowerdom. About 35 per cent of the world's mail, telexes, and cables and about 40 per cent of the world's radio programs are in English, while about 50 per cent of all internet traffic is in English.[3]
- Competitively, a new global business market has created increased productivity and competition, for as the market became world-wide, companies have upgraded their prod-

ucts and improved their technology to cope with increased competition. The United States has led the world in such movements.

- Ecologically, environmental solutions to challenges such as climate change, water and air pollution, and over-fishing are being sought by international co-operation. However, developing countries have competed globally and their factories have increased pollution. Until recently the United States has been a polluter rather than a solver of pollution. This is now changing.
- Culturally, local regions participating in world culture have imported American culture such as Hollywood films. Such imports have increased multiculturalism and cultural diversity, but have often supplanted local culture. The United States has led the world in cultural domination.
- Socially, global political policy has been led by non-governmental organisations, especially those linked to the UN. The United States has led the way in creating these.
- Technically, global telecommunications and trans-border data have improved. The United States has led the world in creating the internet, communication satellites, submarine fibre-optic cable, and wireless telephones.
- Legally, an international criminal court and international justice movements have emerged to cope with global crime-fighting, and a global administrative law has emerged. The United States has led the world in such developments, although out of American self-interest and in the interests of American superiority it has resisted subordinating US troops to the International Criminal Court.

The World State will continue globalisation while recognising that the 2008 world recession wiped 45 per cent off global wealth[4] and many were left behind by the prosperity globalisation has delivered. Populism was an expression of the anger and protest felt by the 'left-behinds', and was a cry to deglobalise.

By implementing the seven goals the World State will deliver a sound, basic, peaceful, clean, healthy, well-nourished and financially-secure context to all humankind and the effect, and impact, of globalisation on the 'left-behinds' will be liberating and welcome. All humankind will be lifted out of poverty.

The World State will deliver 'good globalisation' after a time of what for many has proved 'bad globalisation' that has evoked an insular and isolationist populist response. Under a World State there will be prosperity for all.

Funds diverted to peaceful use

The abolition of war and implementation of disarmament would make an enormous saving. From 2001 to 2018 the War on Terror cost $2,016.5 billion (i.e. $2.0156 trillion)[5] – excluding the cost of oil for the US troops amounting to nearly $3 trillion. The total US spending on national security during the War on Terror from 2001 to 2016 reached $3.6 trillion and was set to reach $4.79 trillion in 2017; and interest alone on funds borrowed to pay those bills could climb to $7.9 trillion by 2053 according to the Costs of War Project based on Brown University's Watson Institute for International and Public Affairs.[6] Some private analysts put the cost of the War on Terror at $4 trillion, and have costed the war in Iraq at over $3 trillion.[7] The wars in Afghanistan and Iraq helped push the American national debt to over $11 trillion (or according to Obama's federal budget $12.7 trillion) by October 2009,[8] and $20.1 trillion by 2017; and the UK national debt to £800.8 billion by July 2009,[9] and £1.73 trillion by 2017.

According to the Stockholm International Peace Research Institute, in 2008 global military spending by nation-states totalled $1,472.7 trillion, of which NATO's spending was $1,049.8 trillion. In 2014 global military spending was $1.78 trillion and in 2015 was $1.676 trillion.[10] According to *The Economist* in 2016, NATO's spending was $918 billion. The EU member states' military spending has been estimated to have been $285 billion. The US's military spending in 2017 was $598.5 billion, the largest national military spending in the world. The cost of the war in Syria to the US could be $1.3 trillion by 2020.[11] (The cost of the

Syrian war to Russia and the UK would also be considerable.)

To this must be added the future cost of renewing deteriorating nuclear weapons and replacing military equipment. It has been estimated by the UK Defence Secretary Michael Fallon[12] that for the UK to replace the *Trident* nuclear missile system and build two large aircraft carriers will cost £205.3 billion. The cost of replacing the world's nuclear weapons can be expected to run to many trillions of dollars. The world already had 15,375 nuclear weapons in 2016, but it is a US, UK and Russian priority to buy bigger and better nuclear weapons with money that could be better spent on raising the standard of living of all humankind.

The vast amounts of taxpayers' money or borrowings spent on wars and nuclear weapons are available to be diverted to more peaceful uses, such as implementing the seven goals. The saving will wipe out the consequences of the 2008 financial crisis, which has cost the world many trillions of dollars, far more than the $3 trillion of bank bail-outs. The abolition of defence spending will release at least $1.676 trillion *each year* to raise the standard of living across the world for a while, to the benefit of all humankind.

There will be no continuation of the War on Terror after a peace accord covering the entire Middle East, including Iraq, Afghanistan, Syria, Iran and Israel, although the World Armed Force may still be patrolling parts of West Asia, coping with outbreaks of insurgency. Internecine wars would be at an end for a while. Islamic terrorism will be disarmed. There will be a borderless world and free movement of peoples subject to local restrictions to prevent any one city or region from being swamped. There will be free trade.

Rising population and natural resources

The world's population will rise despite a containment policy, and there will be no population reduction by war, disease or famine. The defence saving will be available to feed the increased population. The diversion of these defence funds will ensure that there would be no food shortage, and every world citizen will have access to drinking-water. In a redistribution of wealth out of saved defence spending there will be a minimum standard of living for all, basic accommodation and access to utilities and energy. Clearly, this will take time to achieve in parts of Asia and Africa.

There will be a global policy to convey resources and energy to all humankind, and the élitist Syndicate's profit-making role in dispensing resources and energy, and the role of multinationals, will be carefully monitored, regulated and controlled. The Four Horsemen of the Apocalypse – conquest, war, famine and disease – will cease to ride. There will be no spreading of man-made diseases like AIDS or viruses like H1N1, the swine-flu virus, that can start a pandemic. The world will become more multipolar with India and China having more influence.

Under a World State the world's population can be controlled. Without a World State the world's population will increase from 7.5 billion in April 2017 to at least 9.4 billion by 2050[13] (and probably 9.7 billion, see next paragraph), and the 2 billion increase in the world's population, nearly a quarter more mouths to feed, would place a strain on the world's resources, especially food and water. (The US Census Bureau projects that the biggest population gains will be in Africa. Nigeria's population, 16m in 2015 and 191m in 2017, will exceed 400m by 2050, and Ethiopia's population, 104m in 2017, will be 171.8m on one estimate or 278m on another estimate by 2050.)[14]

According to John R. Wilmoth, the director of the United Nations (UN) Population Division, speaking on 10 August 2015, models of demographic change derived from historical experience estimate the global population as 9.7 billion in 2050 (9.8 billion according to a later UN report) and 11.2 billion in 2100, and give a highest estimate of the world's population in 2100 as 16 billion and a lowest estimate as 6 billion, depending on future wars, diseases, famines and fertility rates.[15]

There will be shortages. There will have to be central planning (and perhaps some form of rationing) to cope with such a huge rise in world population, which may double in the course of the 21st century, whereas the availability of food will not double.

Political, Religious, Environmental and Cultural Universalism

With political Universalism focusing on the 13 regions listed on p.185 will come religious Universalism. All religions will draw together. There will be unity in diversity as the common essence of Christianity, Islam, Buddhism, Hinduism, Taoism and other world religions will be emphasised, but in local, regional cathedrals, temples and mosques traditional differentiation and diversity will continue. There will be environmental Universalism as the supranational authority will treat the Earth as one planet and will come up with unified solutions for global agricultural and climate problems. Space exploration on a cost-conscious basis will determine whether it would be possible to colonise the nearest stars.

The supranational pattern will be superimposed on the international pattern which will continue below it. The savings from abolishing military expenditure will slow the pace of economic decline. Foreign occupation will be averted for the time the world is under the supranational authority. The world will be governed by the liberal democracy dreamt of by Kant and Hegel. Education and culture will thrive, along with the arts. There will be money, goods and services for all. There will be sweeping, unified policies and plans to benefit the world. National governments will appear as parochial as local parish councils.

For a while there will be a new Golden Age of the kind that flourished under Augustus's peaceful Roman Empire where one world-wide religion co-existed with local cults which reflected it.

The World President will be based near the World Commission, the World Senators and the World Council of Ministers, initially in New York, but in due course perhaps London. He will have regular live link-ups with the Regional Leaders and World Leaders. His success will be measured by his implementation of the seven goals.

I glimpsed the World President in 1966. I ended my poem 'Archangel' on my visits to China and Soviet Russia during the height of the Cold War that year with a vision I had in Moscow's Cathedral of the Archangel. I saw world elders near a Leaders' Hall in an unknown location. They did not resemble World Commissioners or World Senators, but rather the elders of the World Leaders' Guidance Council in a place that might be Rome, and a "World-Lord":

Indifferent tsars and tyrants,
Compassionate inquisitors;
Can nothing bring together
Enslaving Leader and Saint?
As I stared at the murals' centre
In this Cathedral-tomb,
The Archangel became a Shadow
With a sword and wings outstretched,
And I saw in the second icon
The future of the West,
From the Atlantic to the Urals:
Into the People's Square
From the Cathedral gates,
File in the morning rush-hour
An *élite* of self-made Saints
Each still on the last hour's quest.
They reach the central banner
In the forum of statues and graves,
The great mazed *mandala*
Under which the supplicants wait;
Decades of contemplation
Show in their white-haired peace
As, trusting to perfect feelings,
They value each equal they greet;
Until, whispering on silence,
They glide to the Leaders' Hall,

Their hearts, with a World-Lord's wholeness,
At the centre of life, of all,
Their hearts where all past and future meet.[16]

At the time I located this vision in Europe, foreseeing the end of the Cold War and the reunification of Europe ("From the Atlantic to the Urals"), but the setting I saw led me to speak of the "future of the West", and my glimpse was of peaceful world rulers who have mastered the art of living, and of a "World-Lord".

Peering into the future of the supranational authority, we are peering into a Paradise that will be relatively short-lived but will be the apex of human achievement. It has been estimated that the number of humans who have ever lived is between 100 billion and 115 billion, with 106 billion being a calculation based on 2002.[17] Life for the 9.7 to 10.5 billion living under the World Commission in 2050 will reach a zenith that has never been, and will never be, surpassed. It must be remembered that the Universalist philosophy which is alert to universal being and universal humankind underpins the Universalist political vision, and that there will also be cultural Universalism: a high cultural style unifying local/regional diversity. Communications, the internet, peace and high culture will all combine to raise civilization to its highest-ever point. Its Universalism can bring in a new Renaissance in the arts during a Golden Age of peace and prosperity for all humankind which will mark the highest peak of world culture.

It must be stressed that the supranational authority will only last for a while. It is in the nature of institutions to have a limited duration. As with the Roman Empire, there will always be challenges to the World Commission. Terrorism has always been with us in some form. Change is ever pressing. The Roman Empire which seemed so solid was subject to pressure from outside forces, barbarians, and the British Empire on which the sun would never set was always subject to winds of change.

There will come a time when an established supranational authority will be regarded as intrusive and tyrannical. There will be a kind of mass nationalism that will reassert the international level, and the supranational authority and level will be swept away, as was the Roman Empire.

The rise and fall of civilizations will have continued uninterrupted at the inter-national level, and the collapse of the supranational authority will bring with it a need to rearm, to spend money on limited wars and defence, and will thus accelerate economic decline and foreign occupation. It is reckless to make historical predictions, but my pattern of rising and falling civilizations allows me to overlay living civilizations on dead civilizations and to see what is ahead for the living civilizations. After the fading and fall of the supranational level, the rise and fall of civilizations will continue at the inter-national level, and it will be clear that the world government will not have arrested the course of civilizations, which will have seemed to flow into it. In fact, they will have carried on unhindered beneath the World State at the inter-national level and will be seen to have resurfaced further on.

I have looked into the future and I have seen what is there: regional Unions, the élitist Syndicate's self-interested New World Order whose goal of a federal tyranny can be firmly shackled, and a new Era of Peace that can bring Paradise on Earth for a while along with a new Golden Age. I have had the vision and have described it, and located myself, within the tradition of Plato and Kant. I have seen what I have seen. It is for the political class to implement this universal World State.

The World State offers a vision of hope: an era of universal peace and prosperity that will be recognised in times to come as humankind's greatest achievement. Humankind now has to have the self-belief to bring the vision into actuality.

Epilogue

Global Democracy and a Golden Age

Life under the World State will be good for all humankind. We can glimpse it now.

Life under the World State

War has been abolished, peace is enforced by the World Court of Justice and the World Armed Force and its international bases on every continent. The World Commission moves in a regular roster between 11 cities. Television comprehensively shows the activities of the World Commission, the World Senate and the World Parliamentary Assembly. Gas and oil pipelines supply gas and oil to all nation-states and there is a network of nuclear power stations. The World Cabinet (the World President and Council of Ministers) controls pollution. Diseases are under control, the world's citizens are being moved from conditions of squalor, rehoused and guaranteed access to pure water and medical care. There is no military expenditure; annual world budgets finance economic growth and public spending. There is one global currency and one world-wide central bank. Access to mortgages and jobs is universal. Migration is freely conducted, subject to quotas. The 13 regions based on the world's living civilizations (see p.185) send regional leaders to the Regional Leaders' Meeting, but the main world regions are now: the American Union; the European Union; the West Asian (or Middle Eastern) Union; the Central Asian Union; and the East Asian-Pacific Union.

Life in a sample of regions and nation-states

What is it like to live under a global democracy? Let us consider how people might live in some of the regions and nation-states of the World State, taking account of how they will be represented. (See table on pp.166–170 for individual nation-states' representation in the World Parliamentary Assembly.) The picture is as follows:

- *North America.* The United States has 30 World Representatives in the World Parliamentary Assembly and eight World Senators (two per zone in four zones). As the World State was US-inspired and created as the result of a US initiative, many Americans are in the World Commission's bureaucracy and World Armed Force. There is no stockpile of nuclear weapons, all have been destroyed. Poverty within the United States was abolished soon after the advent of universal health care. All Americans are entitled to a minimum standard of living (dollars per day/housing). Canada has six World Representatives in the World Parliamentary Assembly, six World Senators and one World Commissioner. Canada has moved closer to North America in lifestyle and outlook.
- *Central America/Caribbean.* The region has four World Senators and one World Commissioner. There is no poverty.
- *South America.* There are six World Senators and two World Commissioners. All South-American citizens are entitled to a minimum of $10 per day.
- *China* has 30 World Representatives in the World *Parliamentary* Assembly, eight World Senators and one World Commissioner. Communism is officially dead and China is now a liberal democracy. The death penalty has been abolished. There is a minimum entitlement of $10 per day for all Chinese citizens.
- *India* has 30 World Representatives in the World Parliamentary Assembly, six World Senators and one World Commissioner. There is no famine.
- *Africa* has eight World Senators and two World Commissioners. AIDS and malaria have been eliminated.
- *Europe* has 30 World Representatives, 12 World Senators and four World Commissioners. All European citizens have a minimum entitlement per day/housing.

- *The Russian Federation* has 15 World Representatives in the World Parliamentary Assembly, six World Senators and one World Commissioner. There is no stockpile of nuclear weapons, all have been destroyed.
- *Afghanistan* is within the South-Central Asia region. It has six World Representatives in the World Parliamentary Assembly, shares four World Senators with Central Asia, and shares one World Commissioner with Pakistan. There is a minimum entitlement of $10 per day for all Afghans. Minimum-standard housing has replaced mud huts. All Afghan citizens receive full education.
- *The Middle East*. The region, which includes Syria, has eight World Senators (if Israel and Iran are included) and three World Commissioners. There are no local wars.
- *Central Asia* has four World Senators and one World Commissioner.
- *South-East Asia/Asia* has seven World Senators (one for South-East Asia, two for Central Asia, two for East-Central Asia and two for East Asia) and access to three World Commissioners (for West-Central/South-East Asia, East Asia, and Indonesia).

All of the world's citizens live under conditions of liberty. There are no tyrannies under the World State. There is no élitist Syndicate tyranny of any kind. The New World Order's dream of federal tyranny has been controlled. There is a Universalism (which focuses on all humankind) of minimum standards of living and a context of peace.

Towards a Golden Age

I have set out a conception of a World State that is rooted in the history of the last 5,000 years. I have seen the supranational authority and World State as being *partly* federal in limiting itself to seven goals, and loosely allowing nation-states and civilizations to continue at local, regional level. Such a loose structure will allow a high degree of democracy, with the higher Senate and lower Assembly both directly elected. It will avoid the more drastic United States of the World in which there would be upheavals at the local/regional level, and the New World Order's federal Union of the 13 regions that would be controlled by the élitist Syndicate whose agenda is universal world dominance with very little expansion of democracy.

Such a loose federal model limited at the supranational level to seven goals will leave nation-states and civilizations free to run themselves outside the areas of the seven goals through the democratic process via the World Senate and World Parliamentary Assembly. The loss of sovereignty and disturbance to existing nation-states and civilizations will be minimal. Life outside the areas of the seven goals and elections to the Senate and Assembly will continue, allowing nation-states and civilizations the maximum amount of continuity with their local and regional traditions.

They will surrender sovereignty in the areas of the seven goals, but their minimal loss of sovereignty will be amply compensated for by a gain in a share of world sovereignty and a maximal increase in democracy via the directly-elected Senate and Assembly.

Sceptics will say, "It will never happen. Vested interests are too strong. No nation-state's government will vote for a reduction in its own sovereignty." However, all nation-states' governments may see that their compensatory gain in a share of world sovereignty will bring a peace "dividend", a fund previously spent on defence, that can bring prosperity to their peoples. The UN spends less than one per cent of what is spent by the war industries. The institutions of the old order – national parliaments, banks and financial institutions – have so manifestly failed that it may be timely for governments to consider starting afresh and directing their UN General Assembly members to vote accordingly.

Some will say that a legally-based supranational authority will be ignored by indigenous and foreign insurgents such as the Afghan and Pakistani Taliban, al-Qaeda and the Syrian-Iraqi

IS, and that the situation under a supranational level in Afghanistan will be no different from what it is without the supranational level.

Under a supranational authority the campaign against the likes of the Taliban, al-Qaeda and IS will be directed by the World Armed Force, which will deflect some of the animosity away from the US, British and NATO presence in the region. A world presence will carry more authority among the people in the region who have co-existed with the Taliban, al-Qaeda and IS. Afghanistan-Pakistan and Syria-Iraq are extreme cases. A legally-based supranational authority will not have been ignored in the many other conflicts in the Middle East.

Some will say that all nation-states should act with a strengthened sense of their national interest – what advances it or damages it, what priorities to have and what can be afforded – like Washington, London, Moscow, Delhi and Beijing, and with less bureaucracy. However, many nation-states have already been subsumed into regions or Unions, and the European nation-states have already given up at least 80 per cent of their right to enact laws, and therefore of their sovereignty, to the European Union. And it should not be forgotten that the coming World State will be above the UK post-Brexit nation-state and EU region, and supporters of the EU who have been dismayed by the result of the UK referendum should now look to the coming World State as a new possibility in the process of partly-federal integration.

Some contemporary historians and commentators focus on the conflicts between nation-states at the inter-national level rather than at the supranational level. Samuel Huntington focuses on the inter-national clash between civilizations, and Robert Kagan does likewise in *The Return of History and the End of Dreams*. Seeing that international convergence had failed to materialise after the Cold War, he regards Fukuyama's "end of history" as an illusion without considering the legal power to abolish war that a supranational authority will acquire.

Champions of weakened nation-states must face the fact that

a future based on even stronger national interests will result in many more wars. A UN of even stronger nation-states operating inter-nationally would be powerless to stop another round of local wars in the coming years of the kind that since 1945 have involved 124 countries on one view (see Appendix C6) and 162 countries on another (see Appendix C8). Strengthening nation-states is like abolishing the UN and returning the world to potentially warring nation-states.

My proposal for a World State, which may crown the thinking of Kant, Hegel and Fukuyama, is, as I said on pp.xxiv–xxv, a consequence of political Universalism. The concept of a World State emerged slowly. First came the philosophy of Universalism, then came the need for an expression of political Universalism which proposes a form of government that can enforce peace within the whole of humankind without attacking part of humankind through wars, armies and nuclear warheads. The only such form of government is a World State. At the end of *The Syndicate* I titled the Epilogue 'World Government versus Global Democracy'. The "World Government" was the élitist Syndicate's self-interested brand of world government. The World State includes both world government as it should be and global democracy, and is a benevolent expression of political Universalism.

History has borne humankind from primitive origins to the threshold of a World State. Along the way, Virgil (in the 'Fourth Eclogue'),[1] and Dante (in *De Monarchia*) dreamt of a new order of world peace, and Milton (in *The Ready and Easy Way to Establish a Free Commonwealth*) dreamt of an ideal republic. Universalist history offers the vision of universal history which was so important to Kant: history that is philosophically serious and also empirical.

My vision of a supranational authority that delivers seven goals including peace and disarmament while civilizations continue to rise and fall and nation-states continue their sway at the inter-national level – an authority that enforces international law, democratises the UN, makes global governance accountable and regulates the *élites*' exclusive groups – is a vision (in

Kant's, Hegel's and Fukuyama's sense of the phrase) of the end-point of world history.

I have had the vision and have communicated what I have seen. It is now for others to take it up and make it happen, construct the details, turn the words on these pages into a structure that straddles the world as the Colossus straddled the harbour of Rhodes. A blueprint is a "detailed plan, especially in the early stages of a project or idea", and it is also "a photographic print of the final stage of engineering or other plans in white on a blue background" (*Concise Oxford Dictionary*). Whether it is early or final, a blueprint is an architect's or engineer's plan for builders.

It is now time for the builders to be booked and given the go-ahead, for the benefit of humankind. The old order has collapsed, and is in its death-throes. Humankind is crying out for the supranational structure to be built and for the peace dividend to restore health.

It is time to start building a limited supranational authority that will abolish war, disarm nations and bring in a *Pax Universalis*. Universal peace is Universalism's greatest gift. It is what the world needs to revive, and its resurgence can bring in a coming Golden Age.

A Golden Age of Universalism

We can glimpse the future again. A new Golden Age has dawned. It is a Golden Age of peace, promise, and prosperity. State persecution is unknown – it is of the past. All the bad things of history – plunder, pillage, rapine, air raids, invasion, missile attacks, barbaric hordes, poverty, squalor, disease, blighted crops – have been abolished.

True political Universalism, which sees all humankind as belonging to one political entity, has arrived. No one in the world falls below a minimum standard of living and housing, and there are no avoidable diseases caused by poor environmental conditions. In the past, wars created refugees living in tented squalor that bred diseases. Such conditions no longer apply.

With political Universalism linking all the Earth's regions

into a World State, all religions are drawing together. There will be a religious Universalism, uniting within diversity the essence of Christianity, Islam, Buddhism, Hinduism, Taoism, and other world religions. There will be a spiritual revival. And there will be no wars between religions. Paradise has truly arrived on earth.

However, a World State cannot be built and a Golden Age cannot happen unless the process is set in motion. Someone has to address the UN and propose a World Constitutional Convention to create a new supranational system.

And so I appeal to the UN. Members of the General Assembly, do your duty. Give up a little sovereignty to the supranational level in respect of the seven goals, so there can be universal peace and disarmament on a legally enforceable footing. You will still retain your national or regional sovereignty outside the areas of the seven goals. Have courage and be forward-looking. Bring in the Universalist World State.

9 February – 10 August 2017

Chart of 25 Civilizations and Cultures from One to One

The Fundamental Unity of World Culture

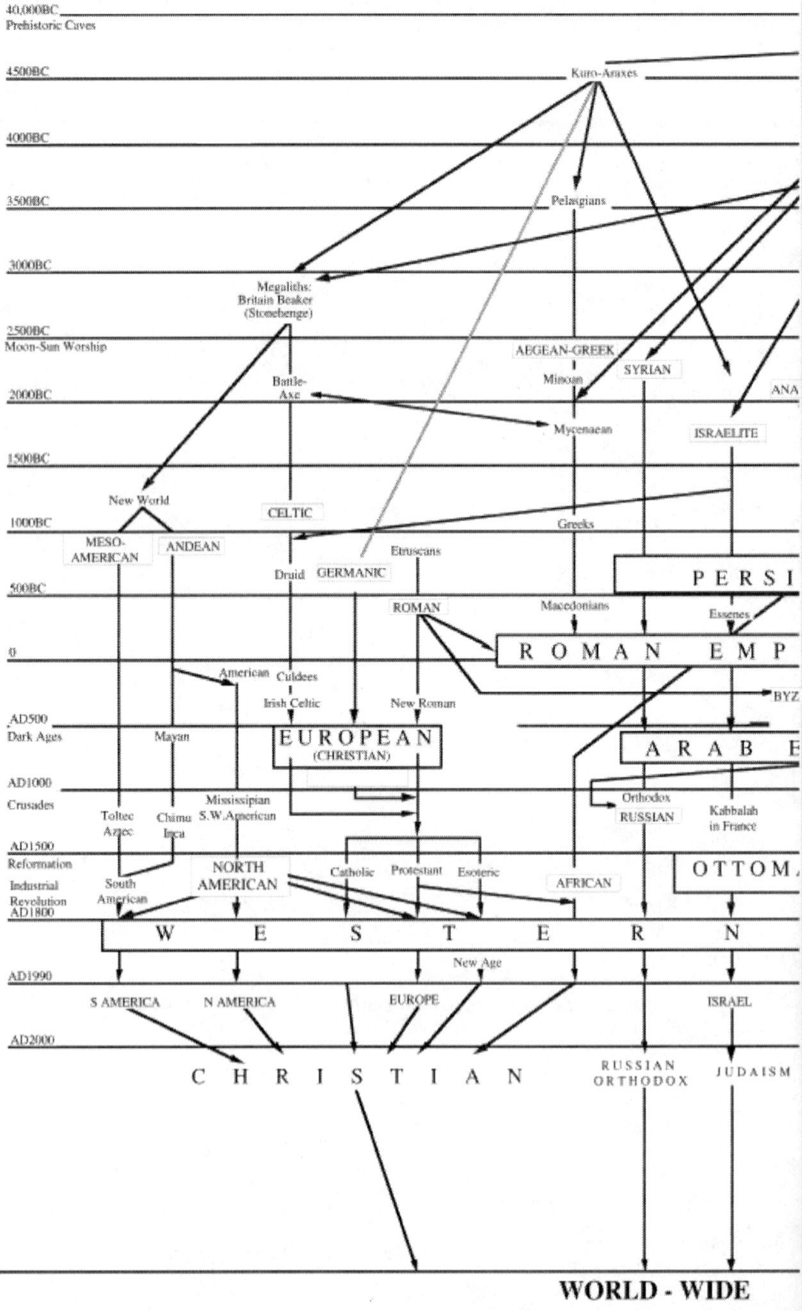

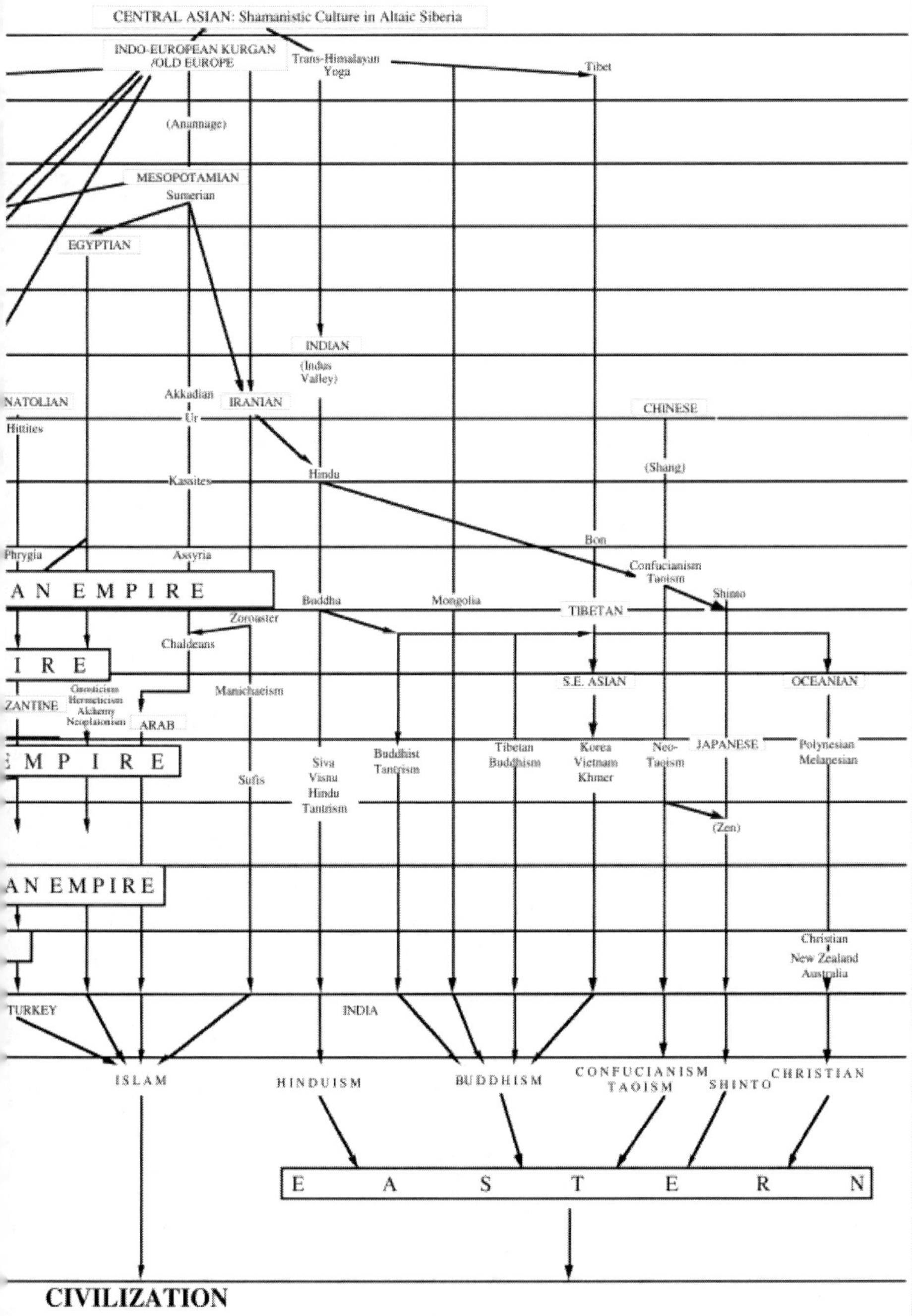
CENTRAL ASIAN: Shamanistic Culture in Altaic Siberia
INDO-EUROPEAN KURGAN /OLD EUROPE
Trans-Himalayan Yoga
Tibet
(Anannage)
MESOPOTAMIAN
Sumerian
EGYPTIAN
INDIAN
(Indus Valley)
NATOLIAN
Hittites
Akkadian
Ur
IRANIAN
CHINESE
Kassites
Hindu
(Shang)
Bon
Phrygia
Assyria
Confucianism Taoism
A N E M P I R E
Buddha
Mongolia
Shinto
TIBETAN
Zoroaster
Chaldeans
I R E
S.E. ASIAN
OCEANIAN
ZANTINE
Gnosticism Hermeticism Alchemy Neoplatonism
ARAB
Manichaeism
Siva Visnu Hindu Tantrism
Buddhist Tantrism
Tibetan Buddhism
Korea Vietnam Khmer
Neo-Taoism
JAPANESE
Polynesian Melanesian
M P I R E
Sufis
(Zen)
A N E M P I R E
Christian New Zealand Australia
TURKEY
INDIA
ISLAM
HINDUISM
BUDDHISM
CONFUCIANISM TAOISM
SHINTO
CHRISTIAN
E A S T E R N
CIVILIZATION

APPENDICES

Evidence and Data:
Evidence on which the need for a World State is based and Data on which World State calculations have been based

A. Confederations, Federations and Unitary States

A1. Confederations

(in chronological order)

(See pp.8–9)

Name of Confederation	Timespan	Details
Toltec Empire	496–1122	Existed as a confederation between the Toltecs and the Chichimeca, and simultaneously as an empire exerting control over places like Cholula
League of Mayapan	987–1461	Mayan league of Itza, Tutui-Xiu and Uxmal
Hanseatic League	13th–17th century	Commercial and defensive federation of guilds and their market towns, begun among N. German towns to protect German trading interests, dominated Baltic trade. At its height it covered 187 cities in 16 countries
Old Swiss Confederacy	1291–1848	Officially, the "Swiss Confederation"
Kalmar Union	1397–1523	Denmark, Sweden, Norway
Aztec Empire	1428–1521	Consisted of the city-states of Tenochtitlan, Texcoco and Tlacopan
Livonian Confederation	1435–1561	Five small states based in present-day Estonia and Latvia, ruled by the Order of Teutonic Knights of Livonia, protected German ascendency against Russian expansion
Pre-Commonwealth, Poland and Lithuania	1501–1569	Shared a monarch (Grand Duke of Lithuania and King of Poland), parliament (*Sejm*) and currency
Denmark-Norway	1536–1814	After Sweden left the Kalmar Union of 1397–1536

Seven United Provinces of the Netherlands	1581–1795	A confederation of seven states: Holland, Zeeland, Gelderland, Utrecht, Friesland, Overijssel and Groningen
Wampanoag Confederacy	1550–1680	A confederacy of about 60 groups or sub-tribes under a head *sachem* or political leader in N. America
Powhatan Confederacy	1550–1684	A confederacy of a group of at least 30 Algonquian-speaking Native American tribes
Illinois Confederation	17th–18th centuries	A confederacy of a group of 12–13 Native American tribes in the Mississippi valley
Confederate Ireland	1642–1649	Irish self-government during the Eleven Years' War after the Irish Rebellion of 1641
New England Confederation	1643–1684	An alliance of the English colonies of Massachusetts Bay, Plymouth, Connecticut and New Haven
Maratha Empire	1674–1818	Ruled much of Indian sub-continent
Aro Confederacy	1690–1902	Parts of present-day Nigeria, Cameroon and Equatorial Guinea
The US under the Articles of Confederation	1781–1789	Confederation of 13 original states of the United States of America
Western Confederacy	1785–1795	Loose confederacy of N. American Natives in the Great Lakes region
Confederation of the Rhine	1806–1813	Formed from 16 German states by Napoleon, had no head of state or government
German Federation	1815–1866	Association of 39 German states in Central Europe after Congress of Vienna
United Provinces of New Granada	1810–1816	A country in S. America, reconquered by Spain in 1816, now part of present-day Colombia
Sweden-Norway	1814–1905	Union of Sweden and Norway with common monarch and foreign policy but separate constitutions, laws, armed forces and currencies

Federation of the Equator	1824	Located in north-eastern Brazil after a rebellion against Brazil's first leader following independence from Portugal
Argentine Confederation	1831–1861	Name of Argentina when its provinces were a confederation without a head of state
Peru-Bolivian Confederation	1836–1839	Loose union of states of Peru and Bolivia in a confederate state under the Bolivian president
Confederation of Central America	1842–1844	Present-day El Salvador, Guatemala, Honduras and Nicaragua
Granadine Confederation	1858–1863	A federal republic replacing the Republic of New Granada, comprising present-day Colombia, Panama and North-West Brazil
Confederate States of America	1861–1865	Southern US secessionist states during the American Civil War
North German Confederation	1867–1871	Confederation of 22 previously independent states of northern Germany, united before the German Empire
Carlist States	1872–1876	Spanish states
USSR	1922–1936	Russian Soviet Federative Socialist Republic, Ukrainian Soviet Socialist Republic, Byelorussian Soviet Socialist Republic and Transcaucasian Socialist Federative Soviet Republic
Arab Federation	1958	Iraq and Jordan
United Arab Republic and the United Arab States	1958–1961	Egypt and Syria, joined by North Yemen
Union of African States	1961–1963	Mali, Ghana and Guinea
Federation of Arab Republics	1972	Egypt, Syria and Libya
Arab Islamic Republic	1974	Libya and Tunisia
Senegambia	1982–1989	Senegal and Gambia

Serbia and Montenegro	1992–2006	Established after the break-up of Yugoslavia, the two republics had separate economic policies and currencies

A2. Federations

(in chronological order)

(See p.9)

Type: Republic (R)/Monarchy (M)

Year est.	Federation	Federating units	Major federating units	Minor federating units	Type
1776	United States of America	Political divisions of the united States	50 states	1 federal district, 16 territories	R
1821	Mexico	States of Mexico	32 federal entities, which are 31 states and its capital Mexico City		R
1848	Switzerland	Cantons of Switzerland	26 cantons		R
1853	Argentina	Provinces of Argentina	23 provinces	1 autonomous city	R
1863	Venezuela	States of Venezuela	23 states	1 federal district, 1 federal dependency	R
1867	Canada	Provinces and territories of Canada	10 provinces	3 territories	M
1889	Brazil	States of Brazil	26 states	1 federal district	R
1901	Australia	States and territories of Australia	6 states	3 federal territories (of which 2 are self-governing) and 7 external territories	M

1918–1991	Russia	Federal subjects of Russia	46 *oblasts*, 22 republics, 9 *krais*, 4 autonomous *okrugs*, 3 federal-level cities, 1 autonomous *oblast*		R
1920	Austria	States of Austria	9 *Länder* or *Bundesländer*		R
1949	Germany	States of Germany	16 *Länder* or *Bundesländer*		R
1950	India	States and territories of India	29 states	7 union territories, including a National Capital Territory	R
1956	Pakistan	Provinces and territories of Pakistan	4 provinces	4 federal territories including a federal capital territory	R
1956	Sudan	States of Sudan	17 states		R
1963	Malaysia	States of Malaysia	13 states	3 federal territories	M
1963	Nigeria	States of Nigeria	36 states	1 federal capital territory	R
1970	Belgium	Divisions of Belgium	3 communities, 3 regions		M
1971	United Arab Emirates	Emirates of the UAE	7 emirates		M
1975	Comoros	Autonomous Islands of the Comoros	3 islands		R

1979	Federated States of Micronesia	Administrative divisions of Micronesia	4 states		R
1983	Saint Kitts and Nevis	The islands Saint Kitts and Nevis	2 islands		M
1995	Bosnia and Herzegovina	Divisions of Bosnia and Herzegovina	2 entities, one of which is itself a federation of 10 cantons	1 district	R
1995	Ethiopia	Regions of Ethiopia	9 regions	2 chartered cities	R
2005	Iraq	Governorates of Iraq	18 provinces		R
2011	South Sudan	States of South Sudan	28 states		R
2012	Somalia	Federal member states of Somalia	18 states		R
2015	Nepal	Provinces of Nepal	7 provinces		R

A3. Unitary States with Devolution

(in chronological order)

(See p.9)

Year	**State**	**Government type**	**Subdivisions**	**Main regional units**	**Other regional units**
1849	Denmark	Constitutional monarchy	Regions of Denmark	5 regions	2 autonomous territories: Greenland and Faroe Islands
1919	Finland	Republic	Regions of Finland	19 regions	Aland Islands
1922	United Kingdom	Common-wealth realm	Countries of the United King-dom (Home Nations)	4 constituent countries, of which 3 have devolved gov-ernments	Gibraltar (overseas territory)
1946	Italy	Republic	Regions of Italy	20 regions, of which 5 have a special degree of autonomy	2 au-tonomous provinces
1947	Japan	Constitutional monarchy	Prefectures of Japan	47 prefectures	
1948	South Korea	Republic	Administrative divisions of South Korea	8 provinces and 6 cities	One special city, one special self-governing city and one special self-governing province

1949	China	People's republic	Administrative divisions of China	22 provinces (Taiwan is claimed as the 23rd province), 5 autonomous regions and 4 municipalities	2 special administrative regions: Hong Kong and Macau
1950	Indonesia	Republic	Provinces of Indonesia	34 provinces of which 5 have special status	Provinces with special status: Aceh, Jakarta, Yogyakarta (De Jure Yogyakarta Region is not a province), Papua, and West Papua
1954	Netherlands	Constitutional monarchy	Provinces of the Netherlands	12 provinces and 3 special municipalities	Aruba, Curaçao and Sint Maarten
1958	France	Republic	Regions of France	18 regions	
1964	Kenya	Presidential republic	Counties of Kenya	47 counties based on 47 districts, with 47 elected governors, recognised by the 2010 Constitution	

1975	Greece	Republic	Administrative divisions of Greece	13 regions	Mount Athos
1975	Papua New Guinea	Common-wealth realm	Provinces of Papua New Guinea	20 provinces	1 capital territory: National Capital District and 1 autonomous region: Bougainville
1976	Portugal	Republic	Administrative divisions of Portugal	308 municipalities	Azores Autonomous Region and Madeira Autonomous Region
1976	Trinidad and Tobago	Republic	Administrative divisions of Trinidad and Tobago	9 regions and 5 municipalities	Tobago
1977	Tanzania	Republic	Regions of Tanzania	30 regions	Zanzibar
1978	Solomon Islands	Common-wealth realm	Provinces of the Solomon Islands	9 provinces	1 capital territory: Honiara
1978	Spain	Constitutional monarchy	Autonomous communities of Spain (nationalities and regions of Spain)	17 autonomous communities of which 2 have a special degree of tax-raising autonomy	2 autonomous cities (Ceuta and Melilla)
1980	Chile	Republic	Regions of Chile	15 regions	

1986	New Zealand	Commonwealth realm	Regions of New Zealand	16 regions	Two territories in free association: Cook Islands and Niue and two dependencies: Tokelau and Ross
1986	Nicaragua	Republic	Departments of Nicaragua	15 departments	Two autonomous regions: North Atlantic and South Atlantic
1987	Philippines	Republic	Administrative divisions of the Philippines	18 regions (including ARMM), 81 provinces, 144 cities, 1,491 municipalities, and 42,028 barangays	Autonomous Region in Muslim Mindanao (ARMM)
1987	Sri Lanka	Republic	Provinces of Sri Lanka	9 provinces	
1991	Colombia	Republic	Departments of Colombia	32 departments	1 Capital District, Bogotá, has the same autonomy and privileges as Colombian Departments

1991	Georgia	Republic	Administrative divisions of Georgia	9 regions (one of them declared *de facto* independence: Abkhazia, 1999), 1 city, and 2 autonomous republics (one of them also declared *de facto* independence: South Ossetia, 2006)	Adjara and South Ossetia (Tskhinvali region)
1991	Moldova	Republic	Administrative divisions of Moldova	32 districts and 3 municipalities	2 provinces: Gagauzia and Transnistria. Transnistria is a *de facto* independent state
1991	Uzbekistan	Republic	Provinces of Uzbekistan	9 provinces and one independent city	Qaraqalpaqstan
1992	Tajikistan	Republic	Provinces of Tajikistan	2 provinces, 1 autonomous province (Gorno-Badakhshan) and a zone of direct central rule (Districts of Republican Subordination)	1 autonomous city

1993	Peru	Republic	Regions of Peru	25 regions	1 province at the first order: Lima
1995	Azerbaijan	Dominant-party presidential state	Administrative divisions of Azerbaijan	10 autonomous regions, 66 rayons and 77 cities	Autonomous republic: Nakhchivan
1996	South Africa	Republic	Provinces of South Africa	9 provinces	
1996	Ukraine	Republic	Administrative divisions of Ukraine	24 *oblasts* (provinces) and one autonomous republic	Crimea
2006	Serbia	Republic	Administrative divisions of Serbia	138 municipalities and 23 cities	Vojvodina and Kosovo and Metohija (Serbia does not recognise the independence of Kosovo)
2009	Bolivia	Constitutional republic	Departments of Bolivia	9 departments	

B. US-Based Documents

B1. Declaration of Independence
July 4, 1776

(See pp.31, 60–62, 85, 130, 140)

When in the course of human events, it becomes necessary for one people to dissolve the political bands which have connected them with another, and to assume among the powers of the earth, the separate and equal station to which the laws of nature and of nature's God entitle them, a decent respect to the opinions of mankind requires that they should declare the causes which impel them to the separation.

We hold these truths to be self-evident:

That all men are created equal; that they are endowed by their Creator with certain unalienable rights; that among these are life, liberty, and the pursuit of happiness; that, to secure these rights, governments are instituted among men, deriving their just powers from the consent of the governed; that whenever any form of government becomes destructive of these ends, it is the right of the people to alter or to abolish it, and to institute new government, laying its foundation on such principles, and organizing its powers in such form, as to them shall seem most likely to effect their safety and happiness. Prudence, indeed, will dictate that governments long established should not be changed for light and transient causes; and accordingly all experience hath shown that mankind are more disposed to suffer, while evils are sufferable, than to right themselves by abolishing the forms to which they are accustomed. But when a long train of abuses and usurpations, pursuing invariably the same object, evinces a design to reduce them under absolute despotism, it is their right, it is their duty, to throw off such government, and to provide new guards for their future security. Such has been the patient sufferance of these colonies; and such is now the necessity which constrains them to alter their former systems of government. The history of the present King of Great Britain is a history of repeated injuries and usurpations, all having in direct object the establishment of an absolute tyranny over these states. To prove this, let facts be submitted to a candid world.

He has refused his assent to laws, the most wholesome and necessary for the public good.

He has forbidden his governors to pass laws of immediate and pressing importance, unless suspended in their operation till his assent should be obtained; and, when so suspended, he has utterly neglected to attend to them.

He has refused to pass other laws for the accommodation of large districts of people, unless those people would relinquish the right of representation in the legislature, a right inestimable to them, and formidable to tyrants only.

He has called together legislative bodies at places unusual, uncomfortable, and distant from the depository of their public records, for the sole purpose of fatiguing them into compliance with his measures.

He has dissolved representative houses repeatedly, for opposing, with manly firmness, his invasions on the rights of the people.

He has refused for a long time, after such dissolutions, to cause others to be elected; whereby the legislative powers, incapable of annihilation, have returned to the people at large for their exercise; the state remaining, in the meantime, exposed to all the dangers of invasions from without and convulsions within.

He has endeavored to prevent the population of these states; for that purpose obstructing the laws for naturalization of foreigners; refusing to pass others to encourage their migration hither, and raising the conditions of new appropriations of lands.

He has obstructed the administration of justice, by refusing his assent to laws for establishing judiciary powers.

He has made judges dependent on his will alone, for the tenure of their offices, and the amount and payment of their salaries.

He has erected a multitude of new offices, and sent hither swarms of officers to harass our people and eat out their substance.

He has kept among us, in times of peace, standing armies, without the consent of our legislatures.

He has affected to render the military independent of, and superior to, the civil power.

He has combined with others to subject us to a jurisdiction foreign to our Constitution and unacknowledged by our laws, giving his assent to their acts of pretended legislation:

For quartering large bodies of armed troops among us;

For protecting them, by a mock trial, from punishment for any murders which they should commit on the inhabitants of these states;

For cutting off our trade with all parts of the world;

For imposing taxes on us without our consent;

For depriving us, in many cases, of the benefits of trial by jury;

For transporting us beyond seas, to be tried for pretended offenses;

For abolishing the free system of English laws in a neighboring province, establishing therein an arbitrary government, and enlarging its boundaries, so as to render it at once an example and fit instrument for introducing the same absolute rule into these colonies;

For taking away our charters, abolishing our most valuable laws, and altering fundamentally the forms of our governments;

For suspending our own legislatures, and declaring themselves invested with power to legislate for us in all cases whatsoever.

He has abdicated government here, by declaring us out of his protection and waging war against us.

He has plundered our seas, ravaged our coasts, burned our towns, and destroyed the lives of our people.

He is at this time transporting large armies of foreign mercenaries to complete the works of death, desolation, and tyranny already begun with circumstances of cruelty and perfidy scarcely paralleled in the most barbarous ages, and totally unworthy the head of a civilized nation.

He has constrained our fellow-citizens, taken captive on the high seas, to bear arms against their country, to become the executioners of their friends and brethren, or to fall themselves by their hands.

He has excited domestic insurrection among us, and has endeavored to bring on the inhabitants of our frontiers the merciless Indian savages, whose known rule of warfare is an undistinguished destruction of all ages, sexes, and conditions.

In every stage of these oppressions we have petitioned for redress in the most humble terms; our repeated petitions have been answered only by repeated injury. A prince, whose character is thus marked by every act which may define a tyrant, is unfit to be the ruler of a free people.

Nor have we been wanting in our attentions to our British brethren. We have warned them, from time to time, of attempts by their legislature to extend an unwarrantable jurisdiction over us. We have reminded them of the circumstances of our emigration and settlement here. We have appealed to their native justice and magnanimity; and we have conjured them, by the ties of our common kindred, to disavow these usurpations which would inevitably interrupt our connections and correspondence. They too, have been deaf to the voice of justice and of consanguinity. We must, therefore, acquiesce in the necessity which denounces our separation, and hold them as we hold the rest of mankind, enemies in war, in peace friends.

We, therefore, the representatives of the United States of America, in General Congress assembled, appealing to the Supreme Judge of the world for the rectitude of our intentions, do, in the name and by the authority of the good people of these colonies solemnly publish and declare, That these United Colonies are, and of right ought to be, FREE AND INDEPENDENT STATES; that they are absolved from all allegiance to the British crown and that all political connection between them and the state of Great Britain is, and ought to be, totally dissolved; and that, as free and independent states, they have full power to levy war, conclude peace, contract alliances, establish commerce, and do all other acts and things which independent states may of right do. And for the support of this declaration, with a firm reliance on the protection of Divine Providence, we mutually pledge to each other our lives, our fortunes, and our sacred honor.

[Signed by] John Hancock [President]

New Hampshire
Josiah Bartlett, Wm. Whipplt, Matthew Thormton.

Massachusetts Bay
Saml. Adams, John Adams, Robt. Treat Paine, Elbridge Gerry.

Rhode Island
Step. Hopkins, William Ellery.

Connecticut
Roger Sherman, Sam'el Huntington, Wm. Williams, Oliver Wolcott.

New York
Wm. Floyd, Phil. Livingston, Frans. Lewis, Lewis Morris.

New Jersey
Richd. Stockton, Jno. Witherspoon, Fras. Hopkinson, John Hart, Abra. Clark.

Pennsylvania
Robt. Morris, Benjamin Rush, Benja. Franklin, John Morton, Geo. Clymer, Jas. Smith, Geo. Taylor, James Wilson, Geo. Ross.

Delaware
Caesar Rodney, Geo. Read, Tho. M'kean.

Maryland
Samuel Chase, Wm. Paca, Thos. Stone, Charles Carroll of Carrollton.

Virginia
George Wythe, Richard Henry Lee, Th. Jefferson, Benja. Harrison, Ths. Nelson, Jr, Francis Lightfoot Lee, Carter Braxton.

North Carolina
Wm. Hooper, Joseph Hewes, John Penn.

South Carolina
Edward Rutledge, Thos. Hayward, Junr., Thomas Lynch, Junr., Arthur Middleton.

Georgia
Button Gwinnett, Lyman Hall, Geo. Walton.

B2. The North Atlantic Treaty
Washington D.C. – 4 April 1949
(See pp.90–91)

The Parties to this Treaty reaffirm their faith in the purposes and principles of the Charter of the United Nations and their desire to live in peace with all peoples and all governments.

They are determined to safeguard the freedom, common heritage and civilisation of their peoples, founded on the principles of democracy, individual liberty and the rule of law.

They seek to promote stability and well-being in the North Atlantic area.

They are resolved to unite their efforts for collective defence and for the preservation of peace and security. They therefore agree to this North Atlantic Treaty:

Article 1

The Parties undertake, as set forth in the Charter of the United Nations, to settle any international dispute in which they may be involved by peaceful means in such a manner that international peace and security and justice are not endangered, and to refrain in their international relations from the threat or use of force in any manner inconsistent with the purposes of the United Nations.

Article 2

The Parties will contribute toward the further development of peaceful and friendly international relations by strengthening their free institutions, by bringing about a better understanding of the principles upon which these institutions are founded, and by promoting conditions of stability and well-being. They will seek to eliminate conflict in their international economic policies and will encourage economic collaboration between any or all of them.

Article 3
In order more effectively to achieve the objectives of this Treaty, the Parties, separately and jointly, by means of continuous and effective self-help and mutual aid, will maintain and develop their individual and collective capacity to resist armed attack.

Article 4
The Parties will consult together whenever, in the opinion of any of them, the territorial integrity, political independence or security of any of the Parties is threatened.

Article 5
The Parties agree that an armed attack against one or more of them in Europe or North America shall be considered an attack against them all and consequently they agree that, if such an armed attack occurs, each of them, in exercise of the right of individual or collective self-defence recognised by Article 51 of the Charter of the United Nations, will assist the Party or Parties so attacked by taking forthwith, individually and in concert with the other Parties, such action as it deems necessary, including the use of armed force, to restore and maintain the security of the North Atlantic area.

Any such armed attack and all measures taken as a result thereof shall immediately be reported to the Security Council. Such measures shall be terminated when the Security Council has taken the measures necessary to restore and maintain international peace and security.

Article 6[1]
For the purposes of Article 5, an armed attack on one or more of the Parties is deemed to include an armed attack:

- on the territory of any of the Parties in Europe or North America, on the Algerian Departments of France,[2] on the territory of or on the Islands under the jurisdiction of any of the Parties in the North Atlantic area north of the Tropic of Cancer;

- on the forces, vessels, or aircraft of any of the Parties, when in or over these territories or any other area in Europe in which occupation forces of any of the Parties were stationed on the date when the Treaty entered into force or the Mediterranean Sea or the North Atlantic area north of the Tropic of Cancer.

Article 7

This Treaty does not affect, and shall not be interpreted as affecting in any way the rights and obligations under the Charter of the Parties which are members of the United Nations, or the primary responsibility of the Security Council for the maintenance of international peace and security.

Article 8

Each Party declares that none of the international engagements now in force between it and any other of the Parties or any third State is in conflict with the provisions of this Treaty, and undertakes not to enter into any international engagement in conflict with this Treaty.

Article 9

The Parties hereby establish a Council, on which each of them shall be represented, to consider matters concerning the implementation of this Treaty. The Council shall be so organised as to be able to meet promptly at any time. The Council shall set up such subsidiary bodies as may be necessary; in particular it shall establish immediately a defence committee which shall recommend measures for the implementation of Articles 3 and 5.

Article 10

The Parties may, by unanimous agreement, invite any other European State in a position to further the principles of this Treaty and to contribute to the security of the North Atlantic area to accede to this Treaty. Any State so invited may become a Party to the Treaty by depositing its instrument of accession with the Government of the United States of America. The Government of the United States of America will inform each of the Parties of the deposit of each such instrument of accession.

Article 11
This Treaty shall be ratified and its provisions carried out by the Parties in accordance with their respective constitutional processes. The instruments of ratification shall be deposited as soon as possible with the Government of the United States of America, which will notify all the other signatories of each deposit. The Treaty shall enter into force between the States which have ratified it as soon as the ratifications of the majority of the signatories, including the ratifications of Belgium, Canada, France, Luxembourg, the Netherlands, the United Kingdom and the United States, have been deposited and shall come into effect with respect to other States on the date of the deposit of their ratifications.[3]

Article 12
After the Treaty has been in force for ten years, or at any time thereafter, the Parties shall, if any of them so requests, consult together for the purpose of reviewing the Treaty, having regard for the factors then affecting peace and security in the North Atlantic area, including the development of universal as well as regional arrangements under the Charter of the United Nations for the maintenance of international peace and security.

Article 13
After the Treaty has been in force for twenty years, any Party may cease to be a Party one year after its notice of denunciation has been given to the Government of the United States of America, which will inform the Governments of the other Parties of the deposit of each notice of denunciation.

Article 14

This Treaty, of which the English and French texts are equally authentic, shall be deposited in the archives of the Government of the United States of America. Duly certified copies will be transmitted by that Government to the Governments of other signatories.

Notes:

1. The definition of the territories to which Article 5 applies was revised by Article 2 of the Protocol to the North Atlantic Treaty on the accession of Greece and Turkey signed on 22 October 1951.
2. On January 16, 1963, the North Atlantic Council noted that insofar as the former Algerian Departments of France were concerned, the relevant clauses of this Treaty had become inapplicable as from July 3, 1962.
3. The Treaty came into force on 24 August 1949, after the deposition of the ratifications of all signatory states.

B3. Project for the New American Century Statement of Principles June 3, 1997

(See p.92)

American foreign and defense policy is adrift. Conservatives have criticized the incoherent policies of the Clinton Administration. They have also resisted isolationist impulses from within their own ranks. But conservatives have not confidently advanced a strategic vision of America's role in the world. They have not set forth guiding principles for American foreign policy. They have allowed differences over tactics to obscure potential agreement on strategic objectives. And they have not fought for the defense budget that would maintain American security and advance American interests in the new century.

We aim to change this. We aim to make the case and rally support for American global leadership.

As the 20th century draws to a close, the United States stands as the world's preeminent power. Having led the West to victory in the Cold War, America faces an opportunity and a challenge: Does the United States have the vision to build upon the achievements of past decades? Does the United States have the resolve to shape a new century favorable to American principles and interests?

We are in danger of squandering the opportunity and failing the challenge. We are living off the capital – both the military investments and the foreign policy achievements – built up by past administrations. Cuts in foreign affairs and defense spending, inattention to the tools of statecraft, and inconstant leadership are making it increasingly difficult to sustain American influence around the world. And the promise of short-term commercial benefits threatens to override strategic considerations. As a consequence, we are jeopardizing the nation's ability to meet present threats and to deal with potentially greater challenges that lie ahead.

We seem to have forgotten the essential elements of the Reagan Administration's success: a military that is strong and ready to meet both present and future challenges; a foreign policy that boldly and purposefully promotes American principles abroad; and national leadership that accepts the United States' global responsibility.

Of course, the United States must be prudent in how it exercises its power. But we cannot safely avoid the responsibilities of global leadership or the costs that are associated with its exercise. America has a vital role in maintaining peace and security in Europe, Asia, and the Middle East. If we shirk our responsibilities, we invite challenges to our fundamental interests. The history of the 20th century should have taught us that it is important to shape circumstances before crises emerge, and to meet threats before they become dire. The history of this century should have taught us to embrace the cause of American leadership.

Our aim is to remind Americans of these lessons and to draw their consequences for today. Here are four consequences:

- we need to increase defense spending significantly if we are to carry out our global responsibilities today and modernize our armed forces for the future;
- we need to strengthen our ties to democratic allies and to challenge regimes hostile to our interests and values;
- we need to promote the cause of political and economic freedom abroad;
- we need to accept responsibility for America's unique role in preserving and extending an international order friendly to our security, our prosperity, and our principles.

Such a Reaganite policy of military strength and moral clarity may not be fashionable today. But it is necessary if the United States is to build on the successes of this past century and to ensure our security and our greatness in the next.

Elliott Abrams
Gary Bauer
William J. Bennett
Jed Bush
Dick Cheney
Eliot A. Cohen
Midge Decter
Paula Dobriansky
Steve Forbes
Aaron Friedberg
Francis Fukuyama
Frank Gaffney
Fred C. Ikle
Donald Kagan
Zalmay Khalilzad
I. Lewis Libby
Norman Pohoretz
Dan Quayle
Peter W. Rodman
Stephen P. Rosen
Henry S. Rowen
Donald Rumsfeld
Vin Weber
George Weigel
Paul Wolfowitz

C. The UN

C1. Overview of the UN Structure

(See p.113)

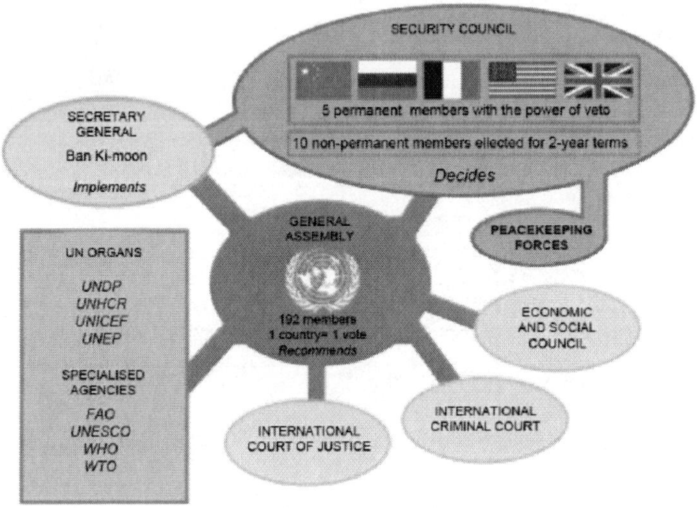

Notes:

1. Ban Ki-moon, Secretary General, has been replaced by António Guterres.
2. In 2011 the UN General Assembly admitted the Republic of South Sudan and in 2017 had 193 members.
3. NB 'ellected' in the Security-Council bubble should read 'elected'.

C2. Structure of the UN Agencies

(See pp.113, 171, 191)

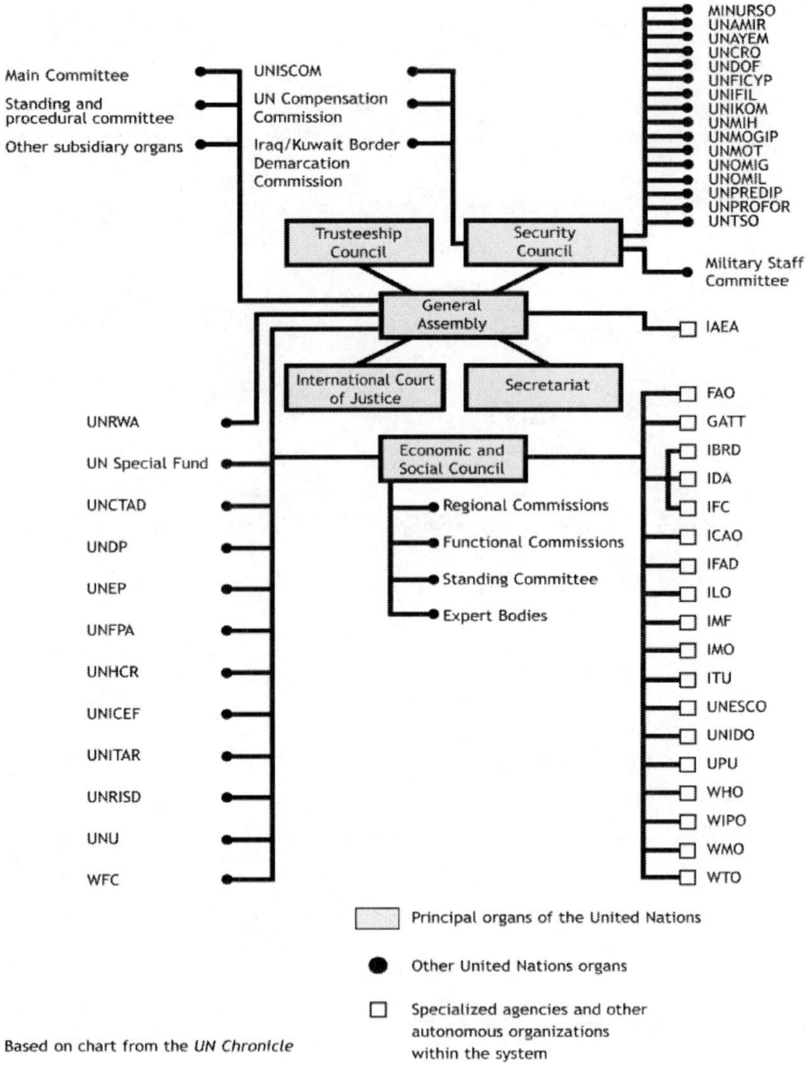

Based on chart from the *UN Chronicle*

C3. UN Organisations
(See pp.113, 171, 191)

* = Exists but not on UN list

Organisations of the General Assembly
- Main committees
- Other session committees
- Standing committees and *ad hoc* bodies

Some of the Programmes and Funds include:
- UNCTAD – United Nations Conference on Trade and Development
  - ITC – International Trade Centre (UNCTAD/WTO)
- UNDCP – United Nations Drug Control Programme*
- UNDP – United Nations Development Programme
  - UNCDF – United Nations Capital Development Fund*
  - UNIFEM – United Nations Development Fund for Women (incorporated into UN WOMEN in 2011)
  - UNV – United Nations Volunteers*
- UNEP – United Nations Environment Programme
- UNFPA – United Nations Fund for Population Activities
- UN-HABITAT – United Nations Human Settlements Programme
- UNHCR – Office of the United Nations High Commissioner for Refugees
- UNHRC – United Nations Human Rights Council*
- UNICEF – United Nations Children's Fund
- UNRWA – United Nations Relief and Works Agency for Palestine Refugees in the Near East
- WFP – World Food Programme

Research and training institutes
- UN WOMEN (including INSTRAW, International Research and Training Institute for the Advancement of Women, incorporated in 2011)

- UNICRI – United Nations Interregional Crime and Justice Research Institute
- UNIDIR – United Nations Institute for Disarmament Research (reports only to the General Assembly)
- UNITAR – United Nations Institute for Training and Research
- UNRISD – United Nations Research Institute for Social Development

Other entities

- COPUOS – United Nations Committee on the Peaceful Uses of Outer Space*
- JIU – Joint Inspection Unit (oversight body of the United Nations system)
- OHCHR – Office of the United Nations High Commissioner for Human Rights
- UNAIDS – Joint United Nations Programme on HIV/AIDS
- UNOOSA – United Nations Office for Outer Space Affairs*
- UNOPS – United Nations Office for Project Services
- UNRRA – United Nations Relief and Rehabilitation Administration (ceased to exist in 1949)
- UNSSC – United Nations System Staff College
- UNU – United Nations University
- UPEACE – United Nations Mandated University for Peace*

Organisations of the Security Council

- 1540 Committee (Committee established pursuant to UN Security Council Resolution 1540, 2004)
- CTC – Counter-Terrorism Committee (Committee established pursuant to UN Security Council Resolution 1373, 2001)
- International Criminal Tribunal for Rwanda (closed in 2015)
- International Criminal Tribunal for the Former Yugoslavia
- Military Staff Committee
- Standing Committee and *ad hoc* bodies

- Peacekeeping Operations and Missions
  - MONUC – United Nations Mission in the Democratic Republic of Congo, changed to:
  - MONUSCO – United Nations Organization Stabilization Mission in the Democratic Republic of the Congo
  - UNAVEM III – United Nations Angola Verification Mission III (operational 1995–1997)
  - UNDOF – United Nations Disengagement Observer Force*
  - UNFICYP – United Nations Peacekeeping Force in Cyprus*
  - UNIFIL – United Nations Interim Force in Lebanon*
  - UNMEE – United Nations Mission in Ethiopia and Eritrea (terminated in 2008)
  - UNMIK – United Nations Interim Administration Mission in Kosovo*
  - UNMIL – United Nations Mission in Liberia*
  - UNMIN – United Nations Mission in Nepal (ceased operations in 2011)
  - UNMIS – United Nations Mission in Sudan (wound up in 2011)
  - UNMOGIP – United Nations Military Observer Group in India and Pakistan*
  - UNMOVIC – United Nations Monitoring, Verification and Inspection Commission (mandate terminated in 2007)
  - UNOMIG – United Nations Observer Mission in Georgia (ended in 2009)
  - UNOMSIL – United Nations Mission of Observers in Sierra Leone (terminated in 1999)
  - UNSMIH – United Nations Support Mission in Haiti (terminated in 1997)
  - UNSMIS – United Nations Supervision Mission in Syria (mandate ended in 2012)
  - UNTSO – United Nations Truce Supervision Organization*

- Former Peacekeeping Operations and Missions
  - ONUMOZ – United Nations Operation in Mozambique
  - UNAMIR – United Nations Assistance Mission for Rwanda
  - UNAMSIL – United Nations Mission in Sierra Leone
  - UNCRO – United Nations Confidence Restoration Operation in Croatia
  - UNIKOM – United Nations Iraq-Kuwait Observation Mission
  - UNMIBH – United Nations Mission in Bosnia and Herzegovina
  - UNMOP – United Nations Mission of Observers in Prevlaka
  - UNMOT – United Nations Mission of Observers in Tajikistan
  - UNSCOM – United Nations Special Commission (Iraq, replaced by UNMOVIC, see above)
  - UNTAC – United Nations Transitional Authority in Cambodia
  - UNTAET – United Nations Transitional Administration in East Timor

Organisations of the Economic and Social Council

Functional commissions

- CCPCJ – Commission on Crime Prevention and Criminal Justice
- Commission on Population and Development
- CSD – Commission on Sustainable Development
- CSocD – Commission for Social Development
- CSTD – Commission on Science and Technology for Development
- CSW – Commission on the Status of Women
- UNFF – United Nations Forum on Forests
- UNSC – United Nations Statistical Commission
- UNODC – United Nations Office on Drugs and Crime

Regional commissions

- ECLAC – United Nations Economic Commission for Latin America and the Caribbean
- ESCAP – United Nations Economic and Social Commission for Asia and the Pacific
- ESCWA – United Nations Economic and Social Commission for Western Asia
- UNECA – United Nations Economic Commission for Africa
- UNECE – United Nations Economic Commission for Europe

Specialised agencies

The specialised agencies are autonomous organisations working with the United Nations and each other through the co-ordinating machinery of the Economic and Social Council.

- FAO – Food and Agriculture Organization
- ICAO – International Civil Aviation Organization
- IFAD – International Fund for Agricultural Development
- ILO – International Labour Organization
- IMF – International Monetary Fund (see Appendix E7)
- IMO – International Maritime Organization
- INCB – International Narcotics Control Board*
- IRO – International Refugee Organization (ceased to exist in 1952)
- ITU – International Telecommunication Union
- PFII – Permanent Forum on Indigenous Issues*
- Sessional and Standing Committees Expert, *ad hoc* and related bodies
- UNESCO – United Nations Educational, Scientific and Cultural Organization
- UNIDO – United Nations Industrial Development Organization
- UNWTO – United Nations World Tourism Organization
- UPU – Universal Postal Union
- WHO – World Health Organization

- WIPO – World Intellectual Property Organization
- WMO – World Meteorological Organization
- World Bank Group
  - IBRD – International Bank for Reconstruction and Development*
  - IDA – International Development Association*
  - IFC – International Finance Corporation*
  - MIGA – Multilateral Investment Guarantee Agency*
  - ICSID – International Centre for Settlement of Investment Disputes*

Organisations of the Secretariat

The United Nations Secretariat is led by the Secretary-General of the United Nations.

- DESA – Department of Economic and Social Affairs
- DGACM – Department of General Assembly and Conference Management
- DM – Department of Management
- DPA – Department of Political Affairs
- DPI – Department of Public Information*
- DSS – Department of Safety and Security*
- EOSG – Executive Office of the Secretary-General
- OCHA – Office for the Coordination of Humanitarian Affairs
- OIOS – Office of Internal Oversight Services
- OIP – Office of the Iraq Programme (closed in 2004)
- OLA – Office of Legal Affairs
- UNODA – United Nations Office for Disarmament Affairs
  DPKO – Department of Peacekeeping Operations
- UNODC – United Nations Office on Drugs and Crime*
- UNOG – UN Office at Geneva
- UN-OHRLLS – Office of the High Representative for the Least Developed Countries, Landlocked Developing Countries and Small Island Developing States*
- UNON – UN Office at Nairobi*
- UNOV – UN Office at Vienna*

- UNSECOORD – Office of the United Nations Security Co-ordinator (formed in 2000)

Related organisations

- CTBTO – Preparatory Commission for the Comprehensive Nuclear-Test-Ban Treaty Organization
- IAEA – International Atomic Energy Agency, reports to the Security Council and the General Assembly
- ICC – International Criminal Court*
- IOM – International Organization for Migration
- ISA – International Seabed Authority*
- ITLOS – International Tribunal for the Law of the Sea*
- OPCW – Organization for the Prohibition of Chemical Weapons
- SHIRBRIG – Standby High-Readiness Brigade (closed in 2009)
- UNFCCC – United Nations Framework Convention on Climate Change
- UNICSC – International Civil Service Commission
- UNISDR – United Nations International Strategy for Disaster Reduction
- UNSOG – Special Operations Group*
- WTO – World Trade Organization

C4. The UN's 193 Member States*

(See pp.7, 55, 113)

A

Afghanistan
Albania
Algeria
Andorra
Angola
Antigua and Barbuda
Argentina
Armenia
Australia
Austria
Azerbaijan

B

Bahamas
Bahrain
Bangladesh
Barbados
Belarus
Belgium
Belize
Benin
Bhutan
Bolivia
Bosnia and Herzegovina
Botswana
Brazil
Brunei
Bulgaria
Burkina Faso
Burundi

C

Cambodia
Cameroon
Canada
Cape Verde
Central African Republic
Chad
Chile
China
Colombia
Comoros
Congo (Brazzaville)
Congo (Kinshasa)
Costa Rica
Côte d'Ivoire
Croatia
Cuba
Cyprus
Czech Republic

D

Denmark
Djibouti
Dominica
Dominican Republic

E

East Timor (or Timor-Leste)
Ecuador
Egypt
El Salvador
Equatorial Guinea
Eritrea
Estonia
Ethiopia

F

Fiji
Finland
France

G

Gabon
Gambia
Georgia
Germany
Ghana
Greece
Grenada
Guatemala
Guinea
Guinea-Bissau
Guyana

H

Haiti
Honduras
Hungary

I

Iceland
India
Indonesia
Iran
Iraq
Ireland
Israel
Italy

J

Jamaica
Japan
Jordan

K

Kazakhstan
Kenya
Kiribati
Korea, North
Korea, South
Kuwait
Kyrgyzstan

L

Laos
Latvia
Lebanon
Lesotho
Liberia
Libya
Liechtenstein
Lithuania
Luxembourg

M

Macedonia
Madagascar
Malawi
Malaysia
Maldives
Mali
Malta
Marshall Islands
Mauritania
Mauritius
Mexico
Micronesia
Moldova
Monaco
Mongolia
Montenegro
Morocco
Mozambique
Myanmar

N

Namibia
Nauru
Nepal
Netherlands
New Zealand
Nicaragua
Niger
Nigeria
Norway

O

Oman

P

Pakistan
Palau
Panama
Papua New Guinea
Paraguay
Peru
Philippines
Poland
Portugal

Q

Qatar

R

Romania
Russia
Rwanda

S

St Kitts and Nevis
St Lucia
St Vincent and the Grenadines
Samoa
San Marino
São Tomé and Principe
Saudi Arabia
Senegal
Serbia
Seychelles
Sierra Leone
Singapore
Slovakia
Slovenia
Solomon Islands
Somalia
South Africa
South Sudan
Spain
Sri Lanka
Sudan
Suriname
Swaziland
Sweden
Switzerland
Syria

T

Tajikistan
Tanzania
Thailand
Togo
Tonga
Trinidad and Tobago
Tunisia
Turkey
Turkmenistan
Tuvalu

U

Uganda
Ukraine
United Arab Emirates
United Kingdom
United States
Uruguay
Uzbekistan

V

Vanuatu
Venezuela
Vietnam

Y

Yemen

Z

Zambia
Zimbabwe

* The US Department of State recognised 195 countries in 2017, including Kosovo and Vatican City

C5. The UN Universal Declaration of Human Rights, 1948 (Adopted by the UN General Assembly on 10 December 1948)

(See pp.38, 39, 55, 150, 157)

PREAMBLE

Whereas recognition of the inherent dignity and of the equal and inalienable rights of all members of the human family is the foundation of freedom, justice and peace in the world,

Whereas disregard and contempt for human rights have resulted in barbarous acts which have outraged the conscience of mankind, and the advent of a world in which human beings shall enjoy freedom of speech and belief and freedom from fear and want has been proclaimed as the highest aspiration of the common people,

Whereas it is essential, if man is not to be compelled to have recourse, as a last resort, to rebellion against tyranny and oppression, that human rights should be protected by the rule of law,

Whereas it is essential to promote the development of friendly relations between nations,

Whereas the peoples of the United Nations have in the Charter reaffirmed their faith in fundamental human rights, in the dignity and worth of the human person and in the equal rights of men and women and have determined to promote social progress and better standards of life in larger freedom,

Whereas Member States have pledged themselves to achieve, in co-operation with the United Nations, the promotion of universal respect for and observance of human rights and fundamental freedoms,

Whereas a common understanding of these rights and freedoms is of the greatest importance for the full realization of this pledge,

Now, Therefore THE GENERAL ASSEMBLY proclaims THIS UNIVERSAL DECLARATION OF HUMAN RIGHTS as a common standard of achievement for all peoples and all nations, to the end that every individual and every organ of society, keeping this Declaration constantly in mind, shall strive by teaching and education to promote respect for these rights and freedoms and by progressive measures, national and international, to secure their universal and effective recognition and observance, both among the peoples of Member States themselves and among the peoples of territories under their jurisdiction.

Article 1
All human beings are born free and equal in dignity and rights. They are endowed with reason and conscience and should act towards one another in a spirit of brotherhood.

Article 2
Everyone is entitled to all the rights and freedoms set forth in this Declaration, without distinction of any kind, such as race, colour, sex, language, religion, political or other opinion, national or social origin, property, birth or other status. Furthermore, no distinction shall be made on the basis of the political, jurisdictional or international status of the country or territory to which a person belongs whether it be independent, trust, non-self-governing or under any other limitation of sovereignty.

Article 3
Everyone has the right to life, liberty and security of person.

Article 4
No one shall be held in slavery or servitude; slavery and the slave trade shall be prohibited in all their forms.

Article 5
No one shall be subjected to torture or to cruel, inhuman or degrading treatment or punishment.

Article 6
Everyone has the right to recognition everywhere as a person before the law.

Article 7
All are equal before the law and are entitled without any discrimination to equal protection of the law. All are entitled to equal protection against any discrimination in violation of this Declaration and against any incitement to such discrimination.

Article 8
Everyone has the right to an effective remedy by the competent national tribunals for acts violating the fundamental rights granted him by the constitution or by law.

Article 9
No one shall be subjected to arbitrary arrest, detention or exile.

Article 10
Everyone is entitled in full equality to a fair and public hearing by an independent and impartial tribunal, in the determination of his rights and obligations and of any criminal charge against him.

Article 11

1. Everyone charged with a penal offence has the right to be presumed innocent until proved guilty according to law in a public trial at which he has had all the guarantees necessary for his defence.
2. No one shall be held guilty of any penal offence on account of any act or omission which did not constitute a penal offence, under national or international law, at the

time when it was committed. Nor shall a heavier penalty be imposed than the one that was applicable at the time the penal offence was committed.

Article 12
No one shall be subjected to arbitrary interference with his privacy, family, home or correspondence, nor to attacks upon his honour and reputation. Everyone has the right to the protection of the law against such interference or attacks.

Article 13
1. Everyone has the right to freedom of movement and residence within the borders of each state.
2. Everyone has the right to leave any country, including his own, and to return to his country.

Article 14
1. Everyone has the right to seek and to enjoy in other countries asylum from persecution.
2. This right may not be invoked in the case of prosecutions genuinely arising from non-political crimes or from acts contrary to the purposes and principles of the United Nations.

Article 15
1. Everyone has the right to a nationality.
2. No one shall be arbitrarily deprived of his nationality nor denied the right to change his nationality.

Article 16
1. Men and women of full age, without any limitation due to race, nationality or religion, have the right to marry and to found a family. They are entitled to equal rights as to marriage, during marriage and at its dissolution.
2. Marriage shall be entered into only with the free and full consent of the intending spouses.

3. The family is the natural and fundamental group unit of society and is entitled to protection by society and the State.

Article 17

1. Everyone has the right to own property alone as well as in association with others.
2. No one shall be arbitrarily deprived of his property.

Article 18

Everyone has the right of freedom of thought, conscience and religion; this right includes freedom to change his religion or belief, and freedom, either alone or in community with others and in public or private, to manifest his religion or belief in teaching, practice, worship and observance.

Article 19

Everyone has the right to freedom of opinion and expression; this right includes freedom to hold opinions without interference and to seek, receive and impart information and ideas through any media and regardless of frontiers.

Article 20

1. Everyone has the right to freedom of peaceful assembly and association.
2. No one may be compelled to belong to an association.

Article 21

1. Everyone has the right to take part in the government of his country, directly or through freely chosen representatives.
2. Everyone has the right of equal access to public services in his country.
3. The will of the people shall be the basis of the authority of government; this will shall be expressed in periodic and genuine elections which shall be by universal and equal

suffrage and shall be held by secret vote or by equivalent free voting procedures.

Article 22

Everyone, as a member of society, has the right to social security and is entitled to realization, through national effort and international co-operation and in accordance with the organization and resources of each State, of the economic, social and cultural rights indispensable for his dignity and the free development of his personality.

Article 23

1. Everyone has the right to work, to free choice of employment, to just and favourable conditions of work and to protection against unemployment.
2. Everyone, without any discrimination, has the right to equal pay for equal work.
3. Everyone who works has the right to just and favourable remuneration ensuring for himself and his family an existence worthy of human dignity, and supplemented, if necessary, by other means of social protection.
4. Everyone has the right to form and to join trade unions for the protection of his interests.

Article 24

Everyone has the right to rest and leisure, including reasonable limitation of working hours and periodic holidays with pay.

Article 25

1. Everyone has the right to a standard of living adequate for the health and well-being of himself and of his family, including food, clothing, housing and medical care and necessary social services, and the right to security in the event of unemployment, sickness, disability, widowhood, old age or other lack of livelihood in circumstances beyond his control.

2. Motherhood and childhood are entitled to special care and assistance. All children, whether born in or out of wedlock, shall enjoy the same social protection.

Article 26

1. Everyone has the right to education. Education shall be free, at least in the elementary and fundamental stages. Elementary education shall be compulsory. Technical and professional education shall be made generally available and higher education shall be equally accessible to all on the basis of merit.
2. Education shall be directed to the full development of the human personality and to the strengthening of respect for human rights and fundamental freedoms. It shall promote understanding, tolerance and friendship among all nations, racial or religious groups, and shall further the activities of the United Nations for the maintenance of peace.
3. Parents have a prior right to choose the kind of education that shall be given to their children.

Article 27

1. Everyone has the right freely to participate in the cultural life of the community, to enjoy the arts and to share in scientific advancement and its benefits.
2. Everyone has the right to the protection of the moral and material interests resulting from any scientific, literary or artistic production of which he is the author.

Article 28

Everyone is entitled to a social and international order in which the rights and freedoms set forth in this Declaration can be fully realized.

Article 29

1. Everyone has duties to the community in which alone the free and full development of his personality is possible.

2. In the exercise of his rights and freedoms, everyone shall be subject only to such limitations as are determined by law solely for the purpose of securing due recognition and respect for the rights and freedoms of others and of meeting the just requirements of morality, public order and the general welfare in a democratic society.
3. These rights and freedoms may in no case be exercised contrary to the purposes and principles of the United Nations.

Article 30

Nothing in this Declaration may be interpreted as implying for any State, group or person any right to engage in any activity or to perform any act aimed at the destruction of any of the rights and freedoms set forth herein.

C6. Wars the UN Failed to Prevent Involving 124 Countries, 1945–2017

(See pp.91, 174, 212, 359)

* = war still continuing in 2017 (72 wars)

Afghanistan

Afghanistan-Pakistan skirmishes, 1949–present*

Civil War, 1978–present*

Herat uprising, 1979

Soviet War in Afghanistan, 1979–1989

Mujahideen v. Democratic Republic of Afghanistan, 1989–1992

Al-Qaeda War in Afghanistan, 2001–present*

Albania

Communist Regime, 1948–1989

Civil War, 1997

Algeria

War of Independence, 1954–1962

Algerian Civil War/Muslim uprising, 1991–2002

Algerian insurgency 2002–present*

Angola

Angolan War of Independence, Portuguese Colonial War v. MPLA, UNITA and others, 1961–1975

Angolan Civil War v. UNITA and FLEC for Cabinda, 1975–present*

Argentina

Overthrow of Juan Peron, 1955

Overthrow of Isabel Peron, 1976

Argentine Civil War and Dirty War, 1976–1983

Falklands War, 1982

Azerbaijan

Nagorno-Karabakh War between Armenia and Azerbaijan, Artsakh Liberation War, 1988–1994

Bangladesh

Bangladesh Liberation War, massacres, 1971

Communist insurgency in Bangladesh, 1972–1975

Chittagong Hill Tracts conflict, 1977–1997

Belgium

Congo Crisis, 1960–1967

Bolivia

Bolivian Revolution, 1952

Junta, 1971–1978

Bosnia and Herzegovina

Bosnian War (v. Serbia and Croatians), 1992–1995

Brazil

Military Regime, 1964–1985
Araguaia guerrilla war, 1967–1974
Rightist terrorism, 1980
Death squads, 1985–1991
Yanomami Indians, 1987–1991

Brunei

Brunei revolt, 1962

Bulgaria

Communist Regime, 1948–1989

Burundi

Rwanda v. Burundi, 1959–1995
Hutu rebellion, 1972
Burundian Civil War, 1993–2005

Cambodia

Cambodian Civil War, 1967–1975
Pol Pot revolution, 1975–1978
Cambodian-Vietnamese War, 1975–1989
Civil War, 1978–1991
Vietnamese (installed Cambodian Government v. Khmer Rouge), 1979–1998
Cambodian-Thai border conflict, 2008–2012

Cameroon

The Cameroonian Independence War, 1955–1960
Cameroon v. Communist UPC (Union of the Peoples of Cameroon), 1955–1970

Canada

Vancouver gang war, 2009

Central African Republic/Empire

Kongo-Wara rebellion, 1928–1931
Excesses of Bokassa Regime, 1965–1979
Bush War, 2004–2007
Sectarian conflict, 2012–present*

Chad

Chadian Civil War, 1965–1979
Chadian war of Muslims v. Christians, 1966–present*
Chadian-Libyan conflict, 1978–1987
Habré regime, 1982–1990
Chad-Libya War, 1987
Chadian Civil War, 2005–2010

Chile

Chilean military *coup*, 1973
Armed resistance in Chile, 1973–1990

China

Chinese Civil War, 1945–1949
Taiwanese revolt and massacre, 1947
Chinese Revolution, 1949
Kuomintang insurgency, 1949–1961
Third Sino-Tibetan War/invasion of Tibet and battle of Chamdo, 1950
Korean War, 1950–1953
Chinese occupation of and wars with Tibet, 1950–present*
First Taiwan Strait Crisis, 1954–1955
Tibetan uprising, 1956–1959
Second Taiwan Strait Crisis, 1958

Campaign at the Chinese-Burmese border, 1960–1961
Xinjiang conflict, 1960–present*
Sino-Indian War, 1962
Sino-Soviet War, 1963–1969
Sino-Soviet border conflict, 1969
Cultural Revolution, 1966–1976
Battle of the Paracel Islands, 1974
Sino-Vietnamese War, 1979
Sino-Vietnamese conflicts, 1979–1990
Tiananmen Square (civil violence), 1989
Third Taiwan Strait Crisis, 1996

Colombia
La Violencia, 1948–1958
Colombian conflict with insurgencies, 1964–present*

Comoros
Invasion of Anjovan, 2008

North Congo (a.k.a. "French Congo", "Congo-Brazzaville", "People's Republic of the Congo")
First Republic of the Congo Civil War, 1993–1994
Coup, 1997
Second Republic of the Congo Civil War, 1997–1999
The Pool War, 2016–present*

South Congo (a.k.a. "Belgian Congo", "Zaire", "Congo-Kinshasa", "Democratic Republic of the Congo")
Congo Crisis, 1960–1966
Katanga insurgency, 1960–present*
Simba rebellion, 1964
Stanleyville revolt, 1964–1965
Stanleyville mutinies, 1966–1967
Mercenary uprising, 1967–1968
Uprisings and repression, 1970s
Shaba I, 1977
Shaba II, 1978
Conflicts, 1992–1994
Hunde v. Hutu, Banyarwanda, 1993–1996
First Congo War, 1996–1997
Overthrow of Mobutu, 1997
Second Congo War, 1998–2003
Ituri conflict, 1999–2003
Civil War, 2003–present*
Kivu conflict, FARDC v. FDLR, 2004–2009
Dongo conflict, 2009
M23 rebellion, 2012–2013
Batwa-Ruba clashes, 2013
Kamwina Naspu rebellion, 2016–present*

Costa Rica
Costa Rican Civil War, 1948
War with Nicaragua, 1955

Croatia
Croatian War of Independence (Croatia v. Serbian irregulars, Krajina, and JNA), 1991–1995

Cuba
Batista regime & Civil War, 1952–

1959
Cuban Revolution, 1953–1959
Escambray rebellion, 1959–1965
Bay of Pigs invasion, 1961
Angola, 1975–1995
Grenada, 1983

Cyprus
EOKA v. UK, 1955–1959
Cyprus Civil War, 1963–1964
Turkish invasion of Northern Cyprus, 1974

Czechoslovakia
Post-WW2 expulsions of Germans, 1945–1947
Uprising/Warsaw Pact invasion of Czechoslovakia, 1968

Dominican Republic
Coup and Dominican Civil War, 1965
US occupation of Dominican Republic, 1965–1966

East Timor (or Timor-Leste)
Indonesian occupation, 1975–1999

Ecuador
War with Peru, 1995–1997

Egypt
Arab-Israeli Wars, 1947–1973
Suez Crisis and Sinai War, 1956
Egyptian troops in North Yemen War, 1962–1970
Egypt v. Israel, 1969–1970
Libyan-Egyptian War, 1977
Sinai insurgency, Islamist militants, 2011–present*

El Salvador
Football War against Honduras, 1969
Salvadorian Civil War v. FMLN, 1979–1992

Equatorial Guinea
Atrocities after Spanish military intervention, 1969–1979

Eritrea
War of Independence, ELF and ELPF v. Ethiopia, 1961–1991
First Eritrean Civil War, 1972–1974
Second Eritrean Civil War, 1980–1981
War with Ethiopia, 1998–present*
Djiboutian-Eritrean border conflict, 2008

Estonia
Anti-Soviet Singing Revolution, 1987–1991

Ethiopia
Attempted *coup*, 1960
Ethiopia v. Eritrean ELF and ELPF, 1961–1991
Bale revolt, 1963–1970
Oromo conflict, Ethiopia v. OLF, 1973–present*
Ethiopia v. Ogadeni rebels, 1976–present*
Ethiopian Civil War v. EPRDF,

1974–1991
Ethiopian-Somali Ogaden War, 1977–1978
Ethiopian-Somali Border War, 1982
Ethiopian War with Eritrea, 1998–2000

France
Indochina War of Independence, 1945–1954
Madagascar, 1947
Malagasy uprising, 1947–1948
Tunisia, 1952–1954, 1961
Morocco, 1953–1956
Algeria, 1954–1962
Chad, 1982–1990
Lebanon, 1983

Gambia
Gambian *coup* attempt, 1981
Invasion of Gambia, 2017

Georgia
Georgian Civil War in South Ossetia and Abkhazia, 1991–1993
Russo-Georgian War, 2008

Ghana
Coup and aftermath, 1981–1993

Greece
Greek Civil War, 1946–1949
Greek junta, 1967–1974

Grenada
US invasion of Grenada, 1983

Guatemala
Guatemalan Civil War, 1960–1996

Guinea
Touré, 1969–1976
Civil War, 2000–present*

Guinea-Bissau
War of Independence, Portuguese Colonial War, 1963–1974

Haiti
Duvalier regime, 1957–1986
Revolt, 1991–1994

Honduras
War with Nicaragua, 1957
Football War with El Salvador, 1969
Death squads, 1980–1988

Hungary
Hungarian uprising, 1956

India
Partition violence, 1947
Integration of Junagadh, 1947
Indian partition Civil War, Communist violence, 1947–1948
First Kashmir War, Indo-Pakistani War, 1947–1948
India v. Communist CPI, 1948–1951
Telangana rebellion and Indo-Hydrabad War/Operation Polo, 1948
Coup of Yanaon/annexation of Dadra and Nagar Haveli, 1954
Indian annexation of Goa, 1961

Sino-Indian War, 1962
Insurgency in North-East India, 1964–present*
Second Kashmir War, Indo-Pakistani War, 1964–1971
Naxalite-Maoist insurgency, 1967–present*
Attack by Naxalites in Kerala, 1968
Bangladeshi War of Independence, 1971
Indo-Pakistani War, 1971
Assam agitation, 1978–1985
India v. Sikh insurgence in Punjab, 1983–1993
Siachen conflict, India v. Pakistan, 1984–1987
Islamic insurgency and Civil War in Jammu and Kashmir (Indian Kashmir), 1989–present*

Indonesia

Indonesian National Revolution, War of Independence, 1945–1949
Darul Islam insurgency, 1949–1962
Makassar uprising, APRA *coup*, 1950
Indonesia v. Republic of South Moluccas, 1950
Permesta rebellion, 1957–1961
PRRI v. Indonesia, 1958–1961
Operation Trikora against Dutch, 1961–1962
Indonesian annexation of West Papua, 1962–1978
Irian Jaya, 1962
Indonesia-Malaysia confrontation, 1963–1966
30 September Movement, 1965
Coup and massacres, 1965–1967
Papua conflict, 1969–present*
Indonesian invasion and occupation of East Timor, 1975–1999
Insurgency in Aceh, 1976–2005
Jakarta, 1998
Conflict in the Moluccas, 1999–2002

Iran

Iran crisis, 1945–1946
Soviet occupation, 1945–1947
Pahlevi regime, 1953–1979
Kurdish revolt in Iran, 1967–1968
Iranian Revolution and overthrow of the Shah, 1978–1979
Khuzestan uprising, 1979
Kurdish rebellion in Iran, 1979–1983
Iran v. rebel groups (MEK, PJAK), 1979–present*
Nojeh *coup* plot, 1980
Iran-Iraq War, 1980–1988
Amol uprising, 1982
KDPI insurgency, 1989–1996
Iran-PJAK conflict, Kurdish separatism, 2004–present*
Sistan and Balochistan conflict, 2004–present*

Iraq

Kurds 1933, 1961–1970, 1980s
14 July Revolution (Qasim's *coup*), 1958
Mosul uprising, 1959
First Iraqi-Kurdish War, 1961–1970
Arif's two Baathist *coups*, 1963

Second Iraqi-Kurdish war, 1974–1975
PUK insurgency, 1975–1979
Saddam's *coup*, 1979
Al-Ansar insurgency, 1979–1988
Iran-Iraq War, 1980–1988
Iraq v. Shiite SCIRI, 1982–1996
Iraq v. Kurdistan (KDP/PUK), 1982–1996
Kurdish rebellion, 1983
Gulf War, 1990–1991
Shia rebellion, 1991–1993
Bombing of Iraq, 1998
US invasion, 2003
Iraq War, 2003–2011
Iraqi insurgency, 2003–present*
ISIL insurgency, 2013–present*
Civil War/military intervention against ISIL, 2014–present*

Ireland
The Troubles in Northern Ireland, 1968–1998

Israel
British Palestine, 1945–1948
Arab-Israeli War, 1948–1949
Arab-Israeli Wars, 1948–present*
Sinai War during Suez Crisis, 1956
Conflict with Palestinians, 1964–1993
Six-Day War, 1967
War of Attrition, 1967–1970
Israel v. Egypt, 1969–1970
Yom Kippur War, 1973
Lebanon, 1982–present*
Gaza, 2008–2009

Italy
Years of Lead, 1968–1982
Reggio revolt, 1970–1972

Ivory Coast
First Ivorian Civil War, 2002–2007
Second Ivorian Civil War, 2010–2011

Jamaica
Violence after election, 1980
Kingston unrest, 2010

Jordan
Arab-Israeli Wars, 1947–1973
Uprising, Black September in Jordan, 1970–1971

Kenya
Mau-Mau uprising, 1952–1960
Border conflict, 1963
Shifta War, 1963, 1967
Ethnic clash, 1992
Mount Elgon insurgency, 2005–2008

North Korea
Conflict with South Korea, 1948–present*
Korean War, 1950–1953

South Korea
Yeosu-Suncheon rebellion, 1948
Jeju uprising, 1948–1949
Pre-Korean War insurgency, 1948–1950
Korean War, 1950–1953
Gwangju uprising, 1980

Kosovo (disputed state)
Kosovo War (Yugoslavia v. NATO and UCK), 1998–1999

Kyrgyzstan
South Kyrgyzstan ethnic clashes, 2010

Laos
French Indochina, 1945–1954
Laotian Civil War, Laos v. Communist Pathet Lao, 1953–1975
Vietnam War, 1963–1975
Cambodian Civil War, 1975–1987
Insurgency in Laos, 1975–2007
Thai-Laotian Border War, 1987–1988

Lebanon
First Lebanon Civil War, 1958
Lebanon crisis, US intervention, 1958
Second Lebanese Civil War, 1975–1990
South Lebanon conflict, Israel v. PLO, 1978
Lebanon War Security Zone conflict, 1982–2000
Southern Lebanon War, 1990–2006
Civil War, 2006
Syrian Civil War, spill-over in Lebanon, 2011–present*

Liberia
First Liberian Civil War, 1989–1996
Second Liberian Civil War, 1999–2003

Libya
Libyan-Egyptian War, 1977
Uganda, 1978–1979
Chadian-Libyan conflict, 1978–1987
US attack, 1986
Kufra conflict, 2008
Libyan Civil War after NATO v. Libyan Arab Jamahiriya, 2011–present*
ISIL insurgency, 2014–present*

Macedonia
Kondovo crisis, 2004–2005

Madagascar
Madagascar rebellion, 1947

Malaysia
First Malayan Emergency, 1947–1960
War with Indonesia, 1962
Communist insurgency in Sarawak, Malaysia, 1962–1990
Second Malayan Emergency, Communist insurgency in Malaysia, 1968–1989

Mali
Tuareg rebellion, 1962–1964
Agacher Strip War, 1985
Conflict in northern Mali, 1990–present*
Mali Civil War, 2012–present*

Mauritania
Western Sahara, 1975–1978
Mauritania-Senegal Border War,

1989–1991

Mexico

Dirty War, 1970–1982

Mexican Drug War, 2006–present*

Moldova

Conflict in Transnistria, 1991–1992

Morocco

Moroccan War of Independence, 1953–1956

Ifni War, 1957–1958

Sand War, 1963

Western Sahara War, Morocco v. POLISARIO Front, 1975–1991

Mozambique

Mozambican War of Independence, Portuguese Colonial War v. FRELIMO, 1964–1974

Mozambican Civil War, 1975–1992

Mozambique v. RENAMO and FRELIMO, 1977–present*

RENAMO insurgency, 2013–present*

Myanmar (Burma)

Burmese v. separatists, Communist guerrillas, 1948–1994

Karin conflict, 1949–present*

Unrest, 1988

Nepal

Nepalese Civil War, 1996–2006

Netherlands

War of Independence against Dutch East Indies, 1945–1946

Irian Jaya, 1962

Nicaragua

War with Costa Rica, 1955

War with Honduras, 1957

Nicaraguan Revolution, 1961–1990

Civil Wars, 1972–1991

Nicaragua v. Sandinistas, 1978–1979

Nicaragua v. Contras, 1981–1990

Niger

Tuareg rebellion, 2007–2009

Nigeria

Nigerian Civil War/Biafra, 1967–1970

Muslim uprising, 1980–1984

Internal conflicts, 1990s

Boko Haram insurgency, 2009–present*

Oman

Jebel Akhdar War, 1954–1958

Dhofar rebellion, 1962–1976

Pakistan

Partition violence, 1947

Afghanistan-Pakistan skirmishes, 1949–present*

Indo-Pakistani War in Kashmir, 1965

Bengali massacres, 1971

Balochistan insurgency, Balochi/Pathan separatists, 1973–1977

Kashmir insurgency and Civil War,

1989–present*
Sindh War, 1990s
Balochistan conflict, 2003–present*
Waziristan War in North-West Pakistan, 2004–present*

Palestine (*de jure* sovereign state)
Civil War in Mandatory Palestine, 1947–1948
Israel, 1947–present*
Palestinian Fedayeen insurgency, 1949–1956
Conflict with Israel, 1964–1993
Jordan, 1970–1971
Lebanon, 1975–present*
Fatah-Hamas conflict, 2006–2011
Israel-Gaza conflict, 2008–2009, 2014

Panama
US invasion of Panama, 1989

Papua New Guinea
Irian Jaya, 1962
Bougainville Civil War, 1988–1998

Paraguay
Paraguayan Civil War v. Rebels, 1947
Stroessner regime, 1954–1989
Aché Indians, 1968–1974
Coup, 1989
Paraguayan People's Army insurgency, 2005–present*

Peru
Uprising, 1965–1966
Peru v. Shining Path (Sendero Luminoso) and MRTA, 1965–present*
Paquisha War with Ecuador, 1981
War with Ecuador, 1995–1997
Peruvian political crisis, 2009

Philippines
Huk rebellion, 1946–1954
Civil conflict/insurgency of the Communist Party of the Philippines/ Moro insurgency, 1969–present*
Rebellion in the south, 2016

Poland
Post-WW2 expulsions of Germans, 1945–1947
Poland and USSR v. Ukrainian partisans, 1945–1947
Poznań uprising, 1956

Portugal
Angola, 1961–1975
Mozambique, 1961–1975
Guinea-Bissau, 1962–1974

Romania
Romanian Revolution, 1989

Russian Federation
First Chechen War, 1994–1996
Second Chechen War, 1999–2009
War in Ingushetia, 2007–2015
Caucasus Emirate insurgency, 2007–present*
Russo-Georgian War, 2008

Rwanda

Rwanda v. Burundi, 1959–1995

First Rwandan Civil War, 1963–1964

Second Rwandan Civil War and genocide, Hutus v. Tutsis, 1990–1993

Saudi Arabia

Fighting in North Yemen Civil War, 1962–1969

Al-Wadiah War against South Yemen, 1969

Grand Mosque seizure, 1979

Senegal

Casamance conflict, 1982–present*

Senegal Civil War, 1990–2014

Mauritania-Senegal Border War, 1989–1991

Invasion of Anjouan, 2008

Serbia

Serbia v. Croatian irregulars, 1991

Serbia in Yugoslav wars, 1991–1997

Croatian War of Independence, 1991–1995

Bosnian War, 1992–1995

Kosovo War, 1998–1999

Insurgency in the Preševo Valley, 1991–2001

Sierra Leone

Ndogboyosoi War, 1982

Sierra Leone Civil War, 1991–2002

Somalia

Ogaden War, 1962–1992

Conflict with Kenya, 1963

Barre regime, 1971–1990

Ethiopian-Somali War, 1977–1978

Ethiopian-Somali Border War, 1982

Somalian Civil War, 1991–present*

Chaos, UN involvement, 1992–1995

South Africa

South Africa v. ANC, 1960–1994

Namibia, 1975–1990

Angola, 1975–1995

South Sudan

Ethnic violence in South Sudan, 2011–present*

South Sudan Civil War, 2013–present*

Spain

Basque conflict, 1959–2011

Sri Lanka

Sri Lanka v. JVP (Janatha Vimukthi Peramuna), 1971–1990

Sri Lankan Civil War, 1983–2009

JVP insurrection, 1987–1989

Sudan

First Sudanese Civil War, 1955–1972

Sudan v. Anya Nya insurgents, 1963–1972

Second Sudanese Civil War, 1983–2005

War in Darfur, 2003–present*

Sudanese nomadic conflicts, 2009–present*

Conflict in South-Koretofan and Blue Nile, Sudan v. SRF, 2011

Suriname

Suriname guerrilla war against Tucayana Amazonas, 1986–1992

Syria

Arab-Israeli Wars, 1947–1973

Syrian Baathist *coup*, 1963

Lebanon, 1976

Muslim Brotherhood Islamist uprising in Syria, 1979–1982

Syrian Civil War, spill-over in Lebanon, 2011–present*

ISIL insurgency, 2013–present*

Tajikistan

Tajikistani Civil War, 1992–1997

Tajikistan Government v. Opposition, 19922011

Tajikistan insurgency, 2010–2012

Tanzania

Zanzibar Revolution, 1964

Uganda-Tanzania War, 1978–1979

Thailand

Palace rebellion, 1949

Manhattan rebellion, 1951

South-Thailand insurgency, 1960–present*

Communist insurgency in Thailand, 1965–1983

Thailand v. CPT (Communist Party of Thailand), 1974–1982

Thai-Laotian Border War, 1987–1988

Cambodian-Thai border conflict, 2008–2012

Tunisia

Tunisian War of Independence, 1952–1956

Bizerte crisis, 1961

ISIL insurgency, 2015–present*

Turkey

Turko-Cypriot War, Turkish invasion of Northern Cyprus, 1974

Political violence in Turkey, 1976–1980

Turkish-Kurdish (PKK) conflict, 1978–present*

Maoist insurgency in Turkey, 1980–present*

Uganda

Civil War, 1966

Uganda-Tanzania War, 1978–1979

Ugandan Bush War (a.k.a. Luwero War), 1981–1986

Ugandan Civil War in north Uganda, 1980–present*

Lord's Resistance Army insurgency, 1987present*

Kasese clashes, 2016

Ukraine

Poland and USSR in West Ukraine, 1945–1947

Pro-Russian unrest in Donbass, 2014–present*

USSR

Soviet war against Baltic partisans (Estonia, Latvia, Lithuania), 1945–1951
Soviet Union and Poland v. Ukrainian partisans, 1945–1947
Occupation of Iran, 1945–1947
Soviet invasion of Hungary, 1956
Sino-Soviet War, 1963–1969
Soviet war in Afghanistan, 1979–1988

United Kingdom

Dutch East Indies, 1945–1946
Palestine, 1945–1948
Malaya, 1948–1960
Korean War, 1950–1953
Mau-Mau uprising in Kenya, 1952–1956
Suez, 1956
Cyprus, 1955–1959
Malaysia, 1962
Aden, 1963–1967
The Troubles in Northern Ireland, UK v. PIRA, 1968–1998
Falklands War, 1982

United States

Conflict with Puerto Rican Nationalist Party (Utuado and Jayuya) uprisings and San Juan Nationalist revolt, 1950
Korean War, 1950–1953
Fighting in Dominican Republic, 1961–1965
Vietnam War, 1965–1975
Lebanon, 1983
Grenada, 1983
Panama, 1989
Gulf War, 1990–1991
Kosovo, 1998
Al-Qaeda War, 2001–present*

Vietnam

War in Vietnam, 1945–1946
Indochina War, 1946–1954
Vietnam War, 1955–1975
Vietnam Civil War (phase 1), 1955–1964
Quỳnh Luu uprising, 1956
North-Vietnamese invasion of Laos, 1958–1959
FULRO (United Front for the Liberation of Oppressed Races) insurgency against Vietnam, 1964–1992
Cambodian-Vietnamese War, 1975–1989
Vietnam's invasion of Cambodia (Kampuchea) and ending of Khmer Rouge, 1978–1979
Fighting in Cambodian Civil War, 1978–1991
Sino-Vietnamese War, 1979

North Yemen (a.k.a. "Kingdom of Yemen", "Yemen Arab Republic")

Yemen Imamate Civil War (Alwaziri or Yahia clan *coup*), 1948
North Yemen Civil War, 1962–1970
NDF rebellion, 1978–1982

Yemenite War, North Yemen v. South Yemen, 1979
North Yemen v. secessionists, 1994
Houthi insurgency, 2004–2015
Yemeni Civil War, 2015–present*

South Yemen (a.k.a. "Aden", "Federation of South Arabia", "People's Republic of Southern Yemen")
Aden Emergency, British intervention, 1963–1967
Yemenite War, South Yemen v. North Yemen, 1979
South Yemen *coup* and Civil War, 1986
South Yemen insurgency, 2009–present*
Yemeni Civil War, 2015–present*

Zimbabwe
Rhodesian Bush War, 1964–1979
War with ZANU and ZAPU, 1967–1979
Entumbane uprising, 1981
Chaos, 2007

Notes:
US OEF-TS anti-drug and counter-terrorism war in Sahara/Sahel (African region) not included as its activities are within 10 trans-Saharan states, 2007–present*.

The Lord's Resistance Army insurgency and Christian cult included under Uganda but not under the other countries where it operates (South Sudan, the Central African Republic, the Democratic Republic of the Congo and Chad), 1987–present*.

C7. 37 Major Conflicts the UN Failed to Prevent after 1945: 689 UN Resolutions and 33,750,000 Deaths

(in chronological order)

Countries involved	**War(s)**	**Deaths**	**No. of UNSC Resolutions**
Israel, Egypt, Syria, Iraq, Jordan, Lebanon, Palestinians, others	Arab-Israeli conflict (1948–present)	5,000,000	221
South Korea, North Korea, People's Republic of China, United Kingdom, United States, others	Korean War (1950–1953, ceasefire)	2,300,000	5
France, National Liberation Front, Front Algérie Française	Algerian War (1954–1962)	600,000	0
Sudan, Anya Nya	First Sudanese Civil War (1955–1972)	500,000	0
United States, South Korea, South Vietnam, North Vietnam, Viet Cong	Vietnam War (1955–1975)	4,200,000	1
Congo, Zaire, South Kasai, United Nations	Congo Crisis (1960–1966)	100,000	6

Philippines, United States, New People's Army, Moro National Liberation Front, Moro Islamic Liberation Front, Abu Sayyaf, Rajah Solaiman Movement, Jemaah Islamiyah	Insurgency in the Philippines (1969–present)	200,000	0
Eritrean Liberation Front, Ethiopia, Cuba	Eritrean War of Independence (1961–1991)	700,000	0
Portugal, African independence movements	Portuguese Colonial War (1961–1974)	140,000	1
Mutawakkilite Kingdom of Yemen, Saudi Arabia, South Kasai, Yemen Arab Republic, Egypt	North Yemen Civil War (1962–1970)	120,000	2
Khmer Rouge, Khmer Republic, United States, Democratic Republic of Vietnam	Cambodian Civil War (1967–1975)	1,000,000	1
Nigeria, Republic of Benin	Nigerian Civil War (1967–1970)	1,200,000	0
Pakistan, Mukti Bahini	Bangladesh Liberation War (March–December 1971)	2,800,000	2

Lebanon, Palestine Liberation Organization, Syria, South Lebanon Army, Israel, Lebanese National Movement	Lebanese Civil War (1975–1990)	250,000	43
MPLA, UNITA, National Liberation Front of Angola, United States, Soviet Union, South Africa, Cuba, Zaire	Angolan Civil War (1975–2002)	600,000	81
FRELIMO, RENAMO, United Nations Operation in Mozambique	Mozambican Civil War (1977–1992)	900,000	3
People's Democratic Party of Afghanistan, Soviet Union, Taliban, al-Qaeda, United States, United Kingdom, Mujahideen, Iran	Civil War in Afghanistan (1978–present)	1,700,000	28
China, Vietnam	Sino-Vietnamese War (February–March 1979)	200,000	0
Iran, Iraq	Iran-Iraq War (1980–1988)	1,000,000	8
Sudan, Lord's Resistance Army, Sudan People's Liberation Army/Movement, Eastern Front (Sudan), al-Qaeda, Egypt, Libya	Second Sudanese Civil War (1983–2005)	1,900,000	7

Sri Lanka, Liberation Tigers of Tamil Eelam	Sri Lankan Civil War (1983–2009)	140,000	0
Armed Forces of Liberia, National Patriotic Front of Liberia, Independent National Patriotic Front of Liberia, United Nations, United Liberation Movement of Liberia for Democracy	First Liberian Civil War (1989–1996)	200,000	18
India, al-Qaeda, Lashkar-e-Taiba, Harkat-ul-Mujahideen, Al-Badr (India), Hizbul Mujahideen, Pakistan	Islamic Insurgency in Jammu and Kashmir (1989–present)	100,000	0
Rwandan Patriotic Front, Rwandan Defence Forces, French Army, Uganda People's Defence Force, other	Rwandan Civil War (1990–1993)	800,000	4
Iraq, Kuwait, Coalition of the Gulf War	Gulf War (August 1990–February 1991)	80,000	19
Somalia, Al-Shabaab, Ethiopia, al-Qaeda, United States, United Nations	Somali Civil War (1991–present)	400,000	54

Sierra Leone, Liberia, West Side Boys, Armed Forces Revolutionary Council, United Kingdom, other	Sierra Leone Civil War (1991–2002)	100,000	24
Federal Republic of Yugoslavia, Croatia, Croatian Republic of Herzeg-Bosnia, Republika Srpska, NATO, other	Yugoslav wars (1991–2002)	130,000	67
Algeria, France, Islamic Salvation Front, Armed Islamic Group	Algerian Civil War (1991–2002)	170,000	0
Burundi, Union for National Progress, National Forces of Liberation	Burundi Civil War (1993–2005)	300,000	0
AFDL, Zaire, Ethiopia, Uganda, Rwanda, other	First Congo War (1996–1997)	200,000	0
Liberia, Liberians United for Reconciliation and Democracy, Movement for Democracy in Liberia, Economic Community of West African States Monitoring Group	Second Liberian Civil War (1999–2003)	150,000	8
Democratic Republic of the Congo, Movement for the Liberation of Congo, Namibia, Zimbabwe, Burundi, other	Second Congo War (1998–2003)	3,900,000	22

Russia, Chechnya, Chechen Republic of Ichkeria, Arag Mujahideen in Chechnya	Second Chechen War (1999–2009)	200,000	0
International Security Assistance Force, Afghanistan, United States, United Kingdom, Taliban, al-Qaeda, Lashkar-e-Taiba, other	War in Afghanistan (2001–present)	70,000	22
Multinational Force – Iraq, United States, United Kingdom, Iraq, Armed Islamic Group, Iraqi Insurgency	Iraq War (2003–2011)	1,000,000	10
Sudan, Janjaweed, Justice and Equality Movement, Sudan Liberation Movement/Army, other	War in Darfur (2003–present)	400,000	32
TOTAL		33,750,000	689

C8. 162 Wars since 1945

(See pp.xx, 56, 89, 91, 116, 174, 195, 212)

A list of all wars in the 20th and 21st centuries, based on data by COW (Correlates of War project), PRIO (Peace Research Institute Oslo) and UCDP (Uniform Collateral Data Portal)
(in reverse chronological order)
* = ongoing, wars still being fought in 2017 (nos. 1–36 and 52)

	Name of War	Dates	Killed
1	Eastern Ukraine War	2014–2015*	4,398
2	South Sudan Civil War	2011–2015*	4,416
3	Libyan Civil War	2011–2015*	3,617
4	Syrian Civil War	2011–2017*	470,000
5	South Yemeni Civil War	2009–2015*	5,981
6	Nigerian Government v. Boko Haram	2009–2015*	13,601
7	Waziristan conflict	2007–2015*	28,542
8	Mexican Drug War	2006–2015*	11,465
9	Iraqi Insurgency	2003–2015*	46,834
10	Afghanistan War	2001–2015*	72,593
11	Turkish Government v. Kurdistan guerrillas (PPK)	1976–2015*	28,651
12	Sudan Government v. militias	1983–2015*	97,221
13	Somalian conflict and Civil War	1982–2015*	51,701
14	Russia v. Chechnyan Secessionists and the Caucasus Emirate	1994–2014*	23,389
15	Indian Government v. Maoist guerrillas	1989–2014*	7,198
16	Algerian Government v. Islamic rebels, GIA, AIS, AQIM	1991–2014*	20,658
17	Nagorno-Karabakh War and conflict	1988–2014*	5,294
18	Northern Mali conflict	1990–2014*	2,784
19	India-Pakistan dispute and intra-state insurgency in Kashmir	1984–2014*	21,929
20	Ethiopian Government v. Ogadeni rebels-WSLF/ONLF/AIAI	1976–2014*	23,382

21	Philippines Government v. Mindanao guerrillas (Moros)	1969–2014*	17,692
22	Philippines Government v. CPP (Communist Party of the Philippines) guerrillas	1969–2014*	24,804
23	Colombian Government v. FARC and ELN guerrillas	1964–2014*	26,877
24	Israel v. Palestine	1948–2014*	15,216
25	Burmese Government v. separatist guerrillas	1948–2014*	53,707
26	Sectarian conflict in the Central African Republic	2012–2013*	5,735
27	Kivu conflict in Democratic Republic of the Congo	2004–2013*	10,449
28	Lou Nuer v. Murle (Jonglei conflict) in South Sudan	2006–2013*	3,362
29	Al-Qaeda v. USA and allies in Afghanistan	2001–2013*	7,649
30	Ugandan Civil War	1980–2013*	127,566
31	Mozambique Government v. RENAMO and FRELIMO	1977–2013*	115,888
32	Ethiopia v. Oromian rebels (OLF)	1973–2013*	2,651
33	Tajikistan Government v. Opposition	1992–2011*	9,145
34	Senegal Civil War	1990–2011*	1,657
35	Iran v. rebel groups (MEK, PJAK, etc.)	1979–2011*	5,015
36	Chad Civil Wars, Muslims v. Christians	1966–2010*	36,078
37	Peruvian Government v. Sendero Luminoso and MRTA	1965–2010	17,250
38	SriLankan Government v. Tamil militants (LTTE)	1983–2009	73,818
39	Burundian Civil War	1993–2005	15,651
40	Nepalese Civil War	1996–2006	12,282
41	Southern Lebanese Wars	1985–2006	1,712
42	Indonesian Government v. Aceh Liberation Movement	1976–2005	3,184
43	Civil War in Côte d'Ivoire	2002–2007	1,371
44	Ituri conflict	1999–2007	5,826
45	Iraq v. US-led Coalition	2003–2003	7,927
46	First and Second Congo Wars	1996–2003	80,018

47	First and Second Liberian Civil Wars	1989–2003	23,249
48	First and Second Republic of the Congo Civil Wars	1993–1999	15,541
49	Angolan Government v. UNITA guerrillas	1975–2002	114,898
50	Sierra Leone Civil War	1991–2002	18,119
51	Eritrea v. Ethiopia	1998–2000	98,192
52	Afghanistan Civil War	1978–2000*	546,703
53	Yugoslavia v. NATO Forces and UCK guerrillas	1998–1999	3,613
54	Indonesian Government v. FRETILIN-East Timor	1975–1999	76,623
55	Cambodian Government v. Khmer Rouge	1979–1998	87,499
56	Northern Ireland, The Troubles	1968–1998	3,010
57	Hunde and allies v. Hutu, Banyarwanda in Democratic Republic of the Congo	1993–1996	3,938
58	Iraq v. Kurdistan (KDP/PUK)	1982–1996	20,849
59	Iraqi Government v. Shiite SCIRI	1982–1996	1,165
60	Iranian Government v. KDPI	1966–1996	2,618
61	Bosnian Government v. Serbian and Croatian insurgents	1992–1995	29,103
62	Croatia v. Serbian irregulars, Republic of Krajina	1991–1995	1,442
63	Guatemalan Civil War	1960–1996	45,392
64	North Yemen v. Secessionists	1994–1994	1,489
65	Rwandan Civil War (Hutus v. Tutsis)	1990–1993	507,754
66	Burmese Government v. Communist guerrillas	1948–1994	17,700
67	Georgian Civil War	1992–1993	2,752
68	Indian Government v. Sikh insurgents in Punjab	1983–1993	14,551
69	Serbian Government v. Croatian irregulars	1991–1991	3,933
70	First Gulf War in Iraq	1990–1991	23,946
71	El Salvador Government v. FMLN guerrillas	1979–1992	51,809
72	Ethiopian Government v. EPRDF	1974–1991	56,003
73	Ethiopia v. Eritrean separatists ELF/EPLF	1961–1991	168,510
74	Nicaraguan Government FSLN v. Contras	1981–1990	29,965
75	Lebanese Civil War	1975–1990	131,104
76	Sri Lankan Government v. JVP	1971–1990	2,018
77	Romanian Revolution	1989–1989	909

78	Panama *coup* and US invasion	1989–1989	920
79	Western Sahara War	1975–1991	12,687
80	South Africa v. ANC	1981–1989	4,087
81	Iran v. Iraq	1980–1988	644,500
82	Sino-Vietnamese War	1979–1990	47,046
83	Namibia v. South Africa	1966–1988	10,000
84	Chad-Libya War (Aouzou Strip)	1987–1987	8,500
85	South Yemen failed *coup*	1986–1986	10,000
86	Falklands War	1982–1982	964
87	Syrian Government v. Muslim Brotherhood	1979–1982	2,075
88	Thai Government v. CPT	1974–1982	3,425
89	Iranian Revolution	1978–1979	1,100
90	Uganda v. Tanzania	1978–1979	3,847
91	Nicaraguan Government v. Sandinistas	1978–1979	10,000
92	Rhodesian Government v. ZANU, ZAPU, PF	1967–1979	27,080
93	Vietnam v. Cambodia (Kampuchea)	1978–1979	32,500
94	Indonesian annexation of West Papua	1962–1978	8,700
95	Balochistan insurgency	1973–1977	8,600
96	Argentine Civil War and Dirty War	1974–1977	4,677
97	Chinese Cultural Revolution	1966–1976	2,050,000
98	Cambodian Civil War	1967–1975	250,000
99	Vietnamese War	1965–1975	2,048,050
100	Angolan War of Independence	1961–1975	79,000
101	Turko-Cypriot War	1974–1974	5,000
102	Mozambique's War of Independence	1964–1974	13,500
103	Chilean military *coup*	1973–1973	2,095
104	Yom Kippur War	1973–1973	6,450
105	Guinea-Bissau War of Independence	1963–1974	15,000
106	Laos Civil War	1953–1975	21,500
107	Hutu rebellion in Burundi	1972–1972	153,000
108	Sudanese Government v. Anya Nya insurgents	1963–1972	10,000
109	Bangladesh War	1971–1971	50,000
110	Second Kashmir War	1964–1971	16,327

111	Israel v. Egypt	1969–1970	5,520
112	Nigerian Civil War	1967–1970	75,000
113	North Yemen Civil War	1962–1970	10,000
114	First Iraqi-Kurdish War	1961–1970	6,600
115	Football War, Honduras v. El Salvador	1969–1969	2,107
116	The Six-Day War	1967–1967	5,413
117	Dominican Republic *coup*	1965–1965	4,027
118	Congo Crisis	1960–1966	7,175
119	First Rwandan Civil War	1963–1964	1,000
120	Vietnamese Civil War	1955–1964	164,923
121	Sino-Indian War	1962–1962	2,105
122	Algerian War of Independence	1954–1962	184,886
123	Bizerte crisis in Tunisia	1961–1961	1,394
124	Cameroon Government v. UPC (1955–1970)	1960–1961	60,000
125	Indonesia v. PRRI, Permesta and Darul Islam	1953–1961	33,965
126	Cuban Revolution	1953–1959	1,205
127	Mosul uprising in Iraq	1959–1959	2,000
128	Cameroon War of Independence	1955–1960	11,700
129	Tibetan uprising	1956–1959	16,000
130	First Lebanese Civil War	1958–1958	1,400
131	La Violencia in Colombia	1948–1958	29,800
132	First Malayan Civil War	1947–1960	10,845
133	Soviet invasion of Hungary	1956–1956	3,171
134	Sinai War	1956–1956	2,142
135	Kenya, Mau-Mau v. UK	1952–1960	12,955
136	Moroccan War of Independence	1953–1956	1,000
137	Tunisian War of Independence	1952–1956	2,000
138	Taiwan Strait Crisis	1954–1955	10,025
139	First Indochina War, Communists v. France	1946–1954	377,523
140	Philippines, Huk rebels v. Government	1946–1954	9,695
141	Korean War	1950–1953	995,025
142	Bolivian Revolution	1952–1952	1,000
143	Indian Government v. Communist rebels CPI	1948–1951	4,000

144	Soviet Union v. Baltic partisans in Estonia, Latvia, Lithuania ("Forest Brethren")	1945–1951	32,400
145	Indonesian Government v. Republic of South Moluccas	1950–1950	1,000
146	Third Sino-Tibetan War	1950–1950	4,000
147	Cheju rebellion in South Korea	1948–1949	17,000
148	Arab-Israeli War	1948–1949	21,111
149	Chinese Civil War	1945–1949	1,200,000
150	Greek Civil War	1946–1949	154,000
151	Yemen Imamate War	1948–1948	4,000
152	Costa Rican Civil War	1948–1948	2,000
153	First Kashmir War	1947–1948	7,500
154	Civil war in Mandatory Palestine	1947–1948	4,009
155	Indian Partition communal violence	1947–1948	200,000
156	Telangana rebellion and Indo-Hyderabad War	1947–1948	4,360
157	Madagascar rebellion	1947–1947	6,952
158	Paraguayan Government v. rebels	1947–1947	4,000
159	Taiwanese revolt	1947–1947	1,000
160	Poland and Soviet Union v. Ukrainian partisans in West Ukraine	1945–1947	59,700
161	Indonesian Independence	1945–1949	5,400
162	World War II	1939–1945	60,000,000

C9. The World's Nuclear Weapons in Early 2017

(See pp.xx, 56, 138)

1. According to the Federation of American Scientists (FAS), in early 2017 the world's deployed/non-deployed nuclear weapons totalled approximately 14,900 (of which 3,960 were deployed strategic weapons):

Country	Deployed Strategic	Reserve/ Non-deployed	Military Stockpile	Total Inventory
Russia	1,910	2,390	4,300	7,000
United States	1,650 (+150 deployed non-strategic)	2,200	4,000	6,800
France	280	10	300	300
China	0	270	270	270
United Kingdom	120	95	215	215
Israel	0	80	80	80
Pakistan	0	120–130	120–130	120–130
India	0	110–120	110–120	110–120
North Korea	0	?	?	?
Total	3,960 (+150 deployed non-strategic)	5,275–5,295 approx. 5,300	9,395–9,415 approx. 9,400	14,895–14,915 approx. 14,900

2. According to the Arms Control Association (ACA), in early 2017 the world's deployed/stockpiled nuclear weapons totalled 12,809 (of which 3,176 were deployed strategic weapons), with 5,410 nuclear weapons having been retired:

Country	**Deployed**	**Stockpiled**	**Total**	**Previously Retired**
Russia	1,765	4,500	6,265	2,510
USA	1,411	4,018	5,429	2,900
France	–	300	300	
China		260	260	
UK		215	215	
Pakistan		140	140	
India		110	110	
Israel		80	80	
DPRK (North Korea)		10	*10	
Total	3,176	9,633	12,809	5,410

* Note: in August 2017 it was reported by US intelligence sources that North Korea had 60 nuclear weapons.

D. Freedom

D1. 125 Electoral Democracies, 2017

(These are asterisked in the Freedom Ratings Table of D3)
(See pp.58, 74–75)

Albania
Andorra
Antigua and Barbuda
Argentina
Australia
Austria
Bahamas
Bangladesh
Barbados
Belgium
Belize
Benin
Bhutan
Bolivia
Bosnia and Herzegovina
Botswana
Brazil
Bulgaria
Burkina Faso
Canada
Cape Verde
Chile
Colombia
Comoros
Costa Rica
Croatia
Cyprus
Czech Republic
Denmark
Dominica
Dominican Republic
Ecuador
El Salvador
Estonia
Fiji
Finland
France
Georgia
Germany
Ghana
Greece
Grenada
Guatemala
Guyana
Hungary
Iceland
India
Indonesia
Ireland
Israel
Italy
Ivory Coast (or Côte d'Ivoire)
Jamaica
Japan
Kenya
Kiribati
Kosovo
Latvia
Lesotho
Liberia
Liechtenstein
Lithuania
Luxembourg
Madagascar
Malawi
Malta
Marshall Islands
Mauritius
Mexico
Micronesia
Moldova
Monaco
Mongolia
Montenegro
Namibia
Nauru
Nepal
Netherlands
New Zealand
Nigeria
Northern Cyprus
Norway
Pakistan

Palau
Panama
Papua New Guinea
Paraguay
Peru
Philippines
Poland
Portugal
Puerto Rico
Romania
St Kitts and Nevis
St Lucia
St Vincent and the Grenadines
Samoa
San Marino
São Tomé and Principe
Senegal
Serbia
Seychelles
Sierra Leone
Slovakia
Slovenia
Solomon Islands
South Africa
South Korea
Spain
Sri Lanka
Suriname
Sweden
Switzerland
Taiwan
Tanzania
Timor-Leste (or East Timor)
Tonga
Trinidad and Tobago
Tunisia
Tuvalu
Ukraine
United Kingdom
United States
Uruguay
Vanuatu

D2. Freedom Ratings, 2017

(See pp.74–75, 189)

Of 209 UN countries and related and disputed territories in 2017, 88 were free, 64 partly free and 57 not free.

Countries are ranked according to political rights and civil liberties on a scale from 1.0 (most free) to 7.0 (least free). The rankings can be found in the column headed Freedom Rating in D3.

The status designation of free, partly free or not free, which is determined by the combination of the political rights and civil liberties ratings, indicates the general state of freedom in a country.

Free

1.0

Andorra
Australia
Austria
Bahamas
Barbados
Belgium
Canada
Cape Verde
Chile
Costa Rica
Cyprus
Czech Republic
Denmark
Dominica
Estonia
Finland
France
Germany
Iceland
Ireland
Italy
Japan
Kiribati
Lithuania
Luxembourg
Malta
Marshall Islands
Micronesia
Netherlands
New Zealand
Norway
Palau
Portugal
St Kitts and Nevis
St Lucia
St Vincent and the Grenadines
San Marino
Slovakia
Slovenia
Spain
Sweden
Switzerland
Taiwan
Tuvalu
United Kingdom
United States
Uruguay

1.5

Belize
Croatia
Ghana
Grenada
Israel
Latvia
Liechtenstein
Mauritius
Mongolia
Poland

2.0

Antigua and Barbuda
Argentina
Benin
Brazil
Bulgaria
Greece
Monaco
Namibia
Nauru
*Northern Cyprus
Panama
Romania
Samoa
São Tomé and Principe
Senegal
South Africa
South Korea
Tonga
Trinidad and Tobago
Tunisia
Vanuatu

2.5

Botswana
El Salvador
Guyana
Hungary
India
Jamaica
Peru
Serbia
Solomon Islands
Suriname

Partly Free

3.0

Albania
Bolivia
Colombia
Dominican Republic
East Timor
Georgia
Indonesia
Lesotho
Malawi
Mexico
Moldova
Montenegro
Papua New Guinea
Paraguay
Philippines
Seychelles
Sierra Leone
Ukraine

3.5

Bhutan
Burkina Faso
Comoros
Ecuador
Fiji
*Hong Kong
*Kosovo
Liberia
†Macedonia
Madagascar
Nepal
Sri Lanka
Tanzania

4.0

Bangladesh
Bosnia and Herzegovina
Côte d'Ivoire
Guatemala
†Honduras
*Indian Kashmir
Kenya
†Malaysia
†Mozambique
†Niger
Nigeria
†Singapore
†Togo
Zambia

4.5

*Abkhazia
Armenia
Lebanon
Mali
Morocco
Nicaragua
Pakistan
Turkey

5.0

Guinea
Guinea-Bissau
Haiti
Jordan
Kuwait
Kyrgyzstan
Maldives
Myanmar
*Nagorno-Karabakh
*Somaliland
Zimbabwe

Not Free

5.5

Algeria
Brunei
Cambodia
Djibouti
Egypt
Gabon
*Gaza Strip
Iraq
Mauritania
Oman
*Pakistani Kashmir
Qatar
Thailand
Uganda
Venezuela

6.0

Afghanistan
Angola
Cameroon
Congo (Brazzaville)
Gambia
Iran
Kazakhstan
Rwanda
Swaziland
*Transnistria
United Arab Emirates
Vietnam
*West Bank

6.5

Azerbaijan
Bahrain
Belarus
Burundi
Chad
China
Congo (Kinshasa)
*Crimea
Cuba
Ethiopia
Laos
Libya
Russia
*South Ossetia
Tajikistan
Yemen

7.0

Central African Republic
Equatorial Guinea
Eritrea
North Korea
Saudi Arabia
Somalia
South Sudan
Sudan
Syria
*Tibet
Turkmenistan
Uzbekistan
*Western Sahara

* denotes related or disputed territories, as opposed to independent countries. Related and disputed territories are also ranked from 1.0 (most free) to 7.0 (least free).

† denotes not regarded as an elected democracy and therefore not on the list of D1. Puerto Rico (on the list of D1) had a rating of 1.0 until 2016 but was excluded from the freedom ratings in 2017. The 125 elected democracies of D1 are all within 1.0 and 4.0 of this list. They exclude Hong Kong and Indian Kashmir (related/disputed territories) and the countries with crosses (Macedonia, Honduras, Malaysia, Mozambique, Niger, Singapore and Togo), which are all 3.5 or 4.0 but are not regarded as electoral democracies. They include Pakistan (now 4.5) and Puerto Rico (on list D1 but not now freedom rated, see above).

D3. Freedom Ratings Table by Countries and Territories, 2017

(See pp.74–75, 189, 296, 298)

The table lists countries and territories in alphabetical order alongside ratings for political rights, civil liberties and freedom.

PR and CL stand for political rights and civil liberties, respectively; 1 represents the most free and 7 the least free rating. The ratings reflect an overall judgment based on survey results.
* indicates a country's status as an electoral democracy.

A. Independent Countries

Country	PR	CL	Freedom Rating	Freedom Status
Afghanistan	6	6	6.0	Not Free
Albania*	3	3	3.0	Partly Free
Algeria	6	5	5.5	Not Free
Andorra*	1	1	1.0	Free
Angola	6	6	6.0	Not Free
Antigua and Barbuda*	2	2	2.0	Free
Argentina*	2	2	2.0	Free
Armenia	5	4	4.5	Partly Free
Australia*	1	1	1.0	Free
Austria*	1	1	1.0	Free
Azerbaijan	7	6	6.5	Not Free
Bahamas*	1	1	1.0	Free
Bahrain	7	6	6.5	Not Free
Bangladesh*	4	4	4.0	Partly Free
Barbados*	1	1	1.0	Free
Belarus	7	6	6.5	Not Free
Belgium*	1	1	1.0	Free
Belize*	1	2	1.5	Free

Benin*	2	2	2.0	Free
Bhutan*	4	5	3.5	Partly Free
Bolivia*	3	3	3.0	Partly Free
Bosnia and Herzegovina*	4	4	4.0	Partly Free
Botswana*	3	2	2.5	Free
Brazil*	2	2	2.0	Free
Brunei	6	5	5.5	Not Free
Bulgaria*	2	2	2.0	Free
Burkina Faso*	4	3	3.5	Partly Free
Burundi	7	6	6.5	Not Free
Cambodia	6	5	5.5	Not Free
Cameroon	6	6	6.0	Not Free
Canada*	1	1	1.0	Free
Cape Verde*	1	1	1.0	Free
Central African Republic	7	7	7.0	Not Free
Chad	7	6	6.5	Not Free
Chile*	1	1	1.0	Free
China	7	6	6.5	Not Free
Colombia*	3	3	3.0	Partly Free
Comoros*	3	4	3.5	Partly Free
Congo, Democratic Republic of	7	6	6.5	Not Free
Congo, Republic of	7	5	6.0	Not Free
Costa Rica*	1	1	1.0	Free
Côte d'Ivoire*	4	4	4.0	Partly Free
Croatia*	1	2	1.5	Free
Cuba	7	6	6.5	Not Free
Cyprus*	1	1	1.0	Free
Czech Republic*	1	1	1.0	Free
Denmark*	1	1	1.0	Free
Djibouti	6	5	5.5	Not Free
Dominica*	1	1	1.0	Free
Dominican Republic*	3	3	3.0	Partly Free

East Timor (a.k.a. Timor-Leste)	3	3	3.0	Partly Free
Ecuador*	3	4	3.5	Partly Free
Egypt	6	5	5.5	Not Free
El Salvador*	2	3	2.5	Free
Equatorial Guinea	7	7	7.0	Not Free
Eritrea	7	7	7.0	Not Free
Estonia*	1	1	1.0	Free
Ethiopia	7	6	6.5	Not Free
Fiji*	3	4	3.5	Partly Free
Finland*	1	1	1.0	Free
France*	1	2	1.5	Free
Gabon	6	5	5.5	Not Free
The Gambia	6	6	6.0	Not Free
Georgia*	3	3	3.0	Partly Free
Germany*	1	1	1.0	Free
Ghana*	1	2	1.5	Free
Greece*	2	2	2.0	Free
Grenada*	1	2	1.5	Free
Guatemala*	4	4	4.0	Partly Free
Guinea	5	5	5.0	Partly Free
Guinea-Bissau	5	5	5.0	Partly Free
Guyana*	2	3	2.5	Free
Haiti	5	5	5.0	Partly Free
Honduras	4	4	4.0	Partly Free
Hungary*	3	2	2.5	Free
Iceland*	1	1	1.0	Free
India*	2	3	2.5	Free
Indonesia*	2	4	3.0	Partly Free
Iran	6	6	6.0	Not Free
Iraq	5	6	5.5	Not Free
Ireland*	1	1	1.0	Free
Israel*	1	2	1.5	Free

Italy*	1	1	1.0	Free
Jamaica*	2	3	2.5	Free
Japan*	1	1	1.0	Free
Jordan	5	5	5.0	Partly Free
Kazakhstan	7	5	6.0	Not Free
Kenya*	4	4	4.0	Partly Free
Kiribati*	1	1	1.0	Free
Kuwait	5	5	5.0	Partly Free
Kyrgyzstan	5	5	5.0	Partly Free
Laos	7	6	6.5	Not Free
Latvia*	1	2	1.5	Free
Lebanon	5	4	4.5	Partly Free
Lesotho*	3	3	3.0	Free
Liberia*	3	4	3.5	Partly Free
Libya	7	6	6.5	Not Free
Liechtenstein*	2	1	1.5	Free
Lithuania*	1	1	1.0	Free
Luxembourg*	1	1	1.0	Free
Macedonia	4	3	3.5	Partly Free
Madagascar*	3	4	3.5	Partly Free
Malawi*	3	3	3.0	Partly Free
Malaysia	4	4	4.0	Partly Free
Maldives	5	5	5.0	Partly Free
Mali	5	4	4.5	Partly Free
Malta*	1	1	1.0	Free
Marshall Islands*	1	1	1.0	Free
Mauritania	6	5	5.5	Not Free
Mauritius*	1	2	1.5	Free
Mexico*	3	3	3.0	Partly Free
Micronesia*	1	1	1.0	Free
Moldova*	3	3	3.0	Partly Free
Monaco*	3	1	2.0	Free

Mongolia*	1	2	1.5	Free
Montenegro*	3	3	3.0	Partly Free
Morocco	5	4	4.5	Partly Free
Mozambique	4	4	4.0	Partly Free
Myanmar	5	5	5.0	Partly Free
Namibia*	2	2	2.0	Free
Nauru*	2	2	2.0	Free
Nepal*	3	4	3.5	Partly Free
Netherlands*	1	1	1.0	Free
New Zealand*	1	1	1.0	Free
Nicaragua	5	4	4.5	Partly Free
Niger	4	4	4.0	Partly Free
Nigeria*	3	5	4.0	Partly Free
North Korea	7	7	7.0	Not Free
Norway*	1	1	1.0	Free
Oman	6	5	5.5	Not Free
Pakistan*	4	5	4.5	Partly Free
Palau*	1	1	1.0	Free
Panama*	2	2	2.0	Free
Papua New Guinea*	3	3	3.0	Partly Free
Paraguay*	3	3	3.0	Partly Free
Peru*	2	3	2.5	Free
Philippines*	3	3	3.0	Partly Free
Poland*	1	2	1.5	Free
Portugal*	1	1	1.0	Free
Qatar	6	5	5.5	Not Free
Romania*	2	2	2.0	Free
Russia	7	6	6.5	Not Free
Rwanda	6	6	6.0	Not Free
Samoa*	2	2	2.0	Free
San Marino*	1	1	1.0	Free
São Tomé and Príncipe*	2	2	2.0	Free

Saudi Arabia	7	7	7.0	Not Free
Senegal*	2	2	2.0	Free
Serbia*	3	2	2.5	Free
Seychelles*	3	3	3.0	Partly Free
Sierra Leone*	3	3	3.0	Partly Free
Singapore	4	4	4.0	Partly Free
Slovakia*	1	1	1.0	Free
Slovenia*	1	1	1.0	Free
Solomon Islands*	3	2	2.5	Free
Somalia	7	7	7.0	Not Free
South Africa*	2	2	2.0	Free
South Korea*	2	2	2.0	Free
South Sudan	7	7	7.0	Not Free
Spain*	1	1	1.0	Free
Sri Lanka*	3	4	3.5	Partly Free
St Kitts and Nevis*	1	1	1.0	Free
St Lucia*	1	1	1.0	Free
St Vincent and the Grenadines*	2	1	1.0	Free
Sudan	7	7	7.0	Not Free
Suriname*	2	3	2.5	Free
Swaziland	7	5	6.0	Not Free
Sweden*	1	1	1.0	Free
Switzerland*	1	1	1.0	Free
Syria	7	7	7.0	Not Free
Taiwan*	1	1	1.0	Free
Tajikistan	7	6	6.5	Not Free
Tanzania*	3	4	3.5	Partly Free
Thailand	6	5	5.5	Not Free
Togo	4	4	4.0	Partly Free
Tonga*	2	2	2.0	Free
Trinidad and Tobago*	2	2	2.0	Free
Tunisia*	1	3	2.0	Free

Turkey	4	5	4.5	Partly Free
Turkmenistan	7	7	7.0	Not Free
Tuvalu*	1	1	1.0	Free
Uganda	6	5	5.5	Not Free
Ukraine*	3	3	3.0	Partly Free
United Arab Emirates	6	6	6.0	Not Free
United Kingdom*	1	1	1.0	Free
United States*	1	1	1.0	Free
Uruguay*	1	1	1.0	Free
Uzbekistan	7	7	7.0	Not Free
Vanuatu*	2	2	2.0	Free
Venezuela	6	5	5.5	Not Free
Vietnam	7	5	6.0	Not Free
Yemen	7	6	6.5	Not Free
Zambia	4	4	4.0	Partly Free
Zimbabwe	5	5	5.0	Partly Free

B. Related Territories

Country and Territory	**PR**	**CL**	**Freedom Rating**	**Freedom Status**
China Hong Kong	5	2	3.5	Partly Free
United States Puerto Rico*	–	–	–	Free

Note: Puerto Rico excluded from 2017 freedom ratings

C. Disputed Territories

Country and Territory	PR	CL	Freedom Rating	Freedom Status
Armenia/Azerbaijan				
Nagorno-Karabakh	5	5	5.0	Partly Free
China				
Tibet	7	7	7.0	Not Free
Ukraine/Russia				
Crimea	7	6	6.5	Not Free
Cyprus				
Northern (Turkish) Cyprus*	2	2	2.0	Free
Georgia				
Abkhazia	4	5	4.5	Partly Free
South Ossetia	7	6	6.5	Not Free
India				
Jammu and Kashmir	4	4	4.0	Partly Free
Israel				
Israeli-Occupied Territories	7	5	6.0	Not Free
West Bank (PA)				
Palestinian Authority-Administered Territories	7	6	5.5	Not Free
Gaza Strip (PA)				
Moldova				
Transnistria	6	6	6.0	Not Free
Morocco				
Western Sahara	7	7	7.0	Not Free
Azerbaijan				
Nagorno-Karabakh	5	5	5.0	Partly Free
Pakistan				
Azad Kashmir	6	5	5.5	Not Free

Russia Chechnya	–	–	–	Not Free
Serbia Kosovo*	3	4	3.5	Partly Free
Somalia Somaliland	5	5	5.0	Partly Free

Note: Chechnya excluded from 2017 freedom ratings

D4. The World's 59 Dictators, 2017

(See p.76)

A "dictator" is a head of state who exercises arbitrary authority over the lives of his citizens and who cannot be removed from power by legal means. The worst dictators commit terrible human-rights abuses. This list draws in part on reports by global human-rights organisations.

	Nation-state	**Dictator**
1	Afghanistan	Ashraf Ghani Ahmadzai
2	Algeria	Abdelaziz Bouteflika
3	Angola	José Eduardo dos Santos
4	Azerbaijan	Ilham Aliyev
5	Bahrain	Hamad bin Isa Al Khalifa
6	Belarus	Alexander Lukashenko
7	Brunei	Haji Hassanal Bolkiah Mu'izzaddin Waddaulah
8	Burundi	Pierre Nkurunziza
9	Cambodia	Hun Sen
10	Cameroon	Paul Biya
11	Central African Republic	Faustin-Archange Touadéra
12	Chad	Idriss Déby
13	China	Xi Jinping
14	Republic of Congo	Joseph Kabila
15	*Crimea	Sergey Valeryevich Aksyonov
16	Cuba	Raúl Castro
17	Djibouti	Ismaïl Omar Guelleh
18	Egypt	Abdel Fattah el-Sisi
19	Equatorial Guinea	Teodoro Obiang Nguema Mbasogo
20	Eritrea	Isaias Afwerki
21	Ethiopia	Hailemariam Desalegn

22	Gabon	Ali Bongo Ondimba is the current President of Gabon
23	Gambia	Adama Barrow
24	*Gaza Strip	Khaled Mashal
25	Iran	Hassan Rouhani
26	Iraq	Muhammad Fuad Masum
27	Kazakhstan	Nursultan Nazarbayev
28	Laos	Bounnhang Vorachith
29	Libya	Nouri Abusahmain
30	Mauritania	Mohamed Ould Abdel Aziz
31	Myanmar	Htin Kyaw
32	North Korea	Kim Jong-un
33	Oman	Qaboos bin Said Al Said
34	*Pakistani Kashmir	Masood Khan
35	Qatar	Sheikh Tamim bin Hamad Al Thani
36	Republic of Congo	Denis Sassou Nguesso
37	Russia	Vladimir Putin
38	Rwanda	Paul Kagame
39	Saudi Arabia	King Salman bin Abdulaziz al-Saud
40	Somalia	Mohamed Abdullahi Mohamed
41	*South Ossetia	Anatoliy Bibilov
42	South Sudan	Salva Kiir Mayardit
43	Sudan	Omar Hassan Ahmad al-Bashir
44	Swaziland	Mswati III
45	Syria	Bashar Hafez al-Assad
46	Tajikistan	Emomali Rahmon
47	Thailand	Prayut Chan-o-cha
48	*Tibet	Che Dalha (Chairman)
49	*Transnistria	Vadim Krasnoselsky
50	Turkmenistan	Gurbanguly Berdimuhamedow
51	Uganda	Yoweri Museveni

52	United Arab Emirates	Sheikh Khalifa bin Zayed Al Nahyan
53	Uzbekistan	Shavkat Mirziyoyev
54	Venezuela	Nicolás Maduro
55	Vietnam	Tran Dai Quang
56	*West Bank	Mahmoud Abbas
57	*Western Sahara (Saharan Arab Democratic Republic)	Brahim Ghali
58	Yemen	Abdrabbuh Mansur Hadi
59	Zimbabwe	Robert Gabriel Mugabe

All the above nation-states were not free in 2017 except for Myanmar and Zimbabwe, which were partly free (both 5.0).

* denotes related or disputed territories, as opposed to independent countries. All are listed as not free in D2.

This list includes the 57 not-free nation-states of D2, plus Myanmar and Zimbabwe, both partly free and 5.0 but still regarded as dictatorships.

E. Regions and Nation-States

E1. Regional Populations as Percentages of World Population, 2017

(See pp.166, 175)

Region	Per cent of Global Population
Asia (including Middle East)	59.6%
Europe	9.8%
North America	4.8%
Latin America/Caribbean	8.6%
Africa	16.6%
Oceania/Australia	0.5%

Note:

Approximate percentages, which total 99.9%

E2. Historical and Predicted Regional Populations as Percentages of World Population

(See pp.166, 175)

World historical and predicted populations (in millions)

Region	1750	1800	1850	1900	1950	1999	2008	2050	2150
World	791	978	1,262	1,650	2,521	5,978	6,707	8,909	9,746
Africa	106	107	111	133	221	767	973	1,766	2,308
Asia	502	635	809	947	1,402	3,634	4,054	5,268	5,561
Europe	163	203	276	408	547	729	732	628	517
Latin America and the Carib-bean	16	24	38	74	167	511	577	809	912
Northern America	2	7	26	82	172	307	337	392	398
Oceania	2	2	2	6	13	30	34	46	51

World historical and predicted populations by percentage distribution

Region	1750	1800	1850	1900	1950	1999	2008	2050	2150
World	100	100	100	100	100	100	100	100	100
Africa	13.4	10.9	8.8	8.1	8.8	12.8	14.5	19.8	23.7
Asia	63.5	64.9	64.1	57.4	55.6	60.8	60.4	59.1	57.1
Europe	20.6	20.8	21.9	24.7	21.7	12.2	10.9	7.0	5.3
Latin America and the Carib-bean	2.0	2.5	3.0	4.5	6.6	8.5	8.6	9.1	9.4
Northern America	0.3	0.7	2.1	5.0	6.8	5.1	5.0	4.4	4.1
Oceania	0.3	0.2	0.2	0.4	0.5	0.5	0.5	0.5	0.5

E3. Nation-States' Populations as Percentages of World Population, 2017

(See pp.161, 166, 175)

The table below is based on the 2016 projections by the United Nations Department of Economic and Social Affairs – Population Division.

Letter on pp. 167-170	Rank	Country/ Territory	Population	Date Last-Updated	Approx % of World-Popu-lation	Source
		World	7,504,975,600	May 16, 2017	100%	US Census – International Programs Department
A	1	China	1,383,200,000	May 16, 2017	18.4%	Chinese population clock
A	2	India	1,315,960,000	May 16, 2017	17.5%	Indian population clock
A	3	United States	324,977,000	May 16, 2017	4.33%	USA population clock
C	4	Indonesia	263,510,000	July 1, 2017	3.51%	UN projection
C	5	Brazil	207,501,000	May 16, 2017	2.76%	Brazilian population clock
C	6	Pakistan	196,448,000	May 16, 2017	2.62%	Pakistani population clock
C	7	Nigeria	191,836,000	July 1, 2017	2.56%	UN projection
C	8	Bangladesh	162,453,000	May 16, 2017	2.16%	Bangladesh population clock

B	9	Russia	146,804,372	Jan 1, 2017	1.96%	Russian estimate
C	10	Japan	126,790,000	April 1, 2017	1.69%	Monthly provisional Japanese estimate
C	11	Mexico	123,518,000	July 1, 2017	1.65%	Official Mexican projection
C	12	Ethiopia	104,345,000	July 1, 2017	1.39%	UN projection
C	13	Philippines	104,032,000	May 16, 2017	1.39%	Philippines population clock
C	14	Egypt	93,007,400	May 16, 2017	1.24%	Egyptian population clock
D	15	Vietnam	92,700,000	July 1, 2016	1.24%	Annual official projection
A	16	Germany	82,800,000	Dec 31, 2016	1.1%	Provisional German annual estimate
D	17	Democratic Republic of Congo	82,243,000	July 1, 2017	1.1%	UN projection
D	18	Iran	80,133,000	May 16, 2017	1.07%	Iranian population clock
D	19	Turkey	79,814,871	Dec 31, 2016	1.06%	Annual Turkish estimate
D	20	Thailand	68,298,000	July 1, 2017	0.91%	UN projection
B	21	France	67,013,000	April 1, 2017	0.89%	Monthly French estimate
B	22	United Kingdom	65,110,000	June 30, 2015	0.87%	Annual UK estimate

A	23	Italy	60,599,936	Nov 30, 2016	0.81%	Italian estimate
D	24	Tanzania	56,878,000	July 1, 2017	0.76%	UN projection
D	25	South Africa	55,908,000	Jul 1, 2016	0.74%	An-nual South African estimate
D	26	Myanmar (Burma)	54,836,000	July 1, 2017	0.73%	UN projection
D	27	South Korea	51,446,201	July 1, 2017	0.69%	Annual South Korean estimate
D	28	Colombia	49,223,200	May 16, 2017	0.656%	Colombian population clock
D	29	Kenya	48,467,000	July 1, 2017	0.65%	UN projection
A	30	Spain	46,812,000	July 1, 2016	0.62%	Spanish estimate
D	31	Argentina	43,850,000	July 1, 2016	0.58%	Annual Argentine projection
D	32	Ukraine	42,541,633	March 1, 2017	0.57%	Monthly Ukrainian estimate
D	33	Sudan	42,176,000	July 1, 2017	0.56%	UN projection
D	34	Uganda	41,653,000	July 1, 2017	0.56%	UN projection
E	35	Algeria	41,064,000	July 1, 2017	0.55%	UN projection
A	36	Poland	38,424,000	Jan 1, 2017	0.51%	Polish estimate
E	37	Iraq	37,883,543	July 1, 2016	0.5%	Annual Iraqi projection

E	38	Canada	36,540,100	May 16, 2017	0.48%	Canadian estimate
E	39	Morocco	34,316,500	May 16, 2017	0.457%	Annual Moroccan projection
E	40	Saudi Arabia	33,710,021	July 1, 2017	0.45%	Saudi Arabian estimate
E	41	Uzbekistan	32,121,000	Jan 1, 2017	0.43%	Uzbekistani population report
E	42	Malaysia	32,062,000	May 16, 2017	0.427%	Malaysian population clock
E	43	Peru	31,826,018	Jul 1, 2017	0.42%	Annual Peruvian projection
E	44	Venezuela	31,431,164	Jul 1, 2017	0.42%	Annual Venezuelan projection
E	45	Nepal	28,825,709	Jul 1, 2017	0.38%	Annual Nepalese projection
E	46	Angola	28,359,634	Jan 1, 2017	0.38%	Angolan estimate
E	47	Ghana	28,308,301	Jul 1, 2016	0.38%	Annual Ghanaian projection
E	48	Yemen	28,120,000	Jul 1, 2017	0.37%	UN projection
E	49	Afghanistan	27,657,145	Jul 1, 2016	0.37%	Annual Afghanistan-ian estimate
E	50	Mozam-bique	27,128,530	Jul 1, 2017	0.36%	Annual Mozambican projection
E	51	Australia	24,459,900	May 16, 2017	0.326%	Australian population clock
E	52	North Korea	24,213,510	Oct 1, 2014	0.32%	2014 census

E	–	Taiwan (China, disputed)	23,545,680	Mar 1, 2017	0.31%	Monthly Taiwanese estimate
E	53	Cameroon	23,248,044	Jan 1, 2017	0.31%	Annual Cameroonian projection
E	54	Côte d'Ivoire	22,671,331	May 15, 2014	0.30%	2014 census
F	55	Madagascar	22,434,363	Jul 1, 2014	0.30%	Madagascar-ian estimate
F	56	Niger	21,564,000	Jul 1, 2017	0.29%	UN projection
F	57	Sri Lanka	21,203,000	Jul 1, 2016	0.28%	Sri Lankan estimate
A	58	Romania	19,760,000	Jan 1, 2016	0.26%	Annual Romanian estimate
F	59	Burkina Faso	19,632,147	Jul 1, 2017	0.26%	Annual Burkina Faso projection
F	60	Syria	18,907,000	Jul 1, 2017	0.25%	UN projection
F	61	Mali	18,875,000	Jul 1, 2017	0.25%	An-nual Malian projection
F	62	Malawi	18,299,000	Jul 1, 2017	0.244%	UN projection
F	63	Chile	18,191,900	Jul 1, 2016	0.24%	Annual Chilean projection
F	64	Kazakhstan	17,975,800	Apr 1, 2017	0.24%	Kazakhstan-ian estimate
A	65	Netherlands	17,121,700	May 16, 2017	0.228%	Dutch population clock
F	66	Ecuador	16,737,100	May 16, 2017	0.223%	Ecuadorian population clock

F	67	Guatemala	16,176,133	Jul 1, 2015	0.22%	Guatemalan estimate
F	68	Zambia	15,933,883	Jul 1, 2016	0.21%	Annual Zambian projection
F	69	Cambodia	15,626,444	Jul 1, 2016	0.21%	Annual Cambodian projection
F	70	Senegal	15,256,346	Jan 1, 2017	0.20%	Annual Senegalese projection
F	71	Chad	14,965,000	Jul 1, 2017	0.20%	UN projection
F	72	Zimbabwe	14,542,235	Jul 1, 2017	0.19%	Annual Zimbabwean projection
K	–	Indian Kashmir (Jammu and Kashmir)	14,280,373	2017	–	Indian census
F	73	Guinea	13,291,000	Jul 1, 2017	0.18%	UN projection
F	74	South Sudan	12,131,000	Jul 1, 2016	0.16%	Anual South Sudanese projection
F	75	Rwanda	11,553,188	Jul 1, 2016	0.15%	Rwandan projection
A	76	Belgium	11,356,191	Mar 1, 2017	0.15%	Monthly Belgian estimate
F	77	Tunisia	11,299,400	Jul 1, 2016	0.15%	Tunisian estimate
F	78	Cuba	11,239,004	Dec 31, 2015	0.15%	Annual Cuban estimate
F	79	Bolivia	11,145,770	Jul 1, 2017	0.15%	Bolivian estimate
F	80	Somalia	11,079,000	Jul 1, 2016	0.15%	UN projection

F	81	Haiti	11,078,033	Jul 1, 2016	0.15%	Haitian projection
A	82	Greece	10,783,748	Jan 1, 2016	0.14%	Greek estimate
F	83	Benin	10,653,654	Jul 1, 2016	0.14%	Beninese projection
A	84	Czech Republic	10,578,820	Dec 31, 2016	0.14%	Czech quarterly estimate
A	85	Portugal	10,341,330	Dec 31, 2015	0.14%	Portuguese annual estimate
F	86	Burundi	10,114,505	Jul 1, 2016	0.13%	Burundian annual projection
F	87	Dominican Republic	10,075,045	Jul 1, 2016	0.13%	Dominican Republic projection
A	88	Sweden	10,053,700	May 16, 2017	0.13%	Swedish population clock
F	89	United Arab Emirates	10,003,223	May 6, 2017	0.13%	UAE annual projection
F	90	Jordan	9,888,600	May 16, 2017	0.13%	Jordanian population clock
F	91	Azerbaijan	9,823,667	Mar 1, 2017	0.13%	Azerbaijanian estimate
A	92	Hungary	9,799,000	Jan 1, 2017	0.13%	Hungarian estimate
G	93	Belarus	9,498,600	Apr 1, 2017	0.127%	Belarusian quarterly estimate
G	94	Honduras	8,866,351	Jul 1, 2017	0.118%	Honduran annual projection
A	95	Austria	8,773,585	Jan 1, 2017	0.117%	Austrian quarterly estimate

G	96	Tajikistan	8,742,000	Jan 1, 2017	0.116%	Tajikistanian estimate
G	97	Israel	8,689,760	May 16, 2017	0.116%	Israeli population clock
G	98	Switzerland	8,417,700	Dec 31, 2016	0.112%	Swiss quarterly estimate
G	99	Papua New Guinea	8,151,300	Jul 1, 2016	0.109%	Papua New Guinean annual estimate
A	–	Hong Kong (China)	7,374,900	Dec 31, 2016	0.098%	Hong Kong estimate
G	100	Togo	7,143,000	Jul 1, 2016	0.095%	Togoese estimate
A	101	Bulgaria	7,101,859	Dec 31, 2016	0.095%	Bulgarian estimate
G	102	Serbia	7,076,372	Jan 1, 2016	0.094%	Serbian annual estimate
G	103	Sierra Leone	7,075,641	Dec 4, 2015	0.094%	2015 census
G	104	Paraguay	6,953,646	Jan 1, 2017	0.093%	Paraguayan estimate
G	105	El Salvador	6,581,940	Jul 1, 2017	0.088%	El Salvadorian projection
G	106	Laos	6,492,400	Mar 1, 2015	0.087%	2015 census
G	107	Libya	6,385,000	Jul 1, 2016	0.085%	Libyan annual projection
K	–	Tibet	6,282,187	2010	–	2010 Chinese census
G	108	Nicaragua	6,262,703	Jan 1, 2015	0.083%	Nicaraguan estimate
G	109	Kyrgyzstan	6,140,200	Jan 1, 2017	0.082%	Kyrgyzstan estimate
G	110	Lebanon	5,988,000	Jul 1, 2016	0.08%	UN projection

A	111	Denmark	5,756,170	Mar 31, 2017	0.077%	Danish quarterly estimate
G	112	Singapore	5,607,300	Jul 1, 2016	0.075%	Singaporean estimate
A	113	Finland	5,503,879	Feb 28, 2017	0.073%	Finnish monthly estimate
G	114	Eritrea	5,482,000	Jul 1, 2017	0.073%	UN projection
A	115	Slovakia	5,435,343	Dec 31, 2016	0.072%	Slovakian estimate
G	116	Norway	5,258,317	Jan 1, 2017	0.07%	Norwegian quarterly estimate
G	117	Central African Republic	5,099,000	Jul 1, 2017	0.068%	UN projection
G	118	Costa Rica	4,890,379	Jun 30, 2016	0.065%	Costa Rican estimate
I	119	Palestine	4,816,503	Jul 1, 2016	0.064%	Palestinian estimate
G	120	New Zealand	4,786,060	May 16, 2017	0.0638%	New Zealand population clock
A	121	Ireland	4,757,976	Jul 14, 2016	0.063%	2016 census
G	122	Turkmeni-stan	4,751,120	Dec 26, 2012	0.063%	2012 census
G	123	Republic of the Congo	4,741,000	Jul 1, 2016	0.063%	UN projection
K	–	Pakistani Kashmir (Azad Kashmir)	4,600,000	2016	–	Pakistani estimate
G	124	Oman	4,573,075	Feb 1, 2017	0.061%	Omani estimate

A	125	Croatia	4,190,669	Dec 31, 2015	0.056%	Croatian annual estimate
G	126	Kuwait	4,183,658	Jun 30, 2015	0.056%	Kuwaiti estimate
G	127	Liberia	4,076,530	Jul 1, 2016	0.054%	Liberian projection
G	128	Panama	3,814,672	Jul 1, 2016	0.051%	Panama estimate
G	129	Mauritania	3,718,678	Jul 1, 2016	0.050%	Mauritanian annual projection
G	130	Georgia	3,718,200	Jan 1, 2017	0.050%	Georgian annual estimate
G	131	Moldova	3,550,900	Jan 1, 2017	0.047%	Moldovan estimate
G	132	Bosnia and Herzegovina	3,531,159	Oct 15, 2013	0.047%	2013 census
G	133	Uruguay	3,480,222	Jun 30, 2016	0.046%	Uruguayan annual estimate
I	–	Puerto Rico (US)	3,411,307	Jul 1, 2016	0.045%	Puerto Rican estimate
G	134	Mongolia	3,147,525	May 16, 2017	0.042%	Mongolian population clock
G	135	Armenia	2,986,500	Jan 1, 2017	0.04%	Armenian quarterly estimate
G	136	Albania	2,876,591	Jan 1, 2017	0.038%	Albanian annual estimate
A	137	Lithuania	2,831,670	Apr 1, 2017	0.038%	Lithuanian monthly estimate
G	138	Jamaica	2,723,246	Dec 31, 2014	0.036%	Jamaican estimate

G	139	Qatar	2,576,181	Jan 31, 2017	0.034%	Qatari monthly estimate
G	140	Namibia	2,324,388	Jul 1, 2016	0.031%	Namibian projection
H	141	Botswana	2,230,905	Jul 1, 2016	0.030%	Botswa-nan annual projection
H	142	Republic of Macedonia	2,071,278	Dec 31, 2015	0.028%	Macedonian estimate
A	143	Slovenia	2,064,241	Jul 1, 2016	0.028%	Slovenian estimate
A	144	Latvia	1,945,500	Apr 1, 2017	0.026%	Latvian monthly estimate
H	145	Lesotho	1,916,000	Jul 1, 2014	0.026%	Lesotho estimate
H	146	Gambia	1,882,450	Apr 15, 2013	0.025%	2013 census
K	–	Kosovo	1,836,978	Jan 1, 2016	0.024%	Kosovo projection
H	147	Gabon	1,811,079	Jun 2, 2016	0.024%	Gabon estimate
H	148	Guinea-Bissau	1,547,777	Jul 1, 2016	0.021%	Guinea-Bissau projection
H	149	Bahrain	1,404,900	Jul 1, 2016	0.019%	Bahrain annual projection
K	–	Chechnya	1,395.678	Jan 2016	–	Chechnyan estimate
H	150	Trinidad and Tobago	1,353,895	Jul 1, 2016	0.018%	Trinidad and Tobago estimate
A	151	Estonia	1,317,797	Jan 1, 2017	0.018%	Estonian estimate
H	152	Mauritius	1,263,747	Jul 1, 2016	0.017%	Mauritian estimate

H	153	Equatorial Guinea	1,222,442	Jul 4, 2015	0.016%	2015 census
H	154	East Timor	1,167,242	Jul 11, 2015	0.016%	2015 census
H	155	Swaziland	1,132,657	Jul 1, 2016	0.015%	Swaziland projection
A	156	Cyprus	938,400	Nov 2015	0.013%	Cypriot estimate
H	157	Djibouti	900,000	Jul 1, 2016	0.012%	UN projection
H	158	Fiji	869,458	Jul 1, 2015	0.0116%	Fijian annual estimate
H	159	Comoros	806,153	Jul 1, 2016	0.011%	Comoros estimate
H	160	Bhutan	786,820	May 16, 2017	0.0105%	Bhutanese population clock
H	161	Guyana	746,900	Jul 1, 2013	0.01%	Guyanese estimate
J	–	Macau (China)	644,900	Dec 30, 2016	0.009%	Macau quarterly etimate
H	162	Solomon Islands	642,000	Jul 1, 2015	0.009%	Solomon Islands annual estimate
H	163	Montenegro	626,388	Apr 29, 2017	0.008%	Montenegro estimate
A	164	Luxembourg	590,667	Jan 1, 2017	0.0079%	Luxembourg population clock
J	–	Western Sahara	584,000	Jul 1, 2016	0.0078%	UN projection
H	165	Suriname	541,638	Aug 13, 2012	0.0072%	2012 census
H	166	Cape Verde	531,239	Jul 1, 2016	0.0071%	Cape Verde annual projection
K	–	Transnistria	475,665	Oct 15, 2015	0.0060%	2015 census

A	167	Malta	429,344	Dec 31, 2014	0.0057%	Maltese estimate
H	168	Brunei	417,200	Jul 1, 2015	0.0056%	Brunei estimate
H	169	Belize	380,010	Oct 1, 2016	0.0051%	Belize estimate
H	170	Bahamas	378,040	Jul 1, 2016	0.0050%	Bahaman projection
H	171	Maldives	344,023	Sep 20, 2014	0.0046%	2014 census
H	172	Iceland	340,110	Mar 31, 2017	0.0045%	Icelandic quarterly estimate
H	–	Northern Cyprus	313,626	June 30, 2014	0.0042%	Northern Cypriot estimate
H	173	Barbados	285,000	Jul 1, 2016	0.0038%	UN projection
H	174	Vanuatu	277,500	Jul 1, 2015	0.0037%	Vanuatu annual estimate
J	–	French Polynesia (France)	271,800	Dec 31, 2014	0.0036%	French Polynesian estimate
J	–	New Caledonia (France)	268,767	Aug 26, 2014	0.0036%	2014 census
K	–	Abkhazia	240,705	Feb 28, 2011	0.0032%	2011 census
H	175	Samoa	194,899	Jan 1, 2016	0.0026%	Samoan projection
H	176	São Tomé and Principe	187,356	May 13, 2012	0.0025%	2012 census
H	177	Saint Lucia	186,000	Jul 1, 2016	0.0025%	UN projection
J	–	Guam (US)	184,200	Jul 1, 2015	0.0025%	Guam annual estimate

J	–	Curaçao (Netherlands)	158,986	Jan 1, 2016	0.0021%	Curaçao annual estimate
K	–	Nagorno-Karabakh Republic	150,932	Dec 1, 2015	0.0020%	2015 census
H	178	Kiribati	113,400	Jul 1, 2015	0.0015%	Kiribati annual estimate
J	–	Aruba (Netherlands)	110,108	Dec 31, 2015	0.0015%	Aruba quarterly estimate
H	179	St Vincent and the Grenadines	109,991	Jun 12, 2012	0.0015%	2012 census
J	–	American Virgin Islands (US)	106,000	Jul 1, 2016	0.0014%	UN projection
H	180	Grenada	103,328	May 12, 2011	0.0014%	2011 census
H	181	Tonga	103,252	Nov 30, 2011	0.0014%	2011 census
H	182	Federated States of Micronesia	102,800	Jul 1, 2015	0.0014%	Micronesian annual estimate
J	–	Jersey (UK)	102,700	Dec 31, 2015	0.0014%	Jersey annual estimate
H	183	Seychelles	94,677	Jun 30, 2016	0.0013%	Seychelles estimate
H	184	Antigua and Barbuda	86,295	May 27, 2011	0.0011%	2011 census
J	–	Isle of Man (UK)	84,497	Mar 27, 2011	0.0011%	2011 census
H	185	Andorra	78,014	Dec 31, 2015	0.001%	Andorran annual estimate
H	186	Dominica	71,293	May 14, 2011	0.00095%	2011 census
J	–	Guernsey (UK)	62,723	Mar 31, 2016	0.00084%	Guernsey estimate

J	–	Bermuda (UK)	61,954	Jul 1, 2013	0.00083%	Bermudan estimate
J	–	Cayman Islands (UK)	60,413	Dec 31, 2015	0.00080%	Cayman Islands estimate
J	–	American Samoa (US)	57,100	Jul 1, 2015	0.00076%	American Samoan annual estimate
J	–	Northern Mariana Islands (US)	56,940	Jul 1, 2015	0.00076%	Northern Mariana Islands annual estimate
J	–	Greenland (Denmark)	56,186	Jul 1, 2016	0.00075%	Greenland annual estimate
H	187	Marshall Islands	54,880	Jul 1, 2015	0.00073%	Marshall Islands annual estimate
K	–	South Ossetia	53,532	Oct 15, 2015	0.00071%	2015 census
J	–	Faroe Islands (Denmark)	49,994	Mar 1, 2017	0.00067%	Faroe Islands monthly estimate
H	188	St Kitts and Nevis	46,204	May 15, 2011	0.00062%	2011 census
J	–	Sint Maarten (Netherlands)	39,410	Jan 1, 2016	0.00053%	Sint Maarten estimate
H	189	Liechtenstein	37,815	Dec 31, 2016	0.0005%	Liechtenstein semi-annual estimate
H	190	Monaco	37,550	Dec 31, 2016	0.0005%	Monaco annual estimate
J	–	Saint-Martin (France)	36,457	Jan 1, 2015	0.00049%	Saint-Martin annual estimate
J	–	Gibraltar (UK)	33,140	Dec 31, 2014	0.00044%	Gibraltar annual estimate

H	191	San Marino	33,121	Sep 30, 2016	0.00044%	San Marino monthly estimate
J	–	Turks and Caicos Islands (UK)	31,458	Jan 25, 2012	0.00042%	2012 census
J	–	British Virgin Islands (UK)	28,514	Jul 1, 2013	0.00038%	British Virgin Islands estimate
J	–	Bonaire (Netherlands)	18,905	Jan 1, 2015	0.00025%	Bonaire estimate
J	–	Cook Islands (New Zealand)	18,100	Mar 1, 2016	0.00024%	Cook Islands quarterly estimate
H	192	Palau	17,950	Jul 1, 2015	0.00024%	Palau annual estimate
J	–	Anguilla (UK)	13,452	May 11, 2011	0.00018%	2011 census
J	–	Wallis and Futuna (France)	11,750	Jul 1, 2015	0.00016%	Wallis and Futuna annual estimate
H	193	Tuvalu	10,640	Nov 4, 2012	0.00014%	2012 census
H	194	Nauru	10,084	Oct 30, 2011	0.00013%	2011 census
L	–	Saint Barthélemy (France)	9,417	Jan 1, 2015	0.00013%	Saint Barthélemy annual estimate
L	–	Saint Pierre and Miquelon (France)	6,286	Jan 1, 2015	0.000084%	Saint Pierre and Miquelon annual estimate
L	–	Saint Helena, Ascension and Tristan da Cunha (UK)	5,633	Feb 7, 2016	0.000075%	2016 census
L	–	Montserrat (UK)	4,922	May 12, 2011	0.000066%	2011 census

L	–	Sint Eustatius (Netherlands)	3,877	Jan 1, 2015	0.000052%	Sint Eustatius estimate
L	–	Falkland Islands (UK)	2,563	Apr 15, 2012	0.000034%	2012 census
L	–	Norfolk Island (Australia)	2,302	Aug 9, 2011	0.000031%	2011 census
L	–	Christmas Island (Australia)	2,072	Aug 9, 2011	0.000028%	2011 census
L	–	Saba (Netherlands)	1,811	Jan 1, 2015	0.000024%	Saba estimate
L	–	Niue (New Zealand)	1,470	Jul 1, 2015	0.00002%	Niue annual estimate
L	–	Tokelau	1,411	Oct 18, 2011	0.000019%	2011 census
J	195	Vatican City	1,000	Jan 1, 2014	0.000011%	Vatican City estimate
L	–	Cocos (Keeling) Islands (Australia)	550	Aug 9, 2011	0.0000073%	2011 census
L	–	Pitcairn Islands	57	Jul 1, 2014	0.00000076%	Pitcairn Islands estimate

*K. 9 disputed territories not recognised by the UN: Indian Kashmir (Jammu and Kashmir), Tibet, Pakistani Kashmir (Azad Kashmir), Kosovo, Chechnya, Transnistria, Abkhazia, Nagorno-Karabakh, South Ossetia.

L. Populations under 12,000 to be represented by colonial power.

The Netherlands Antilles included four island territories: Aruba, Bonaire, Curaçao (ABC), and the Leeward Islands. In 1983, the Leeward Islands were split into Sint Maarten, Saba, and Sint Eustatius (SSS). The above list therefore does not mention the Netherlands Antilles or the Leeward Islands. Of the six Dutch islands, two (Aruba and Curaçao) have populations over 12,000.

E4. 8 Regions and 196 Nation-States

(See pp.176, 179)

(Kosovo, Taiwan and Vatican City were not in the UN in 2017)

Asia (27 nation-states)

Bangladesh
Bhutan
Brunei
Cambodia
China
India
Indonesia
Japan
Kazakhstan
North Korea
South Korea
Kyrgyzstan
Laos
Malaysia
Maldives
Mongolia
Myanmar
Nepal
Philippines
Singapore
Sri Lanka
Taiwan
Tajikistan
Thailand
Turkmenistan
Uzbekistan
Vietnam

Middle East and North Africa (23 nation-states)

Afghanistan
Algeria
Azerbaijan
Bahrain
Egypt
Iran
Iraq
Israel
Jordan
Kuwait
Lebanon
Libya
Morocco
Oman
Pakistan
Qatar
Saudi Arabia
Somalia
Syria
Tunisia
Turkey
United Arab Emirates
Yemen

Europe (48 nation-states)

Albania
Andorra
Armenia
Austria
Belarus
Belgium
Bosnia and Herzegovina
Bulgaria
Croatia
Cyprus
Czech Republic
Denmark
Estonia
Finland
France
Georgia
Germany
Greece
Hungary
Iceland
Ireland
Italy
Kosovo
Latvia
Liechtenstein
Lithuania
Luxembourg

Macedonia
Malta
Moldova
Monaco
Montenegro
Netherlands
Norway
Poland
Portugal
Romania
Russia
San Marino
Serbia
Slovakia
Slovenia
Spain
Sweden
Switzerland
Ukraine
United Kingdom
Vatican City

North America (3 nation-states)

Canada
Mexico
United States of America

Central America and the Caribbean (20 nation-states)

Antigua and Barbuda
The Bahamas
Barbados
Belize
Costa Rica
Cuba
Dominica
Dominican Republic
El Salvador
Grenada
Guatemala
Haiti
Honduras
Jamaica
Nicaragua
Panama
St Kitts and Nevis
St Lucia
St Vincent and the Grenadines
Trinidad and Tobago

South America (12 nation-states)

Argentina
Bolivia
Brazil
Chile
Colombia
Ecuador
Guyana
Paraguay
Peru
Suriname
Uruguay
Venezuela

Africa (48 nation-states)

Angola
Benin
Botswana
Burkina Faso
Burundi
Cameroon
Cape Verde
Central African Republic
Chad
Comoros
Republic of the Congo
Democratic Republic of the Congo
Côte d'Ivoire
Djibouti
Equatorial Guinea
Eritrea
Ethiopia
Gabon
The Gambia
Ghana
Guinea
Guinea-Bissau
Kenya
Lesotho
Liberia

Madagascar
Malawi
Mali
Mauritania
Mauritius
Mozambique
Namibia
Niger
Nigeria
Rwanda
São Tomé and Principe
Senegal
Seychelles
Sierra Leone
South Africa
South Sudan
Sudan
Swaziland
Tanzania
Togo
Uganda
Zambia
Zimbabwe

Australia and Oceania (15 nation-states)

Australia
East Timor
Fiji
Kiribati
Marshall Islands
Federated States of Micronesia
Nauru
New Zealand
Palau
Papua New Guinea
Samoa
Solomon Islands
Tonga
Tuvalu
Vanuatu

E5. 18 Mini-Regions and 210 Nation-States

(See pp.176, 179)

(The 210 nation-states comprise 193 UN nation-states; 16 related and disputed territories; and Taiwan, which was not in the UN in 2017)

AFRICA

Northern Africa

Algeria
Egypt
Libya
Morocco
South Sudan
Sudan
Tunisia
Western Sahara

Western Africa

Benin
Burkina Faso
Cape Verde
Côte d'Ivoire
Gambia
Ghana
Guinea
Guinea-Bissau
Liberia
Mali
Mauritania
Niger
Nigeria
Senegal
Sierra Leone
Togo

Eastern Africa

Burundi
Comoros
Djibouti
Eritrea
Ethiopia
Kenya
Madagascar
Malawi
Mauritius
Mayotte
Mozambique
Reunion
Rwanda
Seychelles
Somalia
Tanzania
Uganda
Zambia
Zimbabwe

Middle Africa

Angola
Cameroon
Central African Republic
Chad
Congo
Congo, Democratic Republic of
Equatorial Guinea
Gabon
São Tomé and Principe

Southern Africa

Botswana	Namibia	Swaziland
Lesotho	South Africa	

AMERICAS

Northern America

Canada	United States

Central America

Belize	Guatemala	Nicaragua
Costa Rica	Honduras	Panama
El Salvador	Mexico	

Caribbean

Antigua and Barbuda	Grenada	Puerto Rico
Bahamas	Guadeloupe	St Kitts and Nevis
Barbados	Haiti	St Lucia
Cuba	Jamaica	St Vincent and the Grenadines
Dominica	Martinique	Trinidad and Tobago
Dominican Republic	Netherlands Antilles	

South America

Argentina	Ecuador	Peru
Bolivia	French Guiana	Suriname
Brazil	Guyana	Uruguay
Chile	Paraguay	Venezuela
Colombia		

ASIA

Western Asia

Armenia	Georgia	Kuwait
Azerbaijan	Iraq	Lebanon
Bahrain	Israel	Oman
Cyprus	Jordan	Palestinian Territory

Qatar
Saudi Arabia
Syria
Turkey
United Arab Emirates
Yemen

South Central Asia

Afghanistan
Bangladesh
Bhutan
India
Iran
Kazakhstan
Kyrgyzstan
Maldives
Nepal
Pakistan
Sri Lanka
Tajikistan
Turkmenistan
Uzbekistan

South-East Asia

Brunei
Cambodia
Indonesia
Laos
Malaysia
Myanmar
Philippines
Singapore
Thailand
Timor-Leste
Vietnam

East Asia

China
China, Hong Kong
China, Macao
Japan
Korea, North
Korea, South
Mongolia
Taiwan

EUROPE

Northern Europe

Channel Islands
Denmark
Estonia
Finland
Iceland
Ireland
Latvia
Lithuania
Norway
Sweden
United Kingdom

Western Europe

Austria
Belgium
France
Germany
Liechtenstein
Luxembourg
Monaco
Netherlands
Switzerland

Eastern Europe

Belarus	Moldova	Russia
Bulgaria	Poland	Slovakia
Czech Republic	Romania	Ukraine
Hungary		

Southern Europe

Albania	Italy	Portugal
Andorra	Kosovo	San Marino
Bosnia and Herzegovina	Macedonia	Serbia
Croatia	Malta	Slovenia
Greece	Montenegro	Spain

OCEANIA

Australia	Kiribati	Papua New Guinea
Federated States of Micronesia	Marshall Islands	Samoa
	Nauru	Solomon Islands
Fiji	New Caledonia	Tonga
French Polynesia	New Zealand	Tuvalu
Guam	Palau	Vanuatu

E6. Club of Rome's 10 Zones

(See p.175)

A revised plan for a world government was outlined in 1973 by the Rockefellerite Club of Rome, which split the world into 10 political/economic regions or zones that would unite the entire world under one government. These were originally called "Kingdoms" to reflect the 10 kingdoms within Atlantis in Plato's account in *Critias*. The word "Kingdoms" was omitted when the plan was published in a book, *Mankind at the Turning Point*, which argued that the world's problems could only be solved "in a global context". These zones are:

1. North America
2. Western Europe
3. Japan
4. The rest of the developed market economies (Israel, Australia, Tasmania, New Zealand, Oceania, South Africa)
5. Eastern Europe include the free Soviet Union
6. Latin America
7. North Africa and the Middle East
8. Main Africa
9. South and South-Eastern Asia including India

10. "Centrally-planned Asia", meaning Communist Asia (Mongolia, North Korea, North Vietnam, and China)

E7. The IMF's 189 Countries, 2017

(See pp.15, 253)

A

Afghanistan, Islamic Republic of
Albania
Algeria
Angola
Antigua and Barbuda
Argentina
Armenia, Republic of
Australia
Austria
Azerbaijan, Republic of

B

Bahamas, The
Bahrain, Kingdom of
Bangladesh
Barbados
Belarus, Republic of
Belgium
Belize
Benin
Bhutan
Bolivia
Bosnia and Herzegovina
Botswana
Brazil
Brunei Darussalam
Bulgaria
Burkina Faso
Burundi

C

Cambodia
Cameroon
Canada
Cape Verde
Central African Republic
Chad
Chile
China, People's Republic of
Colombia
Comoros
Congo, Democratic Republic of the
Congo, Republic of
Costa Rica
Côte d'Ivoire
Croatia, Republic of
Cyprus
Czech Republic

D

Denmark
Djibouti
Dominica
Dominican Republic

E

Ecuador
Egypt, Arab Republic of
El Salvador
Equatorial Guinea
Eritrea
Estonia, Republic of
Ethiopia

F

Fiji
Finland
France

G

Gabon
Gambia, The
Georgia
Germany
Ghana
Greece
Grenada
Guatemala
Guinea
Guinea-Bissau
Guyana

H

Haiti
Honduras
Hungary

I

Iceland
India
Indonesia
Iran, Islamic Republic of
Iraq
Ireland
Israel
Italy

J

Jamaica
Japan
Jordan

K

Kazakhstan, Republic of
Kenya
Kiribati
Korea, Republic of
Kosovo
Kuwait
Kyrgyz Republic

L

Lao People's Democratic Republic
Latvia, Republic of
Lebanon
Lesotho
Liberia
Libyan Arab Jamahiriya, Socialist People's
Lithuania, Republic of
Luxembourg

M

Macedonia, former Yugoslav Republic of
Madagascar
Malawi
Malaysia
Maldives
Mali
Malta
Marshall Islands, Republic of the
Mauritania
Mauritius
Mexico
Micronesia, Federated States of
Moldova, Republic of
Mongolia
Montenegro, Republic of
Morocco
Mozambique, Republic of
Myanmar

N

Namibia
Nauru
Nepal
Netherlands, Kingdom of the
New Zealand
Nicaragua
Niger
Nigeria
Norway

O

Oman

P

Pakistan
Palau, Republic of
Panama
Papua New Guinea
Paraguay
Peru
Philippines
Poland
Portugal

Q

Qatar

R

Romania
Russian Federation
Rwanda

S

Samoa
San Marino
São Tomé and Principe
Saudi Arabia
Senegal
Serbia, Republic of
Seychelles
Sierra Leone
Singapore
Slovak Republic
Slovenia, Republic of
Solomon Islands
Somalia
South Africa
South Sudan
Spain
Sri Lanka
St Kitts and Nevis
St Lucia
St Vincent and the Grenadines
Sudan
Suriname
Swaziland, Kingdom of
Sweden
Switzerland
Syrian Arab Republic

T

Tajikistan, Republic of
Tanzania
Thailand
Timor-Leste, Democratic Republic of
Togo
Tonga
Trinidad and Tobago
Tunisia
Turkey
Turkmenistan
Tuvalu

U

Uganda
Ukraine
United Arab Emirates
United Kingdom
United States
Uruguay
Uzbekistan, Republic of

V

Vanuatu

Vietnam

Venezuela, Republica Bolivariana de

Y

Yemen, Republic of

Z

Zambia

Zimbabwe

E8. Overview of the EU's Institutions

(See p.108)

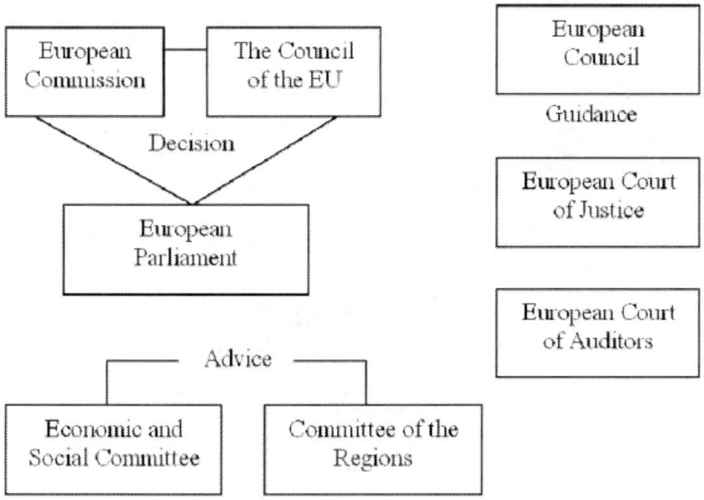

List of Websites Supporting Data in the Appendices

Pages	Website
220–223	A1 Confederations Based on https://en.wikipedia.org/wiki/Confederation
224–226	A2 Federations Based on and put into chronological order https://en.wikipedia.org/wiki/Federation
227–232	A3 Unitary States with Devolution Based on and put into chronological order https://en.wikipedia.org/wiki/Unitary_state
233–238	B1 Declaration of Independence, 1776, taken from Nicholas Hagger, *The Secret Founding of America*
239–243	B2 The North Atlantic Treaty, 1948 http://www.nato.int/cps/en/natolive/official_texts_17 120.htm
244–246	B3 Project for the New American Century, 1997 http://www.rrojasdatabank.info/pfpc/PNAC---statement%20 of%20principles.pdf
247	C1 Overview of the UN Structure http://mpsinfo.files.wordpress.com/2008/12/400px–un_institutio nssvg.png

248	C2 Structure of the UN Agencies Based on a chart from the *UN Chronicle*, originally in http://www.stanford.edu/group/Jonsson/appendb.gif (now defunct). For the 2017 agencies see http://www.un.org/en/aboutun/structure/pdfs/UN%20System%20Chart_ENG_FINAL_MARCH13_2017.pdf
249–255	C3 UN Organisations Originally based on Nicholas Hagger's research, which took account of http://www.un.org/en/peacekeeping/sites/coe/referencedocuments/COE%20Acronyms.pdf and an earlier version of http://en.wikipedia.org/wiki/United_Nations_System (subsequently reorganised). For a 2017 view of the UN organisations see https://www.unsceb.org/directory
256–259	C4 The UN's 193 Member States Based on http://www.encyclopedia.com/reference/encyclopedias-almanacs-transcripts-and-maps/united-nations-members-table
260–267	C5 The UN Universal Declaration of Human Rights, 1948 http://www.un.org/en/documents/udhr/
268–281	C6 Wars the UN Failed to Prevent Involving 124 Countries, 1945–2017 The fully comprehensive list of all wars in 124 countries since 1945 is based on a variety of historical sources and takes account of: http://www.war-memorial.net/wars_all.asp, http://answers.

	google.com/answers/threadview?id=55124 and lists of wars from 1945 to 1989, from 2003 to 2010, and from 2011 to the present: https://en.wikipedia.org/wiki/List_of_wars_1945%E2%80%9389; https://en.wikipedia.org/wiki/List_of_wars_2003%E2%80%9310; and https://en.wikipedia.org/wiki/List_of_wars_2011%E2%80%93present.
282–287	C7 37 Major Conflicts the UN Failed to Prevent after 1945: 689 UN Resolutions and 33,750,000 Deaths http://en.wikipedia.org/wiki/Criticism_of_the_United_Nations#Comparison_of_UNSC_resolutions_on_various_conflicts Note: this website was operational during research and the data has been supplemented and corroborated by additional research.
288–293	C8 162 Wars since 1945 http://www.war-memorial.net/wars_all.asp
294–295	C9 The World's Nuclear Weapons in Early 2017 https://fas.org/issues/nuclear-weapons/status-world-nuclear-forces/ and https://www.armscontrol.org/factsheets/Nuclear-weaponswhohaswhat
296–297	D1 125 Electoral Democracies, 2017 Based on the US Freedom House ratings, see D2 and D3. The 125 electoral democracies have a Freedom Rating of 1.0–4.0, except for Pakistan (4.5) and Puerto Rico (not freedom rated in 2017). https://Freedomhouse.org/report/freedom-world/freedom-world-2017 and https://freedomhouse.org/report/fiw-2017-table-country-scores See also https://en.wikipedia.org/wiki/Freedom_in_the_World

298–301	D2 Freedom Ratings, 2017 Based on the US Freedom House ratings https://Freedomhouse.org/report/freedom-world/freedom-world-2017 and https://freedomhouse.org/report/fiw-2017-table-country-scores
302–310	D3 Freedom Ratings Table by Countries and Territories, 2017 Based on the US Freedom House ratings https://freedomhouse.org/report/fiw-2017-table-country-scores. See also https://en.wikipedia.org/wiki/Freedom_in_the_World
311–313	D4 The World's 59 Dictators, 2017 https://planetrulers.com/current-dictators/. Some of the dictators in this list had died before 2017 and have been replaced by their successors. The list has been updated to include all 57 not-free nation-states (see D2) together with Myanmar and Zimbabwe.
314	E1 Regional Populations as Percentages of World Population, 2017 www.worldometers.info/world-population/population-by-region
315	E2 Historical and Predicted Regional Populations as Percentages of World Population http://en.wikipedia.org/wiki/World_population
316–332	E3 Nation-States' Populations as Percentages of World Population https://en.wikipedia.org/wiki/List_of_countries_and_dependencies_by_population

333–335	E4 8 Regions and 196 Nation-States http://geography.about.com/od/lists/a/officiallist.htm
336–339	E5 18 Mini-Regions and 210 Nation-States Originally based on Nicholas Hagger's research, which took account of http://www.docstoc.com/docs/10157039/2009-World-Population-Data-Sheet (now defunct).
340–341	E6 Club of Rome's 10 Zones No website, taken from Nicholas Hagger's research, published in *The Syndicate*
342–346	E7 The IMF's 189 Countries, 2009 https://www.imf.org/external/np/sec/memdir/memdate.htm
347	E8 Overview of the EU's Institutions http://www.dadalos-europe.org/int/grundkurs4/eu-struktur_1.htm

Notes and Sources

Prologue
The Need for a World State

1. Albert Einstein, 'Towards a World Government' (1946), in *Out Of My Later Years: The Scientist, Philosopher and Man Portrayed Through His Own Words*, New York: Wings Books, 1956.
2. Bertrand Russell, 'The Atomic Bomb and Prevention of War' in the *Bulletin of the Atomic Scientists*, 1 October 1946.
3. In Dennis Laurence Cuddy, *Secret Records Revealed: The Men, the Money & The Methods Behind the New World Order*, p.89.
4. Gandhi, speech, March 1947. In Gandhi, *All Men are Brothers, Autobiographical Reflections*, p.112.
5. The Russell-Einstein Manifesto (1955), issued in London on 9 July 1955 by Bertrand Russell.
6. From 'Atomic Education Urged by Einstein', *New York Times*, 25 May 1946.
7. For Europe's eventual 50 member states, see http://geography.about.com/od/lists/a/officiallist.htm?p=1 for 48 member states, with Azerbaijan and Kazakhstan also in line to become member states. The UK, one of the 48 member states, was preparing to leave the EU at the time of writing. See also Nicholas Hagger, *The Dream of Europa*, p.83.
8. For detailed coverage of the New World Order, see Nicholas Hagger, *The Syndicate*; and *The Secret American Dream*, chs.7 and 8.
9. Nicholas Hagger, *Peace for our Time*, pp.181–183.
10. See Hagger, *Peace for our Time*, p.xvi and source, http://www.war-memorial.net/wars_all.asp.
11. See Hagger, *Peace for our Time*, p.98 and source, https://fas.org/issues/nuclear-weapons/status-world-nuclear-forces/. In autumn 2016 there were 15,375 nuclear weapons, in early 2017 14,900.
12. See https://www.rt.com/news/338086-isis-chemical-lab-mosul/; http://www.independent.co.uk/news/world/middle-

east/isiss-dirty-bomb-jihadists-have-seized-enough-radioactive-material-to-build-their-first-wmd-10309220.html; and http://www.telegraph.co.uk/news/2016/04/01/isil-plotting-to-use-drones-for-nuclear-attack-on-west/.

13. See https://www.theguardian.com/uk-news/2016/apr/01/a-terrorist-dirty-bomb-us-summit-asks-world-leaders-to-plot-response.
14. See *Peace for our Time*, pp.48–49 and elsewhere; and *The Secret American Destiny*, pp.250–253.

PART ONE

Beyond the Nation-State

Epigraph

1. Albert Einstein in an interview with George Sylvester Viereck, 'What Life Means to Einstein', *The Saturday Evening Post*, p.17, 26 October 1929.

1. Transient Forms of Government and the Drift towards a World State

1. For Europe's eventual tally of 48 member states, see http://geography.about.com/od/lists/a/officiallist.htm?p=1.
   For Europe's future enlargement, see http://en.wikipedia.org/wiki/Future_enlargement_of_the_European_Union.
2. Alexander Wendt, 'Why a World State is Inevitable', *European Journal of International Relations*, 9, 4 (2003), pp.491–542.
3. Wendt, *op. cit.*, p.491.
4. Daniel Deudney, 'Nuclear Weapons and the Waning of the *Real*-State', *Daedalus* (journal), 124, 2 (1995), pp.209–231; see also 'Geopolitics and Change' in *New Thinking in International Relations Theory*, M. Doyle and G.J. Ikenberry (eds.), Westview Press, 1997.
5. Wendt, *op. cit.*, pp.505–506.
6. The thinking of Kenneth Waltz.
7. The thinking of Martin Wight and Chris Brown.
8. The thinking of Charles Beitz and Thomas Pogge.
9. The thinking of Michael Walzer.

10. Nicholas Hagger, *The Rise and Fall of Civilizations*.

2. Longings for a World State

1. Abydos Stelae of Tuthmose I described his triumph: "I made the boundaries of Egypt as far as that which the sun encircles" (*ARE* vol. 2, 1998, p.40). An oval cartouche on a hypocephalus (a disc made of linen or papyrus) stated that the Pharaoh ruled "all that the sun-disc encircles". See Max Ostrovsky, *Y=Arctg X: The Hyperbola of the World Order*, p.10.
2. William Hull Botsford, *Papers*, c.1904–1912, 1912: pp.27–28.
3. For a full examination of *rta*, see Jeanine Miller, *The Vision of Cosmic Order in the Vedas*, e.g. p.283.
4. See Jeanne-Marie Gescher, *All Under Heaven: China's Dreams of Order*.
5. Fung Yu-Lan, *The Spirit of Chinese Philosophy*, p.27.
6. *Encyclopedia Britannica*, 15th edition, 'Chinese Philosophy', 4.416.
7. See Ostrovsky, *op. cit.*
8. See http://en.wikiquote.org/wiki/Socrates#Plutarch. Socrates' words seem to contradict his view in *Crito*.
9. Dante, *Convivio* (*The Banquet*, c.1304), in *Readings in Medieval Political Theory 1100–1400*, C.J. Nederman and K.L. Forhan (eds.).
10. Richard Kay, *Dante's Monarchia*, pp.xxiii–xxv, quoted in Barbara Reynolds, *Dante, The Poet, the Political Thinker, the Man*, pp.328–329.
11. Dante, *Monarchia*, pp.13, 15, 21–22, 43–44, xvii and 19, xxxiii for the citings of *Monarchia* in this paragraph. See also another translation, Dante, *Monarchy*, trans. and ed. by Prue Shaw.
12. See John J. Reilly, *The Perfection of the West* and his related essay 'Dante's World Government: *De Monarchia* in the 21st Century', www.johnreilly.info/dwg.htm. Note: this website was operational during research and Reilly's work has been corroborated by additional research.
13. For this and the previous extracts, see the translation of *De*

Monarchia, Dante Alighieri: On World-Government, trans. by Herbert W. Schneider. See also another translation, *Dante: Monarchy*, trans. and ed. by Prue Shaw, who translates the extract from 1:11 as: "Justice is at its strongest only under a monarch; therefore for the best ordering of the world there must be a monarchy or empire."

14. For this extract see Marsilius of Padua, *The Defender of Peace*, trans. by Alan Gewirth.
15. For this extract see, Francesco Petrarch, *Canzoni 128*, trans. by Morris Bishop in *Petrarch and His World*, p.234.
16. Thomas Hobbes, *Leviathan*, p.286.
17. Abbé de Saint-Pierre, *Extrait du projet de paix perpétuelle*, trans. by H.H. Bellot. See also Jean-Jacques Rousseau, *A Lasting Peace through the Federation of Europe and The State of War* (1756), trans. by C.E. Vaughan, pp.61–64.
18. Rousseau, *op. cit.*, pp.91, 93, 112.
19. To find this on the internet, see the version with a slightly different end to the title: Immanuel Kant, *Idea for a Universal History from a Cosmopolitan Point of View* (1784), in *Kant On History*, ed. by Lewis White Beck, http://www.marxists.org/reference/subject/ethics/kant/universal-history.htm. The quotations that follow are taken from the version referred to in notes 20 and 21, *Political Writings*.
20. Immanuel Kant, *Idea for a Universal History with a Cosmopolitan Purpose* (1784) and *Perpetual Peace: A Philosophical Sketch* (1795), in *Political Writings*, trans. by H.B. Nisbet, ed. by Hans Reiss, pp.41, 47, 48 and 105.
21. Kant, *op. cit.* (see note 19), pp.41–53 and 93–130, here citing pp.100, 102, 104, 106, 113 and 114.
22. J. Christopher Harold, *The Age of Napoleon*, p.123.
23. Kant, *op. cit.* (see note 19), p.100.
24. John Rawls, *A Theory of Justice*, pp.11–16.
25. P. Kleingeld and E. Brown, 'Cosmopolitanism', *Stanford Encyclopedia of Philosophy* (Fall 2006 Edition).
26. See http://www.globalpolitician.com/22960-world-government.

27. Joseph E. Schwartzberg, 'Reform of the General Assembly', in *Revitalizing the United Nations: Reform Through Weighted Voting*, Institute for Global Policy, World Federalist Movement, p.3.
28. H.G. Wells, *The Outline of History*, p.1153.
29. Wendell L. Willkie, *One World*, p.165.
30. Emery Reves, *The Anatomy of Peace*, p.247.
31. Einstein, 'Economic War or Peace' in Albert Einstein, *Ideas and Opinions*, p.122.
32. See http://magazine.uchicago.edu/9512/9512Salvation.html.
33. See http://www.worldservice.org/gov.html.
34. For copies of visas, see http://www.worldgovernment.org/visas.html?s=1.
35. Joseph P. Baratta, *The Politics of World Federation*, p.470.
36. E. Adamson Hoebel, *The Law of Primitive Man*, pp.331–333.
37. E. Goodman, 'The Soviet Union and World Government', in *The Journal of Politics* 15, 2 (1953), pp.231–253.
38. See Nicholas Hagger, *Peace for our Time*, ch.5.

3. Attempts at Imposing a World State on the Known World by Conquest

1. For fuller details, see http://www.timelineindex.com/content/select/844/1023,844.
2. See Elli Louka, *Nuclear Weapons, Justice and the Law*, p.341.
3. See https://fas.org/issues/nuclear-weapons/status-world-nuclear-forces/.

4. The Failure of the Old Order

1. Survey conducted by Freedom House, an organisation opposed to tyranny that supports the expansion of freedom in the world since 1972. In the 2017 freedom ratings "free" nations up to a certain ranking were considered to be liberal democracies. See https://freedomhouse.org/report/fiw-2017-table-country-scores. Also https://en.wikipedia.org/wiki/Freedom_in_the_World, where the electoral democracies are asterisked.

2. Kant, *Idea for a Universal History from a Cosmopolitan Point of View* (1784), in *Kant On History*, trans. by Lewis White Beck. See https://www.marxists.org/reference/subject/ethics/kant/un iversal-history.htm. All the quotations regarding the nine theses are taken from this translation.
3. *An Idea for a Universal History from a Cosmopolitan Point of View*, in *Kant On History*, p.16.
4. Francis Fukuyama, *The End of History and the Last Man*, p.66.
5. Jacques Derrida, *Specters of Marx*.
6. See Nicholas Hagger, *The Fire and the Stones, The Light of Civilization* and *The Rise and Fall of Civilizations*.
7. For further details, see Hagger, *The Fire and the Stones, The Light of Civilization* and *The Rise and Fall of Civilizations*.
8. Freedom House Survey of 2017. See https://freedomhouse.org/report/fiw-2017-table-country-scores.
9. See Nicholas Hagger, *The Libyan Revolution*.
10. See https://en.wikipedia.org/wiki/Democracy_Index.
11. *The New Oxford American Dictionary*, 2nd edn., ed. by Erin McKean.
12. For Europe removing 80 per cent of laws from European nation-states, see http://blogs.lse.ac.uk/europpbl og/2012/06/13/europeanization-of-public-policy/. Also see note 15. For the German figure of 84 per cent, see http://www.caef.org.uk/d104germanpresident.html, Roman Herzog and Luder Gerken: "The German Ministry of Justice has compared the legal acts adopted by the Federal Republic of Germany between 1998 and 2004 with those adopted by the European Union in the same period. Results: 84 per cent came from Brussels, with only 16 per cent coming originally from Berlin." For a figure of 85 per cent see http://openeuropeblog.blogspot.com/2009/04/how-many-of-our-laws-aremade-in.html. This website was operational during research. For Pottering's comment see https://forums.skadi.info/archive/index.php/index.php?t-123352.html: "The president of the European Union Parliament, Hans-Gert Pottering, has stated unequivocally that once the Lisbon

Treaty is fully implemented, the EU will be responsible for 'nearly 100 per cent' of all laws made in Europe."

13. For *FREE* see Appendix 7 of Nicholas Hagger, *My Double Life 2: A Rainbow over the Hills*, pp.935–937.
14. Hobbes, *op. cit.*, *Leviathan*, p.188.
15. For Europe making 80 per cent of British laws, see Peter Lilley, House of Commons, *Daily Hansard*, 3 June 2008: "The European Union has supremacy over British Law. 80 per cent of Britain's laws are now made in Brussels and Parliament has no power to reject or amend them." See also note 10.
16. http://www.war-memorial.net/wars_all.asp.
17. The fully comprehensive list of all wars in 124 countries since 1945 (Appendix C6) is based on a variety of historical sources and takes account of: http://www.war-memorial.net/wars_all.asp, http://answers.google.com/answers/threadview?id=55124 and lists of wars from 1945 to 1989, from 2003 to 2010, and from 2011 to the present: https://en.wikipedia.org/wiki/List_of_wars_1945%E2%80%9389; https://en.wikipedia.org/wiki/List_of_wars_2003%E2%80%9310; and https://en.wikipedia.org/wiki/List_of_wars_2011%E2%80%93present.
18. See Nicholas Hagger, *Armageddon*, pp.582–595.
19. Thomas Paine, *The Age of Reason*, p.22.
20. Hagger, *The Fire and the Stones*, pp.3–344. Updated as *The Light of Civilization*.

PART TWO

Supranationalism

5. Beyond Existing Models

1. *Catholic Encyclopedia* (1913), Henry IV.
2. *The Law of War and Peace*, trans. by Francis Kelsey, prol. sect. 28. (The book title does not reflect the Latin *De*, "on" or "concerning".)
3. See Robert Norris and Hans M. Kristensen, 'Global nuclear weapons inventories, 1945–2010', *Bulletin of the Atomic Scientists*, 1 July 2010. The 69,401 figure was in *The Guardian*,

http://www.guardian.co.uk/news/datablog/2009/sep/06/nuclearweapons-world-us-north-korea-russia-iran. (This website is no longer available, and the *Bulletin of the Atomic Scientists'* figures now apply.)

4. See https://www.un.org/sc/suborg/en/sanctions/information.
5. See http://www.war-memorial.net/wars_all.asp.
6. For a much fuller account of the American Constitutional Convention, see Nicholas Hagger, *The Secret Founding of America*, pp.152–158.
7. See http://www.foavc.org/?d=43 and http://www.article-5.org/file.php/1/Articles/TimeToMakeCongressObeyUSConstitution.htm.
8. Anthony and Andrew Cowgill, *The European Constitution in Perspective*, 'The Treaty establishing a Constitution for Europe', p.5.
9. Arthur M. Schlesinger, Jr, *A Thousand Days: John F. Kennedy in the White House*, p.484.
10. See https://www.theguardian.com/business/2014/nov/13/us-wealth-inequality-top-01-worth-as-much-as-the-bottom-90.
11. See https://www.forbes.com/sites/forbespr/2016/10/04/forbes-releases-35th-annual-forbes-400-ranking-of-the-richest-americans/#588a7355502f.
12. See https://www.forbes.com/sites/forbespr/2016/10/04/forbes-releases-35th-annual-forbes-400-ranking-of-the-richest-americans/#588a7355502f.
13. See http://new.euro-med.dk/20161004-how-rothschilds-goldman-sachs-owned-barroso-and-his-eu-and-no-one-protested-until-now.php.
14. See http://new.euro-med.dk/20170113-rothschilds-goldman-sachs-takes-over-trump-and-the-white-house-again.php.
15. See Centre for Research on Globalization, The Federal Reserve Cartel: The Eight Families, http://www.globalresearch.ca/the-federal-reserve-cartel-the-eight-families/25080.
16. See http://www.mining.com/the-richest-man-in-history-a

massed-a-400-billion-fortune-mining-gold-in-africa-80949/ and htt ps://en.wikipedia.org/wiki/List_of_wealthiest_families.

17. See http://www.mining.com/the-richest-man-in-history-amassed-a-400-billion-fortune-mining-gold-in-africa-80949/.
18. For the Bilderberg Group, see Daniel Estulin, *The True Story of The Bilderberg Group, passim*; also Hagger, *The Syndicate*, pp.34–36.
19. Estulin, *op. cit.*, pp.149–165; also Hagger, *The Syndicate*, pp.37–38.
20. *Global 2000: Report to the President*, vol.1, pp.1, 41–42 and *Global Future: Time to Act*, p.50. See also Hagger, *The Syndicate*, pp.267–272.
21. The Kissinger Report, *National Security Study Memorandum 200*, April 1974, on the need for massive population reduction, implying that war, famine and disease can reduce the world's population of "useless eaters" to an acceptable (i.e. cost-effective) level.
22. See http://www.worldometers.info/world-population/.
23. See http://www.worldometers.info/world-population/.
24. Eisenhower, farewell address on radio and TV, 17 January 1961, Public Papers of the Presidents of the United States at http://www.presidency.ucsb.edu/ws/.
25. Charles Griffin, 'New Light on Eisenhower's Farewell Address', *Presidential Studies Quarterly*, 22 (1992), pp.469–479.
26. See http://www.guardian.co.uk/news/datablog/2009/sep/06/nuclear-weapons-world-us-north-korea-russia-iran. The US high for possession of nuclear warheads was in 1965 (32,040), which had come down by 1985 (to 24,401), and the USSR high was in 1985 (45,000).
27. See https://fas.org/issues/nuclear-weapons/status-world-nuclear-forces/.
28. Woodrow Wilson, address to Congress, 8 January 1918, in *Papers Relating to the Foreign Relations of the United States, 1918: Supplement I, The World War* (2 vols., Washington, DC, US Government Printing Office, 1933), I, pp.15–16. See

http://www.historyplace.com/speeches/wilson-points.htm.

29. Hagger, *The Syndicate*, p.41; also Hagger, *The Secret Founding of America*, p.139.
30. A. Ralph Epperson, *The New World Order*, p.xiv; quoting Jean-Michel Angebert, *The Occult and the Third Reich*, p.192.
31. Hermann Rauschning, *Hitler Speaks*, p.87; alternatively translated in Epperson, *op. cit.*, p.xiv, quoting Jean-Michel Angebert, *op. cit.*, p.192.
32. Hagger, *The Syndicate*, pp.120–121, 132.
33. All these quotations about the New World Order are sourced in Hagger, *The Syndicate*, pp.121–122.
34. Hagger, *The Syndicate*, p.23.
35. George Soros, *The Bubble of American Supremacy*, p.vii. For Senator Jay Rockefeller see Hagger, *The Syndicate*, p.185 and *The Secret American Dream*, ch.8.
36. Hagger, *The Secret Founding of America*.
37. See video by Representative Paul Kanjorski, http://www.youtube.com/watch?v=pD8viQ_DhS4, accessed on 9.3.2010.
38. See http://bushstole04.com/monetarysystem/rothschild_bank.htm.
39. James P. Tucker, 'Bilderberg Surreptitiously Pushes Global Treasury Department', *American Free Press*, 22 March 2010.
40. See http://www.i-p-o.org/global-democracy.htm.

6. The Ideal Form of the World State: The United Federation of the World

1. Lenin, *Collected Works*, Progress Publishers, 1974, Moscow, vol.21, pp.339–343, in *Sotsial-Demokrat*, no. 44, August 23, 1915, trans. by Charles Farrell, see http://www.marxists.org/archive/lenin/works/1915/aug/23.htm.
2. Hagger, *The Fire and the Stones*; *The Rise and Fall of Civilizations*.
3. Bank for International Settlements, Triennial Central Bank Survey, December 2007, http://www.bis.org/publ/rpfxf07t.pdf.

7. The Structure of a World State

1. See list http://en.wikipedia.org/wiki/List_of_countries_by_population#cite_note-unpop-3.
2. See http://answers.google.com/answers/threadview?id=55124 for 123 conflicts and http://www.war-memorial.net/wars_all.asp for 162 conflicts.
3. See Hagger, *The Syndicate*, pp.257–260.
4. The 69,401 figure was in *The Guardian*, http://www.guardian.co.uk/news/datablog/2009/sep/06/nuclearweapons-world-us-north-korea-russia-iran. (This website is no longer available, and the Bulletin of the Atomic Scientists' figures now apply.) For the Federation of American Scientists' figures, see https://fas.org/issues/nuclear-weapons/status-world-nuclear-forces/.
5. Hagger, *The Syndicate*, pp.110–111, citing *Spotlight*, 22 April 1996, pp.4–5: "Sources have told the *Spotlight* Chernomyrdin and David Rockefeller are secret partners in Russian energy combines."
6. See https://visit.un.org/sites/visit.un.org/files/FS_UN_Headquarters_History_English_Feb_2013.pdf.
7. For the 2012 figure, see Stockholm International Peace Research Institute figures, http://www.stripes.com/news/despite-cuts-natostill-accounts-for-most-of-world-s-military-spending-1.269882.
8. See http://www.stripes.com/news/despite-cuts-nato-stillaccounts-for-most-of-world-s-military-spending-1.269882.

8. Manifesto for a World State

1. 'Summary of the Annual Review of Developments in Globalization and Regional Integration in the Countries of the ESCWA Region.' See http://fileserver.net-texts.com/asset.aspx?dl=no&id=14347.
2. See https://www.cia.gov/library/publications/the-world-factbook/rankorder/2078rank.html?countryName=United%20States&countryCode=us&regionCode=na&rank=4#us.

3. See http://www.answerbag.com/q_view/53199:http://antrh ow.palomar.edu/language/language_1.htm.
4. See http://www.reuters.com/article/ousiv/idUSTRE52966Z2 00 90310.
5. See https://www.thebalance.com/war-on-terror-facts-costs-tim eline-3306300.
6. See https://news.brown.edu/articles/2016/09/costsofwar2.
7. Joseph Stiglitz and Linda Bilmes, *The Three Trillion Dollar War*.
8. See http://www.cbsnews.com/blogs/2009/03/17/politics/politicalhotsheet/entry4872310.shtml.
9. Office for National Statistics, see http://www.economicshelp.org/blog/uk-economy/uk-national-debt/.
10. See https://www.usatoday.com/story/money/business/2015/04 /25/247-wall-st-countries-war-spending/26308207/.
11. See http://www.cnbc.com/2016/03/08/syria-war-could-cost-country-13t-by-2020-study.html.
12. See https://www.theguardian.com/uk-news/2016/jul/17/trident-renewal-205bn-arguments-for-against.
13. See https://www.populationinstitute.org/resources/populationonline/issue/18/110/.
14. See https://www.healthpolicyproject.com/pubs/724_PROJE CTI NGETHIOPIAN.pdf.
15. See http://www.sciencedaily.com/releases/2015/08/150810 11 0634.htm.
16. Nicholas Hagger, *Collected Poems 1958–2005*, pp.93–94.
17. Carl Haub, 'How Many People Have Ever Lived on Earth?', *Population Today* (Population Reference Bureau), November/December 2002. See http://www.prb.org/pdf/PT_novdec02.pdf.

Epilogue
Global Democracy and a Golden Age

1. Virgil dreamt of a new order in line 5 of the 'Fourth Eclogue': "*Magnus ab integro saeclorum nascitur ordo*", "The great order of the ages is born afresh". (See p.110.)

Bibliography

Abbé de Saint-Pierre, *Extrait du projet de paix perpétuelle*, trans. by H.H. Bellot, London, 1927; republished by Kessinger Publishing, 2009.

Angebert, Jean-Michel, *The Occult and the Third Reich*, Macmillan Publishing Company, 1974.

Armstrong, George, *The Rothschild Money Trust*, California: Omni Publications, 1940.

Baratta, Joseph P., *The Politics of World Federation, United Nations, UN Reform, Atomic Control*, 2 vols., Westport, Connecticut: Praeger, 2004.

Bishop, Morris, *Petrarch and His World*, Indiana University Press, 2002.

Dante, *Convivio* (*The Banquet*, c.1304), in *Readings in Medieval Political Theory 1100–1400*, ed. by C.J. Nederman and K.L. Forhan, Indianapolis: Hackett, 1993.

Derrida, Jacques, *Specters of Marx*, Routledge, 1st edition, 1994.

Einstein, Albert, *Ideas and Opinions*, New York: Bonanza Books, Crown Publishers, 1954.

Einstein, Albert, 'Towards a World Government' (1946), in *Out Of My Later Years: The Scientist, Philosopher and Man Portrayed Through His Own Words*, New York: Wings Books, 1956.

Epperson, A. Ralph, *The New World Order*, Publius Press, 1990.

Estulin, Daniel, *The True Story of The Bilderberg Group*, TrineDay LLC, 2009.

Fukuyama, Francis, *The End of History and the Last Man*, Hamish Hamilton, 1992.

Gandhi, Mahatma, *All Men are Brothers: Autobiographical Reflections*, ed. by Krishna Kripalani, New York: Continuum, 1982.

Gescher, Jeanne-Marie, *All Under Heaven: China's Dreams of Order*, Kaduba House, 2015.

Global Future: Time to Act, Council on Environmental Quality, 1981/ University of Michigan Library, reprint.

Global Report to the President – Entering the Twenty-First Century, Council on Environmental Quality, 1981/Penguin, 1982.

Hagger, Nicholas, *Armageddon*, O-Books, 2010.

Hagger, Nicholas, *Collected Poems 1958–2005*, O-Books, 2006.

Hagger, Nicholas, *My Double Life 2: A Rainbow over the Hills*, O-Books, 2015.

Hagger, Nicholas, *Peace for our Time*, O-Books, 2017.

Hagger, Nicholas, *The Dream of Europa*, O-Books, 2015.

Hagger, Nicholas, *The Fire and the Stones*, Element, 1991.

Hagger, Nicholas, *The Libyan Revolution*, O-Books, 2009.

Hagger, Nicholas, *The Light of Civilization*, O-Books, 2006.

Hagger, Nicholas, *The Rise and Fall of Civilizations*, O-Books, 2008.

Hagger, Nicholas, *The Secret American Destiny*, Watkins, 2016.

Hagger, Nicholas, *The Secret American Dream*, Watkins, 2011.

Hagger, Nicholas, *The Secret Founding of America*, Watkins Publishing, 2007.

Hagger, Nicholas, *The Syndicate*, O-Books, 2004.

Hagger, Nicholas, *The World Government*, O-Books, 2010.

Hagger, Nicholas, *World Constitution: Constitution for the United Federation of the World*, O-Books, 2018.

Harold, J. Christopher, *The Age of Napoleon*, The American Heritage Library, 1963.

Hobbes, Thomas, *Leviathan*, Penguin, 1986.

Hoebel, E. Adamson, *The Law of Primitive Man*, Harvard University Press, 1954.

Kant, Immanuel, *Idea for a Universal History from a Cosmopolitan Point of View* (1784), in *Kant On History*, The Bobbs-Merrill Co., 1963.

Kant, Immanuel, *Idea for a Universal History with a Cosmopolitan Purpose* (1784) and *Perpetual Peace: A Philosophical Sketch* (1795), in *Political Writings*, trans. by H.B. Nisbet, ed. by Hans Reiss, 2nd edn., New York: Cambridge University Press, 1991.

Kant On History, ed. by Lewis White Beck, Indianapolis: Bobbs-Merrill, 1963.

Kay, Richard, *Dante's Monarchia*, PIMS, 1998.

Loftus, John and Aarons, Mark, *The Secret War against the Jews*, New York: St. Martin's Press, 1994.

Louka, Elli, *Nuclear Weapons, Justice and the Law*, Edward Elgar Publishing, 2012.

Marsilius of Padua, *The Defender of Peace*, trans. by Alan Gewirth, Harper & Row, 1957.

Miller, Jeanine, *The Vision of Cosmic Order in the Vedas*, Routledge & Kegan Paul, 1985.

Ostrovsky, Max, *Y=Arctg X: The Hyperbola of the World Order*, Lanham: University Press of America, 2007.

Paine, Thomas, *The Age of Reason*, Dover Publications Inc., 2004.

Piketty, Thomas, *Capital in the Twenty-First Century*, Harvard University Press, 2014.

Rawls, John, *A Theory of Justice*, Harvard University Press, 1999.

Reilly, John J., *The Perfection of the West*, Xlibris Corporation, 2003.

Reves, Emery, *The Anatomy of Peace*, Penguin, 1947 (first published in USA in 1945).

Reynolds, Barbara, *Dante: The Poet, the Political Thinker, the Man*, I.B. Tauris, 2007.

Rousseau, Jean-Jacques, *A Lasting Peace through the Federation of Europe and The State of War* (1756), trans. by C.E. Vaughan, London: Constable and Co., 1917.

Schlesinger, Arthur M., Jr, *A Thousand Days: John F. Kennedy in the White House*, Andre Deutsch, 1965.

Schwartzberg, Joseph E., *Revitalizing the United Nations: Reform through Weighted Voting*, Institute for Global World Federalists, 2004.

Soros, George, *The Bubble of American Supremacy*, W&N, 2004.

The New Oxford American Dictionary, 2nd edn., ed. by Erin McKean, 2051 pages, Oxford University Press, 2005.

Toynbee, Arnold J., *A Study of History*, Oxford University Press, 1987.

Wells, H.G., *The Outline of History*, Cassell & Co., 8th revision, 1927.

Willkie, Wendell L., *One World*, Cassell & Co., 1943.

Yu-Lan, Fung, *The Spirit of Chinese Philosophy*, Routledge & Kegan Paul, 1962.

Index

Page numbers for diagrams and charts appear in italics. Entries are mainly in alphabetical order but in some cases, where they describe a narrative, in chronological or page order.

BOOKS

O-BOOKS

SPIRITUALITY

O is a symbol of the world, of oneness and unity; this eye represents knowledge and insight. We publish titles on general spirituality and living a spiritual life. We aim to inform and help you on your own journey in this life.

If you have enjoyed this book, why not tell other readers by posting a review on your preferred book site?